Understanding and Treating the Psychopath

Dennis M. Doren

JASON ARONSON INC.
Northvale, New Jersey
London

THE MASTER WORK SERIES

First softcover edition 1996

Copyright © 1996 by Jason Aronson Inc.

Library of Congress Cataloging-in-Publication Data

Doren, Dennis M.
    Understanding and treating the psychopath / Dennis M. Doren.
      p. cm. — (Master work series)
    Originally published: New York : Wiley, c1987.
    Includes bibliographical references and index.
    ISBN 1-56821-791-9 (alk. paper)
    1. Antisocial personality disorders. I. Title. II. Series.
    [DNLM: 1. Antisocial Personality Disorder. WM 190 D696u 1987a]
    RC555.D67   1996
    616.85'82 — dc20
    DNLM/DLC
    for Library of Congress   95-26700

Manufactured in the United States of America. Jason Aronson Inc. offers books and cassettes. For information and catalog write to Jason Aronson Inc., 230 Livingston Street, Northvale, New Jersey 07647.

To the memory of my father,
Louis S. Doren, DDS

Preface to the Softcover Edition

Since this book was first published, the amount of research about psychopaths has expanded significantly, especially in the areas of assessment, diagnosis, and description of their dynamics. For instance, Robert Hare completed his measure of the disorder, the Psychopathy Checklist—Revised. Hare and his colleagues have accumulated a substantial body of research that demonstrates the validity of that instrument for making certain predictions, such as of violence and recidivism with incarcerated populations. Similarly, Carl Gacono and Reid Meloy's research has shown the utility of using the Rorschach for assessment purposes involving psychopathic clients. From a formal diagnostic perspective, the main manual (*DSM-III-R*) has been refined once again (though the new volume, *DSM-IV*, still fails to acknowledge the existence of many Antisocial Personality Disorder subtypes). Elsewhere I have delineated the numerous subtypes of that formal diagnostic category, including four other types besides the psychopath. Work is also progressing in documenting at least one biological underpinning of psychopathy. Specifically, research has indicated that the brain functioning of psychopaths differs from that of nonpsychopaths by responding less, and with less organization, to verbal and emotional cues. A lot has been accomplished in a relatively few years.

Unfortunately there are still few resources, beyond my work, to assist mental health clinicians in the practical task of treating psychopathic clients effectively. The new research has enabled us to differentiate with greater reliability which clients are psychopaths, predict their violence with better certainty, and assess their individual attributes with an increased knowledge base. We can now describe psychopaths' dynamics and characteristics more clearly and fully than we could when this book was first published. It still seems, however, that the book contains the most comprehensive set of treatment guidelines for how to accomplish behavioral changes in psychopathic clients.

Over the past few years I have spoken to many people about treating psychopaths. In all of those discussions one topic seems by far the most commonly raised. How do I explain why clinicians fail with psychopathic clients, given my view that psychopaths are treatable? There are two answers to that question, neither one of which is comforting to those of us who have experienced such failure.

The first answer is that we typically set the wrong goal for treatment. Commonly, for instance, the treatment plan goals expected by clinicians reflect their belief that these clients should engage in complete personality change. We write those goals in terms like "will develop empathy" and "will develop remorse." In effect, we strive to make psychopaths into nonpsychopaths. When we strive for overall characterological change in psychopathic clients as our measure of success—however desirable that goal may be—we are demanding more of them than we expect from our other clients, such as substance-abusing, paraphiliac, eating-disordered, phobic, mood-disordered, or thought-disordered clients. We do not typically designate treatment success to be the total change of who they are. Rather, our goals reflect our expectations that clients will improve so that they are no longer debilitated by their symptoms and, if applicable, no longer harmful to others. When we work with psychopathic clients, our treatment goals should be similar—that they will no longer be debilitated by their symptoms and no longer harmful to others. These more modest goals can be accomplished, and, most typically and importantly, address the primary reason the client is in treatment. The lofty goal of complete characterological change is not reachable and leads to the treatment failure so often experienced with psychopathic clients.

The second answer to the question of why clinicians fail with psychopathic clients is that we give up on these clients before they have had an opportunity to make the desired behavioral changes. Let's face it. The reaction many therapists have to seeing one of these clients walk through their door is, metaphorically speaking, to hold up a cross, string up lots of garlic, and look for a wooden stake. Other therapists initially find these clients quite charming, only to become disenchanted rather soon afterwards. Neither of these reactions facilitates effective long-term treatment. We all know that the process of achieving significant behavioral change in personality-disordered individuals takes a long time, usually months and years. Over that time period it is easy even for the best clinicians among us to get burned out from the constant "battles" instigated by psychopathic clients. We see little treatment progress in return for our valiant efforts, at least within the shorter time frames we unilaterally and emotionally set. As a result, we give up, refer the client to some other hapless soul, and proclaim the client was untreatable. To remedy this situation, my hope has been, and still is, that this book will help mental health practitioners persevere long enough with psychopathic clients so that success can and will happen. Knowing what to expect from such clients and how best to respond to them under adverse conditions (items described in detail in this book) goes a long way toward maintaining the necessary endurance. As one reviewer stated about this book, it does not so much teach the reader how to *do* therapy but how to *survive* doing therapy with psychopathic clients.

My conversations with a multitude of mental health practitioners have shown me that there are many professionals and paraprofessionals attempting to help psychopathic clients live more productive and less harmful lives. I hope that this book will continue to assist in that endeavor.

Preface

There are few mental health practitioners who enjoy practicing their craft with psychopathic clients. One's expectation for a successful outcome with these clients is frequently less than that for others, and the frustration at watching one's patient persistently perform destructive and self-defeating behaviors can be substantial. Yet there are still numbers of us who try. I count myself among some of the more optimistic clinicians in working with these clients. Dare I say that I even find satisfaction and some success when working with psychopaths?

This book is designed to help other professionals in their endeavors involving psychopathic clients. The first half of the book describes what we know about psychopaths, both empirically and theoretically. Four research-based theories of psychopathy are initially reviewed. A new formulation concerning the etiology of the psychopath based on our current knowledge is then offered both as a source of understanding for practitioners and as a set of hypotheses to be tested by researchers.

The second half of the book is a description of what can be expected when performing therapy with psychopathic clients. The typical psychological treatment issues of these clients are explicated in detail. Similarly, the guidelines for successful therapy are discussed from a practical perspective. Finally, an enumeration of a host of specific, problematic psychopathic behaviors is offered as the basis of a discussion of how the psychopath can be successfully treated. Countertransference issues and methods by which they can be effectively avoided, always major concerns when working with psychopathic clients, are described for each of the client's problematic behaviors listed.

A comment needs to be made concerning the manner in which psychopaths are referred to in this book. Based on the empirical finding that most psychopaths are male, only the pronoun "he" will be employed when describing the psychopath in general, rather than the cumbersome "he or she" or the confusing periodic alternation from "he" to "she" and back again. I mean no slight to women or sexist implication whatsoever by this choice of pronoun.

I wish to express my sincere thanks to a special person, Susan B. McDonald, for her exceptional assistance with this book. Her persistent attempts to dispute my theoretical formulations served to force me to strengthen virtually all of my arguments. Similarly, her editorial skills greatly aided in making this a readable book for researchers, theoreticians, and clinicians. This book would not have been nearly as polished without her help. Thanks are also extended to Edwin I. Megargee, PhD. His suggestions pertaining to the writing style and topic organization were very useful. Similarly, his knowledge of various research findings and theoretical issues facilitated the comprehensiveness of the literature review herein. Finally, my appreciation is given to Alexander Bassin, PhD, Daniel R. Boroto, PhD, John C. Brigham, PhD, and George Weaver, PhD, for their instructive comments and debate on the issues discussed here. I believe I gained much from their input which I can now pass on to the reader.

I also wish to express my appreciation to the following for permission to reprint material that appears in this book: Plenum Press and author Herbert C. Quay, for a figure from Dr. Quay's chapter, "Psychopathic Behavior: Reflections on Its Nature, Origins, and Treatment," that appeared in *The Structuring of Experience,* edited by I. Užgiris and F. Weizmann, Plenum Press, 1977; the *Tallahassee Democrat,* for material from an article entitled "He was such a pro he even conned the FBI," July 24, 1981; and the *Wisconsin State Journal,* for material from an article entitled "Imposter professor wins students, loses job," January 27, 1985. This book is more complete with these additions.

DENNIS M. DOREN

Madison, Wisconsin
December 1986

Contents

Understanding
and Treating
the Psychopath

PART ONE
Theoretical Issues

CHAPTER 1

The Definition of Psychopathy and Criteria for the Evaluation of Theory

With less than one month to serve on an 18-month term for fraud, Donald feigned illness and escaped from the prison hospital. Through his own negligence, he was apprehended some months later and sentenced to serve another three years.*

> After losing parole, [Max] became constantly unruly in petty ways, often insulting the nurses and attendants, and several times egged on mildly psychotic patients to fight each other or to resist the personnel on the ward. On being questioned about this conduct by physicians, he glibly denied all and showed little concern at being accused.
>
> *(Cleckley, 1964, p. 48)*

A report about another person states that

> Although he had never had a fever or evidence of an infection, he received penicillin. Although the patient was in a hospital that virtually never gave narcotics, even to patients with painful illness, he had received phenobarbital, codeine, pentobarbital (Nembutal), methodone hydrochloride, and chloral hydrate — all after his withdrawal period was completed. He also received 34 other medicines including meprobamate, imipramine hydrochloride, chlorpromazine, methamphetamine hydrochloride, chlordiazepoxide hydrochloride, and hydroxyzine hydrochloride.
>
> *(Vaillant, 1975, p. 179)*

---

* Based on the case history of Donald S. reported by Hare (1970).

3

When dispassionately describing three murders, William said:

The two kids started crying, wanting water. I gave them some and she [their mother] drove a while — and I turned around and started shooting in the back seat and then turned back and shot her. She fell over against me and onto the floor.

(Symkal & Thorne, 1951, p. 311)

There was no apparent sense of guilt about his actions.

During his evening wanderings through Piccadilly, Dever met the woman whom he later married. Once given a discharge from the army, however, he headed back to America, leaving his wife on the day she gave birth to their first child. Several months later, she traced him to New York, followed him there, and forgave him after he swore eternal faithfulness. The next week, he left for Florida without notifying her. When later referring to the incident, he explained that he simply forgot. He had other things to do.*

All of the vignettes presented were based on the lives of persons who were diagnosed as psychopaths. The stories were considered typical. Impulsive actions, perpetual lying, manipulation of others, guiltlessness, aggression, and lovelessness are characteristic descriptions of these people.

What causes people to behave in these irrational, self-defeating, destructive, and uncaring ways? What did these people believe they had to gain from their actions? What ultimately sets the psychopath apart from the rest of humanity? If societies knew what caused the psychopaths' atypical and destructive behaviors, perhaps their behavior could be brought under control and many people, including the psychopaths, could be spared much pain.

Our current understanding of the psychopath is the topic of the first section of this book. After discussions in this chapter concerning the definition of psychopathy and the criteria to be used to evaluate explanatory theories of the syndrome, a review will be conducted in successive chapters of selected research-based sociological (Gough, 1948), psychobiological (Eysenck, 1964; Quay, 1965, 1977), and biological (Hare, 1970) theories that attempt to explain why

---

* Based on the case history of Howard Dever reported by McCord and McCord (1964).

psychopaths differ from the rest of us. The theories' assertions and their empirical support and contraindications will be presented. Each theory's strengths and weaknesses will be identified. By integrating the strengths from all of the theories and adding a few ideas, a new formulation will be described that can advance our understanding of the psychopathic phenomenon.

Before endeavoring to accomplish those ends, however, I wish to express my sincere admiration to those researchers whose theories are reviewed here. These theorists' work, their hours upon hours of highly skilled labor, has made the integration theory in Chapter 6 possible.

DEFINITION OF PSYCHOPATHY

The first order of business in explaining any phenomenon is to define the phenomenon clearly. This chapter therefore presents a brief integration of definitions of psychopathy. Psychopaths are defined herein both by what they are and what they are not. To place the definition of psychopathy in context, a short historical review of the concept's etiology follows.

Although history and literature show that psychopaths have been with us since ancient times, the diagnostic classification of psychopathy probably began during the early 1800s by the French psychiatrist Pinel. He employed the original label of *manie sans delire* for people who demonstrated notably atypical and aggressive actions. (Pinel's work has been described in detail by McCord & McCord, 1964.) Dr. J.C. Pritchard in England soon extended Pinel's work and coined the phrase "moral insanity" to designate those in whom

> the moral and active principles of mood are strongly perverted or depraved; the power of self-government is lost or greatly impaired and the individual is found to be incapable, not of talking or reasoning upon any subject proposed to him, but of conducting himself with decency and propriety in the business of life.*

* Pritchard, J.D. *A treatise on insanity.* Philadelphia: Haswell, Barrington, & Haswell, 1835. As quoted by D. Henderson, *Psychopathic States.* New York: Norton, 1939.

Near the end of the nineteenth century, however, the term "moral insanity" elicited many strong objections. Religious groups rallied against the implication that certain individuals could not, by nature, do the Lord's work, while the legal community would not accept that people could be labeled insane outside of a court of law.

Hence, in 1888, Koch replaced "moral insanity" with the term "psychopathic inferiority" to quell the objections to the former concept. With those objecting societal forces quieted, psychiatrists and psychologists were free to expand the inclusiveness of the term, which later developed into the "psychopathic personality." An influential book by Kahn (1931), for instance, described psychopaths in a manner which by present standards included "a bewildering variety of hysterics, compulsives, sex deviants, and borderline psychotics" (McCord & McCord, 1964, p. 28). A substantial portion of the psychological community dismissed the concept of psychopathy as unworkable, meaningless, and moralistic because of such expansive writings.

Through the individual efforts of many researchers (see McCord & McCord, 1964), however, the concept of the psychopathic personality eventually became more specifically delineated and widely accepted. Additionally, the name of the syndrome underwent alterations from "aggressive psychopath," "hysteric psychopath," "schizoid psychopath," and "sociopath" to its present form of "antisocial personality disorder," each name expressing its own implications and connotations (American Psychiatric Association, 1952, 1968, 1980). Nevertheless, each of these terms seems to have been used to describe the same people. For the sake of simplicity, the most common term, psychopath, is employed in this book.

The mental health professional's belief in psychopathy as a meaningful diagnostic category has not always been steadfast. Some people perceived psychopathy as a classification designed to be used against aggressive people whom we do not like (a criticism described by McCord & McCord, 1964). To discover an updated professional opinion, Gray and Hutchison (1964) surveyed the beliefs and practices of a large number of Canadian psychiatrists. A questionnaire was sent to 937 psychiatrists; the results showed that 89.3 percent of the 677 responding psychiatrists believed in the meaningfulness of the concept of psychopathic personality. The main portion of the questionnaire listed 29 traits and features commonly used to describe psychopathy. When requested to rank 10 of 29 items the professionals viewed as most critical in the diagnosis of psychopathy, the following features were considered (in rank order) the most significant characteristics of the disorder:

1. Does not learn from experience
2. Lacks a sense of responsibility
3. Unable to form meaningful relationships
4. Lacks control over impulses
5. Lacks moral sense
6. Chronically or recurrently antisocial
7. Punishment does not alter behavior
8. Emotionally immature
9. Unable to experience guilt
10. Self-centered.

These features are similar to the descriptive characteristics of the psychopath enumerated by Cleckley (1941), an early expert on the subject. He described the psychopath as possessing (1) superficial charm and good intelligence, (2) absence of delusions or other signs of irrational thinking, (3) absence of "nervousness" or neurotic manifestations, (4) unreliability, (5) untruthfulness and insincerity, (6) lack of remorse or shame, (7) antisocial behavior without apparent compunction, (8) poor judgment and failure to learn from experience, (9) pathologic egocentricity and incapacity to love, (10) general poverty in major affective reactions, (11) specific loss of insight, (12) unresponsiveness in general interpersonal relations, (13) fantastic and uninviting behavior with drink and sometimes without, (14) suicide threats rarely carried out, (15) sex life which is impersonal, trivial, and poorly integrated, and (16) failure to follow any life plan.

Hare has described the psychopath as

unable to show empathy or genuine concern for others. He manipulates and uses others to satisfy his own demands; yet, through a glib sophistication and superficial sincerity, he is often able to convince those he has used and harmed of his innocence or his motivation to change. . . . Most clinical descriptions of the psychopath make some sort of reference to his egocentricity, lack of empathy, and inability to form warm, emotional relationships with others — characteristics that lead him to treat others as objects instead of as persons and prevent him from experiencing guilt and remorse for having done so. After an extensive review of the literature, McCord and McCord (1964) concluded that the two essential features of psychopathy are *lovelessness* and *guiltlessness*. Similarly, Craft (1965) considered the primary features of psychopathy to be a lack of feeling, affection, or love for others and a tendency to act on impulse and without forethought. Secondary features, stemming from those two, are aggressiveness, lack of shame or guilt, inability to profit from experience, and a lack of appropriate motivation.

(Hare, 1970, p. 5)

The most recent professional source defining the disorder of psychopathy is the *Diagnostic and Statistical Manual of Mental Disorders, Third Edition* (DSM-III) (American Psychiatric Association, 1980). The diagnostic criteria listed there for the antisocial personality disorder are described by the following.

Even though the person must be at least age 18 to receive the diagnosis of antisocial personality disorder, he must have demonstrated an antisocial history before reaching age 15. Specific behaviors and occurrences of importance in this category are enumerated in the DSM-III to assist in the interpretation of what constitutes "antisocial" history. For instance, significant amounts of truancy, excluding the person's last year of school, is considered an indicator. So is expulsion or suspension from school for misbehavior. Legal infractions such as thefts, vandalism, and general delinquency (referring to arrests or juvenile court referrals because of misbehavior) are included as definitional of "antisocial" history. Interpersonal transgressions considered indicative include persistent lying, repetitive sexual intercourse in a casual relationship, and the initiation of fights. Finally, irresponsibility such as significant underachievement in school and repeated drunkenness or substance abuse are enumerated to round out the behavioral definition of "antisocial" history.

After age 18, and for at least 5 years previous to the time of the diagnosis, the individual must also have demonstrated a significant propensity toward antisocial activity. The DSM-III defines this adult form of the condition as including any set of four of the following categories:

1. Poor consistency in work behavior
2. Poor responsibility as a parent (as demonstrated by a child's suffering in any of various enumerated ways)
3. Illegal behavior
4. Poor ability to maintain enduring interpersonal relationships
5. Irritability and aggressiveness
6. Failure to honor financial obligations
7. Impulsivity, or failure to plan ahead
8. Lying, "conning," or the use of aliases
9. Recklessness.

Of importance to the DSM-III diagnosis of antisocial personality disorder is that the antisocial behavior cannot have been due to severe mental retardation, schizophrenia, or manic episodes.

Utilizing those criteria, the prevalence of psychopathy seems to be about 3 percent for American men and about 1 percent for American women (American Psychiatric Association, 1980). The symptomatology usually becomes obvious in men in early childhood, whereas women typically show their first signs during puberty. To give the reader a more complete understanding of the disorder, the following description of the typical antisocial personality disorder is offered:

The essential feature is a Personality Disorder . . . in which there is a history of continuous and chronic antisocial behavior in which the rights of others are violated, persistence into adult life of a pattern of antisocial behavior that began before the age of 15, and failure to sustain good job performance over a period of several years. . . . The antisocial behavior is not due to either Mental Retardation, Schizophrenia, or manic episodes.

Lying, stealing, fighting, truancy, and resisting authority are typical early childhood signs. In adolescence, unusually early or aggressive sexual behavior, excessive drinking and use of illicit drugs are frequent. In adulthood, these kinds of behavior continue, with the addition of inability to sustain consistent work performance or to function as a responsible parent and failure to accept social norms with respect to lawful behavior. After age 30 the more flagrant aspects may diminish, particularly sexual promiscuity, fighting, criminality, and vagrancy.

The disorder is often extremely incapacitating, resulting in failure to become an independent, self-supporting adult and in many years of institutionalization, more commonly penal than medical. It is possible, however, for individuals who have some of the features of the disorder to achieve political and economic success; but these people virtually never present the full picture of the disorder, lacking in particular the early onset in childhood that usually interfered with educational achievement and prohibits most public careers.

(American Psychiatric Association, 1980, p. 317)

A common error must be clarified here. All too frequently, people have inaccurately equated psychopathy with criminality. Craft (1966) outlined in detail, however, that "just as not all psychopaths are criminals, so all criminals are not psychopaths" (p. 3). He stated that there exists a substantial overlap between the two, but they are not synonymous and neither term is inclusive of the other. This issue is of particular importance in the appropriate selection of research subjects deemed to be psychopathic (Hare & Schalling, 1978).

According to some researchers, psychopaths can be meaningfully divided into two groups: primary (or classic) psychopaths and secondary (or neurotic) psychopaths. The distinction, although made many years ago, can be exemplified by the results of a recent investigation by Widom (1978). She set out to form an empirical classification of female offenders based on psychometric and demographic variables. Her findings included four separate types of female offenders, two of which are of interest here. One group, totaling 6.1 percent of her sample, showed themselves to be hostile, poorly socialized, impulsive, aggressive, and exhibiting relatively low anxiety. A second cluster comprising 18.2 percent of the sample was impulsive and undersocialized, but high in anxiety, depression, and other subjective disturbances. Widom suggested that this latter group was guilt prone, unlike the former group of subjects. Her interpretation of the study's results was that the nonanxious subjects were similar to primary psychopaths and the anxious subjects were best described as secondary psychopaths. (A similar investigation by Blackburn, 1975, using male offenders yielded comparable results.) The difference between primary and secondary psychopaths lies in their relative experience of anxiety and depression. They share impulsivity and undersocialization.

The first part of this book, concerning theories of psychopathy, concentrates on the primary psychopath. While some theorists assume that the same psychological, etiological process underlies both primary and secondary psychopathy, this assumption is disputed by other theorists, such as those arguing from an analytic orientation. I will take a conservative stance and not make any assumption about a similarity in etiology between primary and secondary psychopathy.

CRITERIA FOR THE EVALUATION OF THEORY

Each theory reviewed in the next five chapters will be assessed by using the six criteria of a "good" theory specified by Hall and Lindzey (1970). Therefore, each of these six considerations is briefly described below for the reader's scrutiny.

First, a theory should lead to "the collection or observation of relevant empirical relations not yet observed" (p. 12). Any theory should function to increase our knowledge concerning the phenomenon under investigation by specifying through statements, hypotheses, or predictions (which are subject to empirical test) the interrelatedness of events or variables. Without venturing beyond the known relationships or observables, a theory has little purpose.

Secondly, a theory is best evaluated according to its utility, not by its truth or falsity. Hall and Lindzey divided this category into the issues of verifiability, comprehensiveness, and the heuristic influence of the theory. "Verifiability refers to the capacity of the theory to generate predictions which are confirmed when the relevant empirical data are collected. Comprehensiveness refers to the scope or completeness of the derivations" (p. 12). A theory which generates predictions that are often confirmed but which deal with only a few aspects of the relevant phenomenon cannot rightfully be considered as generally useful. Finally, the heuristic influence of the theory describes the capacity of the theory to generate research through the arousal of disbelief or resistance or simply by suggesting ideas beyond the explicit propositions. Hall and Lindzey pointed out that at the present stage of development within psychology, this type of influence must still be valued highly.

Third, no theory should fail to accomplish the "incorporation of known empirical findings within a logically consistent and reasonably simple framework" (p. 13). An adequate theory is one which is both consistent with current knowledge and able to integrate that knowledge in a logical and understandable manner. Any theory which does not adhere to this guideline is likely to generate hypotheses or predictions which will not be verified by empirical scrutiny. Therefore, this third function of a theory can be thought of as related to the question of its utility.

Fourth, simplicity or, as it is sometimes called, parsimony, is an evaluative criterion of a theory. When two theories describe a phenomenon in different ways, but forecast exactly the same events, then the simpler theory is to be preferred. To the extent that the two theories generate different hypotheses, the issue of verification must be considered primary before the relative parsimony of each.

Fifth, clarity and explicitness must be considered. A theory is useful only to the degree that each reader reaches the same understanding of what has been stated. Although the limiting case of explicitness is mathematical notation, virtually all psychological theories have used verbal means of descriptions. Within the context of the present state of theorizing, the question of clarity can be interpreted as the extent to which the theory deals in observables (e.g., overt behaviors) rather than the purely conjectured (e.g., abstract concepts).

Sixth, any useful theory should prevent "the observer from being dazzled by the full-blown complexity of natural or concrete events" (p. 14). Although we are all aware of the great complexity of our world, a theory should simplify phenomena so as to focus our attention on the most crucial aspects of the events. "A useful theory will detail rather explicit instructions as to the kinds of data that should be collected in connection with a particular problem" (p. 14).

Through the employment of the six considerations, the following chronologically ordered theories of psychopathy will be evaluated. Although theoretical conceptions exist which employ hereditary, neurological, environmental, neurosocial, and sociological approaches (see McCord & McCord, 1964), the theories chosen for review were limited to those by Gough (1948), Eysenck (1964), Quay (1965, 1977), and Hare (1970). These specific theories were selected because they are substantially founded in research rather than conjecture. After the critiques of the four theories are presented, a new integrative theory of psychopathy will be described that is designed to incorporate what we have learned from the previous theorizing, thereby improving our overall understanding of the psychopathic disorder.

CHAPTER 2

Gough's Theory — The Psychopath as Deficient in Role-Playing Abilities

In 1948, Harrison G. Gough formulated a sociological theory of psychopathy that described psychopaths as suffering a "deficiency in role-playing ability which is particularly liable to manifestation in social relationships" (Gough, 1948, p. 366). Two major facets of this theory need elaboration here: (1) what is meant by role-playing ability, and (2) how that aspect of an individual's personality could possibly cause all of the other behavioral manifestations of the disorder (at least within a social context).

In explanation of the term role-playing, Gough acknowledged his debt to George H. Mead in enumerating the following propositions:

> First of all, the basis for individual sociality is social interaction, and this interaction is effective in so far as the individual can look upon himself as an object or can assume various roles. This role-taking ability provides a technique for self-understanding and self-control. Learned prohibitions (and all social interdictions must be learned) may be observed by "telling one's self" not to behave in a certain way. Or speech may be editorially "reviewed" as it is emitted, and the inadmissible deleted. Role-playing, or putting one's self in another's position, enables a person to predict the other's behavior. Finally, role-playing ability makes one sensitive in advance to reactions of others; such prescience may then deter or modify the unexpressed action.
>
> *(Gough, 1948, p. 363)*

From this perspective, Gough defined a deficiency in role-playing as "the capacity to look upon one's self as an object . . . or to identify with another's point of view" (p. 363). Psychopaths were seen as pathologically deficient in role-taking skills. Hence they cannot adequately anticipate the reaction of others or comprehend the role of the generalized other, society, in their daily lives.

How does the concept of a role-taking skill deficiency explain the variety of behavioral characteristics typical of psychopaths (i.e., how comprehensive is the theory)? Although Gough (1948) did not directly answer this question, some ideas can be gleaned from his work. A corollary of the previously discussed perspective on psychopathy, for instance, was Gough's statement that "the psychopath can verbalize all the moral and social rules, but he does not seem to understand them in a way that others do" (p. 361). Psychopaths know society's expectations, but in some ways are insensitive to them. This insensitivity can be used to explain their untrustworthiness and, possibly to a lesser degree, their impulsivity. Similarly, psychopaths' inability to learn from experience may be traced to their insensitivity to that which is expected of them. Gough mentioned a few other behavioral manifestations of psychopathy (improvidence, poor judgment, and shallow emotionality), though he did not offer clues about how they were related to a role-playing deficiency. Interestingly, although Gough's theory was originally formulated in 1948, a recent communication from Gough found him to be clearly in support of that which he wrote over three decades earlier.*

RESEARCH SUPPORT AND CONTRAINDICATIONS

Two avenues of research have been pursued in testing Gough's concept of the role-playing deficiency of psychopaths. The first of these centers around the Socialization (So) scale of the California Psychological Inventory (CPI) (Gough, 1957). The second group of studies more directly tests the psychopath's lack of role under-standing.

The So scale of the CPI was derived from the theory of role-taking (Gough & Sandhu, 1964). Underlying the scale is the assumption that the less socialized individual is "less adept at sensing and interpreting

---

* Gough, H.G. Personal Communication, August 1980.

the nuances and subtle cues of the interpersonal situation, and hence less able to evolve reliable and trustworthy residual control systems" (Gough & Sandhu, p. 544). Therefore, items on the scale reflect (in part) the degree to which an individual considers the effect of his behavior on others before acting and the extent to which the person shows optimism and trust in others [e.g.: "Before I do something I try to consider how my friends will react to it"; "I have been in trouble one or more times because of my sex behavior"; "Life usually hands me a pretty raw deal"; "I find it easy to 'drop' or 'break with' a friend" (Gough, 1957)]. (See Stein, Gough and Sarbin, 1966, for further description of scale content categories.) In essence, the So scale was designed to measure the extent to which society's values have been internalized and employed in the daily life of the individual (Gough, 1965a).

Megargee (1972), in a review of the extensive literature on the So scale, found substantial support for the scale's concurrent, predictive, construct, and cross-cultural validity. In testing the scale's validity, virtually all of the studies reviewed utilized a delinquent or adult offender status versus a nondelinquent or nonoffender status as the criterion measure. (The So scale was originally published as the Delinquency scale by Gough and Peterson in 1952. The name was changed when the scale was included in the CPI and the keying was reversed.)

The resulting empirical outcomes indicate that the scale's ability to differentiate delinquent groups from nondelinquents is indeed impressive. Studies have demonstrated the validity of the scale when used with children (Reckless, Dinitz, & Kay, 1957), adolescents (Jaffee & Polansky, 1962), parolees (Deuel Vocational Institution, Pilot Intensive Counseling Organization, 1956–1958), prison inmates (Cohen, 1959, as cited by Gough & Sandhu, 1964), reformatory inmates (Donald, 1955, as cited by Gough & Sandhu), and juvenile offenders (Peterson & Quay, 1959). All of the foreign research cited by Megargee (1972) (from 12 countries) demonstrated not only significant differences on the scale between delinquents and nondelinquents, but differences large enough to be of potential predictive utility (see Megargee). One exemplary set of point-biserial correlations between delinquency status and the So scale scores reported by Gough (1965b) was 0.43 for 3209 males and 0.56 for 1099 females, all subjects being foreign to the United States.

Consistent results have been found when comparing (1) delinquents against nondelinquents in the United States and abroad, (2) offenders versus nonoffenders in military samples, and (3) in differentiating socialization levels within both delinquent samples and nondelinquent samples (Megargee, 1972). "In short . . . there seems little doubt that the So scale is one of the best validated and most powerful personality scales available" (Megargee, 1972, p. 65).

The So scale strongly appears to substantiate the concept that delinquents and adult offenders suffer from an egotistic inability to perceive the effects of their behavior on others. Of importance to note, however, is that none of the studies reviewed by Megargee sampled psychopaths and nonpsychopaths as the subject group. Rather groups of criminals were employed to validate a scale originally based on a theory of psychopathy. Only one study was found that successfully differentiated psychopaths from nonpsychopaths using the So scale (Widom, 1976, using Cleckley's criteria for classification of subjects). No other such comparisons seem to exist. Therefore, the degree to which the So scale substantiates the role-playing theory of psychopathy (versus criminality) remains unclear.

A more direct set of tests of the theory come from the studies which investigate the degree to which psychopathic people actually demonstrate a relative inability to perceive another's role in a given situation. One of the earliest investigations of this kind was by Reed and Caudra (1957). Student nurses undergoing training at a Veterans Administration neuropsychiatric hospital were subjects. Each was requested to describe herself, describe the other three members of a four-person group, and finally to predict how the other members would describe her. Each description utilized an adjective checklist. A point was scored for an adjective predicted about oneself if in fact at least two of the three peers had checked that adjective. The total predictive accuracy score was the sum of those points. After the subjects were administered the CPI, a correlation of +0.41 between the So scale scores (the measure of psychopathy) and the predictive accuracy scores was obtained which is a value significantly beyond the .01 level. The greater the predictive ability, the higher was the So scale. One criticism of this study, however, is that student nurses probably do not represent a sample with even a moderate number of psychopaths, suggesting that this study may not have studied psychopathy at all.

More recently, Moss (1975) and Smith (1976) studied the role-playing deficiency theory from a different angle. In both studies, groups of psychopaths were first delineated from a group of nonpsychopaths. Moss, for instance, formed three separate groups of persons in the U.S. Disciplinary Barracks at Fort Leavenworth, Kansas: primary psychopaths, secondary psychopaths, and nonpsychopaths (differentiated using the criteria enumerated by Cleckley, 1964). Using a variety of stimulus materials, he found that nonpsychopaths were significantly more adept at "postdicting" the behaviors of stimulus persons than were either primary or secondary psychopaths. Confounding the results, however, was a factor of differential intelligence (favoring the nonpsychopaths) which may have played a prominent role in influencing the outcome.

Smith controlled intelligence (as well as subject race) when he formed his groups of male prisoner psychopaths and male non-prisoner, nonpsychopaths (selected through the combined use of case history and Minnesota Multiphasic Personality Inventory data). Starting with the hypothesis that psychopaths should show *greater* person perception accuracy than others in coordination with their exploitative behavior (i.e., they have an increased ability to "size people up"), Smith expected to find results contrary to those predicted by Gough's role-playing deficiency theory. The findings, however, supported the role-playing deficiency conception. Normal males were again discovered to demonstrate greater accuracy than psychopaths in anticipating others' reactions.

In both Moss's and Smith's studies, psychopaths and non-psychopaths were not found to differ on measures of cognitive complexity when the stimulus presented was totally devoid of human or social content. When that element was not removed, psychopaths showed a relative deficiency in the constructs they were able to utilize in an impression formation task (Moss, 1975). This result can be interpreted as supporting Gough's suggestion that psychopaths' relative inability to anticipate others' reactions manifests itself particularly in social contexts.

A recent study of the psychopath's role-taking skills was performed by Jurkovec and Prentice (1977). In that research, psychopathic youths were differentiated from other groups using Quay's classification system for delinquents (see Quay & Parsons, 1971). Using a modification of the role-taking task devised by Flavell, Botkin, Fry, Wright, and Jarvis (1968), the investigators found that "the results on role-taking . . . lend support to theorists (e.g., Gough, 1948) who consider psychopaths generally incapable of anticipating the reactions of others to their own behaviors" (p. 419). Again, Gough's theory was substantiated.

In my review of the literature, few studies were uncovered which did not support the role-taking deficiency theory. One such investigation was that done by Palumbo (1976). The psychopaths in that study did not differ from normals in their ability to (1) emit and receive positive social reinforcement, and (2) emit behaviors appropriate to the roles of task and social–emotive leaders. This research, however, was not viewed as a strong test of Gough's theory because the investigator looked only at the role of "leader" in a game situation. Psychopaths were not particularly required to understand the other players' motives. Similarly, the employment of only a single role position left open a variety of alternative explanations of what occurred. For example, psychopaths perhaps react "appropriately" when in a position of control or influence.

In summary, two types of research directions have been pursued in testing Gough's theory of psychopathy. Studies pertaining to the scale's validity and those concerned with directly investigating the role-playing deficiency of psychopaths both show substantial support for Gough's original conceptualizations. Even so, as described in the following section, some writers do not accept the role-playing theory as a sufficient or even necessary theory of psychopathy.

CRITICISMS FROM OTHER RESEARCHERS

Reviewers of Gough's theory tend to acknowledge its empirical support. Major criticisms have been made, however, of the theory's comprehensiveness and clarity. Hare (1970), for instance, described the role-playing deficiency theory as lacking an explanation of why psychopaths lack role-taking skills. A variety of etiological possibilities were suggested by Hare, such as (1) an autonomic nervous system failure to allow the construction of an "emotional facsimile" of other people's feelings and attitudes; that is, a biologically based lack of empathy (based on Ax, 1962,); (2) they are congenitally low in person orientation such that their behaviors are little influenced and rarely directed toward others (based on Bell, 1968); or (3) they lived a specific family experience involving a stern, remote father and an indulgent, frivolous mother both of whom were overly concerned with outward appearances; this lifestyle resulting in a kind of "show-window display" role-playing child (based on Greenacre, 1945). No matter which of these hypotheses may prove useful, Hare's comments about them demonstrate that Gough's theory is incomplete as it stands. What is needed, according to Hare, is a delineation of that which underlies defective role-playing in psychopaths.

Smith's (1978) major criticism of Gough's theory was the ambiguity of the terminology. The employed constructs of "role-playing," "self-consciousness," and "empathy" were attacked by Smith as "slippery" and full of surplus meanings, thereby making consistent empirical investigations of the theory difficult. Ultimately, by objecting to the lack of explicitness of the theory, Smith called into issue the theory's verifiability and heuristic influence (i.e., its utility).

ADDITIONAL COMMENTS

In agreement with Hare's evaluation of the role-playing deficiency theory, I perceive the theory as substantially incomplete. Although much of what Gough stated about psychopaths has been supported empirically, there have been a variety of relevant research findings since publication of the theory that the theory does not address.

For instance, as detailed in the critiques which follow, psychopaths have been found to differ physiologically from normal individuals. Specific physiological characteristics which seem to differentiate psychopaths from the general public are crucial to the theories of

Eysenck, Quay, and Hare (reviewed in following chapters), yet Gough makes no mention of those differences. Psychometric indexes of extraversion and stimulation seeking also appear to yield consistent differential results between psychopaths and nonpsychopaths (see the reviews of Eysenck's and Quay's theories respectively). Although data supportive of the statements just discussed were not available when Gough formulated the role-playing deficiency theory of psychopathy, the fact remains that the theory as it presently stands cannot account for those data.

In addition, a variety of commonly listed psychopathic personality features are difficult to explicate using Gough's theory. The often cited guiltlessness, the psychopath's superficial charm, manipulative abilities, and hedonistic sensation seeking are characteristics that do not easily fit into Gough's formulations.

My conclusion is that the role-playing deficiency theory is not a sufficient theory of psychopathy, even though what Gough postulated has been well supported. Keeping in mind that the theory was formulated over 35 years ago, its failure to be comprehensive in light of more recent research is not particularly surprising. In the 1980s, however, we need a more complete accounting for the syndrome and behaviorial manifestations of that which we call psychopathy.

SUMMARIZING THE REVIEW OF GOUGH'S THEORY OF PSYCHOPATHY

The role-playing deficiency theory of psychopathy was generally found to be well supported from two different avenues of research. Relatively little research seemed to contraindicate Gough's theory. Additionally, the theory appeared to be parsimonious. Two criticisms of the theory, however, were that it involves ambiguous constructs and lacks sufficient comprehensiveness. These reasons for disapprobation seriously limit the theory's utility.

CHAPTER 3

Eysenck's Theory—The Psychopath as a Genetically-Predisposed Deficient Learner

Hans J. Eysenck's (1964) theory of psychopathy was based on a three dimensional model of personality. In explaining Eysenck's theory, a digression outlining that model will be made.

In essence, the model specified

> That there are certain major personality variables, independent of each other; that these are in great measure genetically determined; and that in conjunction they can be used to allocate a given person (whether psychiatrically well or ill) to a particular point in this multidimensional space.
>
> *(Eysenck & Eysenck, 1978, p. 198)*

Initially Eysenck utilized a two dimensional model. The first axis, called extraversion–introversion (E), represented an individual's degree of gregariousness and excitability. Eysenck (1977) described idealized cases of the extravert as

> Sociable, likes parties . . . craves excitement, takes chances, acts on the spur of the moment . . . generally likes change . . . carefree, easygoing . . . tends to be aggressive and loses his temper quickly . . . and he is not always a reliable person.
>
> *(p. 50)*

At the other extreme, the idealized introvert tends to be introspective, reserved, distrusting of the impulse of the moment, emotionally controlled and reliable.

An axis termed neuroticism–stability (N) represented the second dimension of personality. The person high on the neurotic side of this dimension tends to overreact to stimuli, either overtly (extraverts) or covertly (introverts).

> The place of neuroticism in the general theory of . . . psychopathy is essentially one of a drive variable acting as an amplifier. . . . This is a simple extension of the Hullian principle according to which habit multiplies with drive to produce excitatory potential; the drives of introverts and extraverts determine their habitual activities as laid down in terms of their arousal level; these are then multiplied manifold in persons high on N, while in persons low on N there is no such multiplication, leaving such persons much better able to adjust integratively to reality.
>
> *(Eysenck & Eysenck, 1978, p. 214)*

Eysenck termed a third factor beyond extraversion and neuroticism, that of psychoticism (P), in order to be more comprehensive in his description of personality while simultaneously acknowledging a concomitant loss of the theory's parsimony. He likened this third dimension to that which had previously been called "toughmindedness" (Eysenck, 1977). Psychoticism was his preferred term, however, because Eysenck viewed psychopathy as "a half-way stage to psychosis . . . a dimension of personality which leads from outright psychosis through psychopathy to normality" (Eysenck, 1977, p. 57). Based on empirical investigations, persons high on this dimension tend to be characterized by the following traits:

> (1) solitary, not caring for other people; (2) troublesome, not fitting in; (3) cruel, inhumane; (4) lack of feeling, insensitive; (5) lacking in empathy; (6) sensation-seeking, avid for strong sensory stimuli; (7) hostile to others, aggressive, (8) liking for odd and unusual things; (9) disregard for dangers, foolhardy; (10) likes to make fools of other people, and to upset them.
>
> *(p. 58)*

[Eysenck's use of the term psychoticism to represent these characteristics is not in keeping with the usual psychiatric meaning of the term. Usually, psychoticism connotes a mental disorder involving "delusions, hallucinations, incoherence, loosening of associations, markedly illogical thinking, or behavior that is grossly disorganized or catatonic" (American Psychiatric Association, 1980).]

What does this three-factor model have to do with psychopathy? Eysenck's contention was that psychopaths (and criminals) could be expected to lie in the area defined by high E, high N, and high P. Specifically, persons

> who are situated near the P axis would be likely to be diagnosed as primary psychopaths, while those on the plane marked out by E and N, but remote from P, would be likely to be diagnosed as secondary psychopaths. Those in between, or nearer to the origin (i.e., with less elevated scores on these dimensions) would present considerable difficulties of diagnosis, and create the well-known problem of unreliability of psychiatric classifications.
>
> *(Eysenck, 1977, p. 58)*

The brief description just described encapsulizes Eysenck's general conceptual framework of personality and, more specifically, the psychopath. Eysenck's theory, however, was more than simply a general model of personality. (See Figure 1 for a schematic overview of the theory.) Eysenck designed his theory to specify hypotheses about the *reasons* for the behaviors we observe. To accomplish this goal, Eysenck postulated a set of biological causal relations as anchors to his dimensions of personality. The following biologically oriented conjectures are the essence of his theory.

Eysenck viewed the neuroticism factor as one which dealt with the strength or weakness of emotional reactions (Eysenck, 1977). (Eysenck's use of the term neuroticism may have been idiosyncratic, as he did not imply a high degree of anxiety accompanied high N.) People who react with strong emotions in situations not eliciting such affective intensity from the average person (i.e., people high on N compared to the average person) were said by Eysenck to have been endowed with a sympathetic nervous system and limbic system which

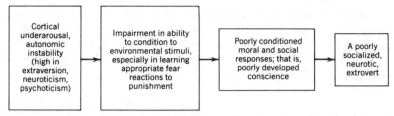

FIGURE 1.   Schematic representation of Eysenck's conception of the development of psychopathy.

are particularly reactive to external stimuli. The opposite was said to be true of people who react with little emotional strength (persons with low N). This dimension of personality was hypothesized to represent the intensity by which one reacts emotionally to external stimuli irrelevant of the specific, personal manifestation of the reaction.

Extraversion, on the other hand, was hypothesized to be related to a particular state of the individual's cortex, referred to as the arousal state. The difference between the experience of the states of drowsiness, sleepiness, general unresponsiveness and the states of high arousal, eagerness, high motivation, and general alertness is something we all understand. Besides differentiating these states introspectively, the electroencephalograph (EEG) has also been useful in this regard. While employing the EEG, researchers have found that the brain can be thought of as possessing a characteristic "idling speed," with high and low levels of arousal occurring as differentially mediated by the reticular activating system (a segment of the brain stem). Differences in people's idling speed appear to be related to their degree of extraversion. Extraverted people are characterized by a low idling speed (low arousal) while introverted people typically demonstrate a high idling speed (high arousal) (e.g., Gale, 1973).

Such findings may appear backward to some readers. Extraverts, people who are physically active, impulsive, and bustling, do not seem to be poorly aroused. Similarly, introverts, as restrained, inhibited people, sound more poorly aroused than highly aroused. Confusion about this state of affairs, however, tends to lie in the difference between two types of arousal, that of the cortex and that of overt behavior.

The major function of the cortex is to coordinate and inhibit the activities of the lower centres; an active aroused cortex is more effective in inhibiting activity than a poorly aroused one. Consequently, high cortical arousal leads to inhibited physical activity; low cortical arousal allows the lower centres to function without constraint or restraint.

(Eysenck, 1977, p. 87)

Putting together the physiological characteristics of the high N, high E person, we find an individual who reacts strongly to external stimulation, tends to be poorly aroused during rest periods in his daily life, and is therefore easily distracted and relatively uninhibited. Eysenck viewed the psychopath in this way. No physiological substrate to the P dimension has been postulated by Eysenck, so that component of the psychopath's personality has not been included here.

The crux of Eysenck's theory lies in his conjecture that the effect of a characteristically underaroused state is the impairment of one's ability to condition to environmental stimuli (i.e., to learn temporal stimuli associations and behavioral consequences). This impairment is especially relevant to the learning of appropriate fear reactions to environmentally punishing contingencies.

That is not to say that extraverts cannot learn as well as introverts. Rather their differing degrees of optimal stimulation (i.e., the intensity or frequency of stimulation at which one learns most efficiently) appear to allow introverts to learn at lower stimulation intensities and hence more readily than extraverts. As Eysenck (1977) stated:

Conditions in real life are seldom optimal, and usually rather poor; thus in real-life situations we may predict that introverts are much more likely than extraverts to form strong conditioned responses, and to form them quickly.

(p. 95)

Briefly stated, Eysenck viewed psychopaths as highly extraverted, highly neurotic individuals who, because of their hereditarily based characteristically low level of cortical arousal, condition poorly to environmental contingencies. The specific failure of highly extraverted, highly neurotic people to develop conditioned moral and social responses (i.e., an appropriate conscience) was postulated by Eysenck to culminate in psychopathy (Eysenck, 1977). Without the conditioned fear to avoid punisment, the psychopath tends periodically to behave in ways contrary to our society's laws and mores.

RESEARCH SUPPORT AND CONTRAINDICATIONS

Research pertaining to only three facets of Eysenck's theory will be reviewed here: (1) the statement that psychopaths are high in extraversion (E), neuroticism (N), and psychoticism (P); (2) the hypothesis of underlying biological correlates of specific arousal and emotional reactivity levels; and (3) the conclusion that psychopaths are deficient in their conditionability. Although Eysenck's theory was conceptually richer than these three aspects imply, other issues (e.g., the three dimensional model of personality, the heritability of psychopathy) were considered of tangential relevance.

Extraversion, Neuroticism, and Psychoticism

Are psychopaths actually high on measures of extraversion, neuroticism, and psychoticism? One commonly employed instrument to answer this question is the Eysenck Personality Questionnaire (EPQ) (Eysenck & Eysenck, 1975), a test that gives scores on E, N, and P, as well as a Lie scale (a measure of the degree to which the subject responded with the socially desirable answer in mind). Eysenck and Eysenck (1978), for instance, presented data using the EPQ on 2070 male criminals and 2442 male controls which highly supported the investigators' theoretical contention. After controlling for the subjects' age, the researchers found that criminals tended to be higher on each dimension (E, N, and P) than the controls. Additionally, the influence of the three factors was discovered to be additive in the sense that increments to a $E + N + P$ score monotonically increased the probability of antisocial behavior. These results were considered by the investigators to be in agreement with their previous empirical findings (e.g., Eysenck 1974; Eysenck & Eysenck, 1973; Eysenck & Eysenck, 1970, 1971a, 1971b).

A serious criticism of the cited studies (e.g., Hare & Schalling, 1978), however, was the use of criminal, instead of specifically psychopathic groups of subjects and the generalization of the results as supportive of a theory of psychopathy. Eysenck and Eysenck's (1978) counterargument to that criticism stated that

> both groups are characterized by the fact that their behavior is antisocial . . . [and] that a much higher proportion of criminals falls into the "psychopathic" ellipsoid postulated in our personality theory than would be true of a control group; this would then enable us to use criminals to test hypotheses concerning psychopaths, with the proviso that a more purified group would show the same effects rather more convincingly and clearly.
>
> *(p. 215)*

Although the researchers' argument might appear logical, it may not be totally correct. The amount of variance contributed by the psychopaths in the Eysencks' studies may have been negligible compared to the variance contributed by all of the subjects' criminality, thereby measuring criminality instead of, and not in addition to, psychopathy. This perspective was supported by Berg (1963, as cited by Hare, 1970) and Schoenherr (1964, as cited by Hare, 1970) who employed the Maudsley Personality Inventory (MPI) (Eysenck, 1959), an earlier version of the EPQ, which also measured extraversion and neuroticism. Using groups of psychopathic criminals, neurotic criminals, and normal noncriminals, those researchers found their psychopaths' extraversion and neuroticism scores virtually the same as those generally obtained from normal populations. One explanation of these negative findings, compared to the Eysencks' results, may be based on the different measure of E and N utilized, the MPI versus the EPQ. The inconsistency of results, however, may also reflect the alteration of subject samples, from psychopaths to criminals.

Cortical Arousal and Emotional Reactivity Levels

Do the dimensions of extraversion and neuroticism represent manifestations of underlying biological processes involving arousal and emotional reactivity levels? Some fascinating empirical results have been found while addressing this question.

Relatively "direct" evidence in support of Eysenck's theory has come from research with physiological measures known to mirror the degree of arousal of the cortex, especially EEG activity. (Although measurement of the activity of the reticular formation would be more satisfactory, that methodology has not been feasible in the intact human being up to the time of this review.) Hare (1970), for instance, reviewed

> evidence that psychopaths exhibit excessive amounts of slow-wave activity [(e.g., Hill, 1952)] and that they give smaller than normal cortical evoked potentials to the second of two stimuli [(e.g., Shagass & Schwartz, 1962), both findings being] consistent with the hypothesis that [psychopaths] are in a state of low cortical arousal.
>
> *(Hare, 1970, p. 64)*

Related evidence comes from a study (Rose, 1964, as cited by Hare, 1970) employing the two-flash threshold (TFT) as an indicant of cortical arousal. The TFT is the minimum time interval required for two brief flashes of light to be seen as a double instead of a single flash. An alert, aroused subject is more able than a less aroused subject to perceive two flashes when the interval between flashes is small. In other words, the higher the level of arousal, the lower the TFT is likely to be. Rose found

> That psychiatric patients with a low TFT tended to be anxious, agitated, and depressed, while those with a high TFT tended to be less anxious, more impulsive, and psychopathic. Thus, psychopathy was related to low cortical arousal as determined by the TFT.
>
> *(Hare, 1970, p. 64)*

This evidence supports a link between psychopathy and low cortical arousal. This finding alone is of great interest. More pertinent to Eysenck's theory, however, is evidence of a direct relationship between extraversion and low cortical arousal. In fact, direct tests of the hypothesized connection between E and arousal have supported the theory. Eysenck (1977) reviewed research which found that (1) recordings of the electric activity of the skin tend to demonstrate that spontaneous fluctuations occur more frequently in introverts than extraverts, and may be regarded as evidence of greater arousal in the former, and (2) introverts tend to have larger pupils than extraverts when both are in a resting state, arousal being indexed here by pupillary dilation. After reviewing other research, Eysenck drew the conclusion about the relationship between E and arousal that

> there are a number of . . . findings which do not prove the theory right, but which all tend in the same direction, and thus support it sufficiently to state that to date it has a reasonably good batting average, as far as validation is concerned. Direct validation of psychological theories which invoke physiological functions is notoriously difficult; this is perhaps as much as one can reasonably expect.
>
> *(p. 89)*

The indirect evidence for the relationship between extraversion and arousal stems from the research investigating certain behaviors known to be facilitated by high or low arousal. As much of this work relates to the conditionability of the psychopath, the relevant research will be reviewed when the topic is addressed in the following section. Let it suffice here to say that the theoretical statements concerning extraversion have been generally supported by the conditionability studies.

When searching for empirical evidence to support the contention that neuroticism represents emotional lability or instability, I found only contraindications. The research described in the following section, in fact, tends to show that the postulate's opposite may be more accurate.

Hare (1968), for instance, divided inmates of a federal penitentiary into three groups depending on how well they met Cleckley's (1964) criteria of psychopathy: (1) psychopaths, (2) mixed group (who met some of the criteria, but about whom there remained doubt), and (3) nonpsychopaths. The experiment was in two segments, a resting phase and an experimental phase. During the baseline rest period, physiological measures of respiratory activity and palmar electrodermal activity were taken. No significant differences among the groups in respiratory activity were found. The psychopaths and mixed groups, however, showed significantly lower levels of resting skin conductance than did the nonpsychopathic group (i.e., the psychopathic groups demonstrated a lower resting state of sympathetic nervous system arousal). Additionally, the psychopaths showed the least frequency of nonspecific galvanic skin response (GSR) activity of the three groups, though the differences were not statistically significant. (Nonspecific GSRs are transient increases in skin conductance that occur in the absence of any specific eliciting stimuli.) These results were consistent with those obtained in other investigations (Fox & Lippert, 1963; Hare, 1965a, 1965b; Lippert & Senter, 1966). Together, these studies suggest

> that psychopaths tend to be characterized by a somewhat lower level of nonspecific GSR activity than that found in nonpsychopaths. Since this index of electrodermal activity, like skin conductance, appears to be positively related to the degree of sympathetic arousal, we might take this to be further evidence that psychopaths are sympathetically underaroused while in a state of relative quiescence.
>
> *(Hare, 1970, p. 42)*

The second phase of Hare's (1968) investigation studied psychopaths' physiological reaction to stimuli. After the resting period, subjects listened to a series of 15 identical tones followed by a sixteenth tone lower in frequency and intensity than the others. Skin conductance, digital vasoconstriction changes (i.e., alterations in the contraction of blood vessels of the fingers) and cardiac reactivity to the last tone were recorded. (Each measure was viewed as representing sympathetic arousal levels.) Neither of the first two measures demonstrated significant differences among the groups in either magnitude or in the rate of habituation to the repetitive tone. When cardiac responsivity was considered, however, the psychopaths demonstrated a lower response magnitude and a substantially smaller reaction to the novel (first and sixteenth) tones. Hare's tentative conclusion was that the psychopath is somewhat less attentive to changes in environmental stimulation than is the normal individual. The researcher found ancillary evidence for his position from work studying the orienting response (e.g., McDonald, Johnson, & Hord, 1964).

More intense stimuli than normal range tones have been employed to explore the same relationship. For instance, cardiac, respiratory, and galvanic skin responses have been measured as electric shock was administered. Most often, psychopaths were found not to differ from normal subjects in their responsivity to the physical stress [Hare, 1965b, 1965c, both using Cleckley's (1964) criteria of psychopathy; Lindner, 1942, using unclear diagnostic criteria]. Occasionally psychopaths were found to react with smaller GSRs to shock than nonpsychopathic subjects [e.g., Lykken, 1957, employing Cleckley's (1941) criteria]. As indicated by Hare (1970), however, all of the cited research using shock employed a classical conditioning paradigm; that is, the shock followed a warning signal. Evidence exists (e.g., Kimmel, 1966) that responses to noxious stimuli which follow a warning can be expected to be smaller than responses without a warning. Additionally, the inhibitory effects of signals may be greater for psychopaths than for nonpsychopaths (e.g., Hare, 1965a). Therefore, the conclusion that psychopaths react to stimulation with equal or less emotional lability than do normal subjects must be considered tentative.

In summary, no research supporting Eysenck's view that psychopaths react with greater emotional instability was found. To the extent that psychopaths differ from nonpsychopaths on this dimension at all, they tend to react less to environmental stimulation. Although psychopaths may score high on psychometric indexes of neuroticism, one cannot rightly assume the hypothesized emotional instability underlying that score.

Conditionability Deficiency

The final research issue concerns the true crux of Eysenck's theory: to what extent do psychopaths show a deficiency in their capacity to condition to environmental contingencies, especially in their capacity to develop a fear-like response to an aversive stimulus? This problem has been investigated using a variety of methodological paradigms: (1) classical conditioning, (2) instrumental conditioning, (3) probability learning, and (4) social learning. Each will be reviewed briefly, the research results described, and overall conclusions concerning the support for Eysenck's postulate offered.

One research design employs a classical conditioning paradigm. The procedure involves a form of learning in which one stimulus acquires the capacity to elicit part of the response normally elicited by another stimulus because of specific temporal and stimulus characteristics. An example is that after the sound of a bell has been repeatedly followed closely in time by the presentation of meat to a dog, the dog's salivation (its unconditioned response to the meat) will eventually be elicited by the sound alone.

In studies of psychopathy, noxious stimuli (in place of the meat in the example) are often utilized to elicit unconditioned responses from subjects: (1) puffs of air to the eyes cause eye blinks or (2) electric shock to cause specific galvanic skin responses. Warren and Grant (1955), for instance, selected their subjects using the Psychopathic Deviate (Pd) scale of the Minnesota Multiphasic Personality Inventory, grouping high scorers versus low scorers. (This method of selecting psychopathic subjects has been criticized by Hare, 1970, and Hare & Schalling, 1978, as not usually accomplishing the goal of appropriate subject selection.) The researchers employed puffs of air to the eye as their noxious stimulus. All subjects were exposed to 60 pairings of one stimulus (S1) followed by the puff of air, culminating in no difference between the groups on how quickly they learned to blink in response to the presentation of S1. However, when a second stimulus (S2) was randomly interspersed during the 30 more pairs of S1 and puffs of air, the low Pd subjects (i.e., nonpsychopaths) learned to discriminate between the stimuli (i.e., they only blinked after the presentation of S1 and not after S2), while high Pd subjects (i.e., psychopaths) blinked indiscriminately in response to either S1 and S2. The investigators concluded that psychopaths, having learned to avoid a noxious stimulus, fail to develop conditioned discrimination because of their tendency to avoid discomfort (associated with a puff of air) by blinking indiscriminately. A partially conscious attempt by the psychopaths to avoid discomfort was suggested. Miller (1966) replicated the initial result that psychopaths and nonpsychopaths do not significantly differ in their ability to learn in a simple classical conditioning eye blink experiment. Eysenck would have predicted differently. The outcomes only partially support Eysenck's contentions.

Results more clearly in support of Eysenck's theory have been found using electric shock to condition GSRs. Lykken (1957) employed shock in a procedure similar to Warren and Grant's in that both studies utilized simple conditioning followed by differential conditioning. In Lykken's investigation, seven 5-second tones were presented to the subjects. An electric shock was administered to the subjects just before the termination of each sound. After those trials, during the discrimination learning trials, four unreinforced presentations of a new tone were interspersed among four reinforced presentations of the original tone. Extinction trials were then run with both tones by presenting each without being paired with shock. During all tone presentations, the subjects' GSRs were monitored. Utilizing several measures of conditioning, Lykken found that psychopaths [selected according to Cleckley's (1941) criteria of psychopathy] conditioned more slowly and extinguished (reduced their degree of GSR responding when the shock was no longer presented) more rapidly than did neurotic criminals (inmates once diagnosed as psychopathic, but not meeting Cleckley's criteria) and normal noncriminals (matched college and high school students). The investigator concluded that psychopaths acquire conditioned fear responses slowly based on the assumption that GSR activity is a measure of subjects' anxiety.

With some improvements on Lykken's procedure, Hare (1965b) also employed painful electric shock and GSRs with psychopathic and nonpsychopathic criminals [selected through a particularly careful application of Cleckley's (1964) criteria of psychopathy]. Hare's results replicated Lykken's findings in that psychopaths showed less conditioning to the original stimulus and less generalization of their conditioned response than did nonpsychopaths. These findings, however, contradict Hare's (1965a) conclusion that psychopaths learn to inhibit behavior more readily than nonpsychopaths when a stimulus signal for an aversive stimulus is presented.

In summary, classical conditioning experiments seem to have shown that psychopaths are deficient in their capacity to learn when an autonomic measure (GSR) is used, but not to the same degree when a skeletal-muscular measure (eye blink) is employed. Hare (1970) explained the discrepancy by the facts that (1) different physiological systems are involved, (2) eye blink conditioning can be affected by voluntary factors, and (3) the same relationship between eye blink and GSR conditioning has been found with groups of normal subjects (e.g., Martin, 1963). The research to date, however, seems to suggest that psychopaths usually acquire conditioned emotional responses (fear, as measured by GSR) less readily than do other individuals.

A second research paradigm, that of instrumental conditioning, has been used more extensively than classical conditioning. Instrumental conditioning refers to the presentation of some form of reinforcing or punishing stimulus to the subject, dependent on the subject's responding in certain ways. This differs from classical conditioning, where the stimulus is presented virtually independently of the subject's behavior.

Most investigators using instrumental conditioning paradigms employ noxious stimuli, either as something to escape (negative reinforcers) or as punishers. An early study by Lykken (1957) employed three groups of subjects defined by Cleckley's (1941) criteria of psychopathy: primary psychopaths, neurotic psychopaths, and nonpsychopaths. Starting with an assumption similar to Eysenck's that psychopaths are defective in their ability to develop conditioned anxiety (in response to appropriate warning signals), Lykken tested his subjects with a maze consisting of 20 choices among four levers. The selection of one lever on each trial was answered with a shock and a signal light indicating the choice was incorrect. The choice of either of two of the levers on any given trial simply resulted in the "incorrect" signal light without shock. The remaining fourth light on each trial was the correct one, its selection leading to the lighting of a different "correct" signal and the "movement" of the machine to the next choice point in the maze. Thus, within this maze, subjects had two tasks to learn, to make the correct choice to move along in the maze and to avoid the shock from one of the three incorrect choices on any turn.

All three subject groups learned to complete the maze with equal skill. The psychopaths, however, demonstrated a deficiency in their ability to avoid the shock compared to the other groups. The failure of psychopaths in this regard was viewed by Lykken as based in the abnormally low anxiety level of those individuals. Similar results and conclusions had been reached in more recent investigations (Bachand, 1978; Nygard, 1975; Schachter & Latané, 1964; Schmauk, 1968, as reported by Hare, 1970; Schoenherr, 1964, as reported by Hare, 1970), each using a "maze" and electric shock. Interestingly, psychopaths who are injected with the hormone adrenaline to increase their sympathetic arousal level no longer show this deficit in avoidance learning. With the same injection, neurotic psychopaths and nonpsychopaths show no improvement in their ability to avoid the shock (Schachter & Latané, 1964). Apparently one can increase the psychopath's ability to learn from an instrumental task involving aversive stimulation by hormonally compensating for their low sympathetic arousal level.

The research results seem to indicate that psychopaths are deficient in their ability to avoid a punishing stimulus, at least shock. An explanation differing from Eysenck's is that the experimental behavioral consequences need to be made more relevant to the psychopaths' value system for them to bother reacting. Salience to their desires for reward may be critical. For instance, psychopaths have shown the same willingness and ability as nonpsychopaths to avoid monetary loss (Martinez, 1976; Schmauk, 1968, as cited by Hare, 1970).

Consistent with psychopaths' difficulty in avoiding an aversive stimulus, one would expect that they should show a deficiency in their ability to anticipate a future punishing stimulus. Indeed, much research supports this contention (Hare, 1965c; Lippert & Senter, 1966; Schalling & Levander, 1967; these studies using a variety of operational definitions of psychopathy). Additionally, when subjects are placed into conditions in which they know electric shock is certain, psychopaths demonstrate less concern and smaller physiological arousal than nonpsychopaths while anticipating the shock (Cook & Barnes, 1964, using nonpsychopaths; Hare, 1966a, 1966b, using a particularly careful application of Cleckley's criteria of psychopathy).

All of the previously mentioned research using the instrumental conditioning paradigm have utilized electric shock as the reinforcing or punishing stimulus. Under these experimental conditions, psychopaths have been found to show a relative lack of ability to avoid or anticipate the stimulus compared to the ability of nonpsychopaths.

The employment of positive reinforcement within instrumental conditioning designs with psychopaths has been relatively rare. In one study by Hutchinson (1977), incarcerated psychopaths were found to be as responsive to anticipated rewards as incarcerated nonpsychopaths. This result seems to be in keeping with the lack of difference on maze completion skill mentioned previously. When working toward obtaining a desired stimulus (versus avoiding an aversive stimulus), the psychopath does as well as the nonpsychopath.

The results of a study by Johns and Quay (1962) appear to contradict that conclusion. Those investigators employed four groups of subjects in a verbal conditioning design employing social reward. Psychopaths and neurotics were obtained using military stockade prisoners and their scores on Psychopathy and Neuroticism scales from an instrument developed by Peterson, Quay, and Cameron (1959) and Peterson, Quay, and Tiffany (1961). Prisoners scoring above the group mean on Psychopathy and below the group mean on Neuroticism were designated as psychopaths. If the subject's scores were above the group mean on Neuroticism and below the group mean on Psychopathy, then he was assigned to the group of neurotics. Experimental and control groups of subjects were made from each of the two major subject classifications, forming four subject groups in total. All subjects were shown a series of index cards each containing a verb and six personal pronouns. Subjects were instructed to construct a sentence using their choice of pronoun and the indicated verb. The experimenter responded in a flat tone with the word "good" each time an experimental subject started a sentence with the pronoun "I" or "We." No verbal reinforcement was ever used by the experimenter in response to the control subject's sentences. The crucial variable was how well each group of experimental subjects conditioned to respond with "I" or "We," the learning being quantified by the frequency of such verbalizations over the four blocks of 20 trials.

Although Johns and Quay concluded that the experimental neurotic subjects learned more than the experimental psychopaths, and hence supported the view that psychopaths are relatively deficient learners, the results were less than definitive. Significant differences among the groups had been found on the pronoun frequency measure during a baseline, nonreinforced condition, including such a difference between experimental neurotics and their own control group. Whatever factors caused such differences could have very easily affected the degrees to which the groups would condition to the later verbal reinforcement. Similarly, psychopaths tended to score higher than neurotics on the frequency measure during the baseline period. The fact that psychopaths conditioned less could therefore be explained by a "ceiling effect"; that is, they had little more they could learn under the test conditions. Finally, the investigators made no mention of the fact that the experimental psychopathic subjects ended the study with the highest scores of any of the groups, a finding that makes the statement that the psychopaths learned less than neurotics rather misleading. In all, the results from this study were unconvincing and the conclusions highly refutable.

Bernard and Eisenman (1967) used a similar verbal conditioning research procedure and found that female psychopaths (i.e., female prisoners with significant elevations on scales Pd and Ma of the MMPI, a somewhat questionable classification procedure according to Hare, 1970, and Hare & Schalling, 1978) conditioned more readily than did a group of female nurses (with no MMPI elevations beyond a T-score of 65). Johns and Quay's study notwithstanding, the psychopath's deficiency in instrumental learning seems to lie mostly in realms associated with anxiety or fear about impending hardship and pain, and probably not in situations where they can be rewarded for their actions.

What about those situations where the probability of punishment is uncertain? A third research paradigm termed probability learning has been designed to address that question. Little empirical work has been reported using that paradigm with psychopaths, though an early study by Painting (1961) touched on it. In that investigation, psychopathic criminals [postnarcotic drug addicts with an Internalization Ratio (Welsh, 1952) indicating anxiety is expressed toward the environment rather than toward themselves], neurotic criminals (postnarcotic drug addicts with an Internalization Ratio indicating anxiety is expressed toward themselves), and normal college students were requested to predict which of two lights would be lit during each of 200 trials. Some subjects were rewarded for correct predictions while other subjects were punished for incorrect predictions (through the gain or loss of cigarettes, respectively). Which light was correct on any given trial varied according to predetermined sequences. Three different sequences of correct light selections were employed with each subject: (1) random, (2) a 75 percent probability that the last correct response would be incorrect on the present trial, and (3) the correct response would be opposite the correct response two trials earlier. During the first set of trials (i.e., the random sequence), psychopaths showed a tendency to repeat the correct response from the preceding trial, a strategy Painting referred to as rigid and stereotyped and Hare (1970) described as "going along with the winner." In the second condition, where the best strategy would be to choose the response that was incorrect on the last trial, psychopaths did somewhat better than did the subjects in either of the other two groups. The third sequence, the most complicated one of the three, resulted in a substantial decrement in the psychopaths' performance compared to that of the other subjects. The psychopaths appeared to manifest deficiencies in the ability to perceive the relationship between past events and present behavioral consequences. One explanation is that the psychopaths lacked the motivation to attend to complicated contingency situations, even when punishment was involved.

A more explicit test of probability learning in psychopaths was performed by Siegel (1978). His three subject groups, each consisting of 25 people, included psychopathic criminals, nonpsychopathic criminals [both formed at a treatment center for sexually dangerous persons using three separate applications of Cleckley's (1964) criteria of psychopathy], and normal noncriminals (undergraduates and Veterans Hospital staff workers). Ten different probability levels of punishment were utilized in a game where the subjects could win or lose chips redeemable for money. Siegal hypothesized that the psychopaths would demonstrate less suppression of behavior as a function of punishment at varying levels of probability than would subjects in either of the two remaining groups. The researcher's operational definition of suppression of behavior was the subject's ability to win money; that is, his ability to adapt to situational contingencies. In support of Siegel's hypothesis, the psychopaths produced less suppression and hence lower winnings than either of the other two groups. Siegel argued that psychopaths engage in cognitive distortion of a magical or superstitious quality that leads them to react to the uncertainty of punishment by surmising that they will somehow be immune. Of importance, Siegel acknowledged the effect of partial reinforcement as an alternative explanation. This latter perspective views the psychopath as affected in a different way from nonpsychopaths by situations involving both reinforcement and punishment. Psychopaths may persist through aversive conditions as long as they believe something positive awaits them. (This concept plays a major role in the theory described in Chapter 6.)

A few tentative conclusions can be drawn from the scanty research using the probability learning paradigm with psychopaths. Under simple conditions, psychopaths tend to fare at least as well as nonpsychopaths. Complexity, however, may substantially lower the psychopath's capacity for constructive behavior, possibly due to poor attention or motivation capabilities. Given situations varying in their probabilities of punishment, psychopaths can be expected to produce less positive results than nonpsychopaths. This latter condition can be viewed as one of a complex nature, either because of the uncertainties involved or because of the partial reinforcement learning schedule inherent in the research design.

The final research paradigm to be reviewed here comes from a social learning perspective. These are investigations that have explored the degree to which subjects are able to learn simply by watching and imitating others who experience rewards and punishment for their actions. Only one study was uncovered that used this paradigm with psychopaths. Using groups of primary psychopathic male prisoners and nonpsychopathic male prisoners (psychopathy being determined using a variety of criteria), Matthey (1974) had his subjects watch a 15-minute interview in which a confederate was seen in one of four conditions involving varying degrees of perceived gain and social reinforcement. Contrary to what Eysenck (and Gough) may have anticipated, Matthey's results indicated the psychopaths were superior to the nonpsychopaths in observational learning and imitation. No difference was found between the two groups of subjects in the observed influence of the type of perceived gain and social reinforcement. (Of importance, the point can be argued that social learning is not conditioning and therefore should not be considered in evaluating Eysenck's theory of psychopathy.

In summary, one must conclude that Eysenck's theory of condition-ability deficit has been supported using only some paradigms. Strong verification has come from the work using an instrumental learning paradigm, especially utilizing shock. Investigations employing a classical conditioning design were less clear in their outcome. The degree of complexity (hence the necessary additional attention to detail) involved in probability learning seems to be a critical factor in that the more complex the task, the greater the likelihood of finding a psychopathic deficiency. Social learning, at least that using positive rewards instead of the usual aversive stimuli, may occur more readily in psychopaths than nonpsychopaths, contrary to Eysenck's contentions.

CRITICISMS FROM OTHER RESEARCHERS

Criticisms of Eysenck's theory have concentrated on two central issues: (1) the quality of the supportive findings and (2) a perceived lack of empirical verification. Attacks within the first rubric involve mostly questions about the validity of psychometric devices utilized in testing Eysenck's theory and concerns about the appropriate homogeneity of people who constitute subject pools. The second set of criticisms emphasize inconsistencies discovered in research results and hence the theory's empirical base. Each of these issues is discussed below.

While reviewing the literature on the personality dimension of introversion–extraversion, Jackson and Paunonen (1980) assessed the validity of two of Eysenck's psychometric instruments, the

Eysenck Personality Inventory (EPI) and the more recent Eysenck Personality Questionnaire (EPQ). Those tests have been used often to substantiate Eysenck's postulates about the extraversion and neuroticism of psychopaths. However, there have been many questions about the scales' validity.

For instance, the factor structure of the EPI was found to be inappropriate given certain theoretical constraints by both Guilford (1975, 1977) and Velicer and Stevenson (1978). Those researchers concluded that the EPI is severely inadequate in measuring extraversion and neuroticism.

Reviews of the EPQ have also been discouraging. Block (1978) pointed out that even though the EPQ Extraversion scale was advanced as an improved version of the EPI scale, the relationship between the two scales remained uncertain. Arbitrary deletions and additions of items from the original measure, as well as the absence of any report describing the EPQ scale's construction or superiority to the EPI, were noted by Block. Stricker (1978) also found the degree of operation of "socially desirable" response determinants in the scale unknown and an acquiescence bias a distinct possibility. Finally, Loo (1979) was not able to reproduce the factors of Neuroticism or Psychoticism using the items from the EPQ. The factor analysis did substantiate a small Extraversion dimension, but it did not resemble the same factor as previous analyses of the EPI. Jackson and Paunonen (1980) concluded from their review that

> these data urge caution in contrasting results from studies that have utilized the EPQ with results based on EPI test scores. More importantly, the data bespeak the difficulty of attempting to relate EPI and EPQ test responses to a general underlying introversion–extraversion construct.
>
> (p. 542)

(Interestingly, although extraversion was the only personality dimension of the three, including neuroticism and psychoticism, Eysenck defined in a conventional fashion, Jackson and Paunonen severely questioned the validity of the EPI and EPQ because of problems in measuring extraversion.)

A second criticism involving research methodology concerns the subjects employed. As stated, Eysenck (and other investigators) employed criminals as participants in his studies of psychopathy with the rationale that both criminals and psychopaths are antisocial and any results found with criminals (a group consisting of both psychopaths and nonpsychopaths) would only be found more reliably if a purer group of psychopaths were employed. Other researchers, however, have taken issue with Eysenck's stance.

Smith (1978), for example, has stated that Eysenck has in effect extended his theory to one of criminality, not psychopathy. "By broadening to 'criminal' from the already imprecise 'psychopath,' the theory inevitably must include neurotic and psychotic offenders" (p. 49). The danger, as pointed out by Hare (1970), is that

> terms such as secondary and neurotic "psychopath" . . . imply individuals so labeled are basically psychopaths. However, this is likely to be misleading because the motivations behind their behavior, as well as their personality structure, life history, response to treatment, and prognosis, are very different from those of the psychopath.
>
> (p. 8)

By grouping primary and secondary psychopaths with nonpsychopaths within a heterogeneous set of criminals, Eysenck may have studied criminality instead of (and not in addition to) psychopathy. This view has been substantiated by the fact that Eysenck's work supporting neuroticism in his criminal subjects was contradicted by the physiological studies employing more homogeneous groups of psychopaths (often being defined as a specific subset of general criminal populations).

The theory has also been criticized because of empirical contraindications. As mentioned, Hare (1970) has stated that little evidence supports Eysenck's contention that psychopaths are emotionally labile (i.e., high in "neuroticism"). On the contrary, psychopaths appear to be autonomically underreactive. In explanation, Hare attributes the discrepancy between Eysenck's postulates and the research results by asserting that "what Eysenck refers to as psychopaths are, in fact, neurotic delinquents" (p. 63).

This perspective is in keeping with viewing Eysenck's theory as descriptive of criminality and not specifically psychopathy. Within the context of Eysenck's theory, Hare believes that psychopaths should be viewed as stable extraverts as opposed to neurotic extraverts as postulated.

Smith (1978) also concluded that Eysenck's theory is ill-supported. In his literature review, Smith cited (1) research showing psychopaths to be more introverted than extraverted (Cochrane, 1974), (2) research (by Warburton) which Eysenck reported in support of his case (Eysenck, 1964) which later was shown to confirm psychopathic prisoners' anxiety but not their extraversion (Taylor, 1975), and (3) research under Eysenck's own auspices which found no conclusive evidence for constitutional or personality deficiencies able to explain antisocial behavior (Field, 1960, as cited by Taylor, 1975). These contraindications coupled with the lack of empirical support from the studies of psychopaths' neuroticism seem to suggest flaws with Eysenck's theoretical formulations.

ADDITIONAL COMMENTS

My overall impression of Eysenck's work was that a few large flaws exist in an otherwise relatively comprehensive, testable, and intellectually appealing theory. The empirical contraindications stemming from the work on physiological correlates of emotional lability (i.e., neuroticism) and rewarded learning capabilities, and the questions concerning criminality versus psychopathy leave at least certain major aspects of the theory open to serious doubt.

The subject characteristics most appropriate to test Eysenck's theory have been hotly debated. Issues beyond the appropriate portion of criminal groups that should be employed, however, have been relatively ignored. For instance, the setting in which subjects are tested, especially experimentally, may affect their performance. Prisoners may have different motivational sets from those of people in the community simply because of the situational demands and expectations. Many times this situational difference has also differentiated experimental and control groups of subjects, potentially confounding the results. (This difficulty can be, and has been overcome in some studies by using two control groups, one criminal and one noncriminal.) Other motivational factors have not been clearly equated between experimental and control groups which can affect the results of conditioning studies. Criminal groups, for example, may be highly motivated to work for a small reward which people in the community find trivial, thereby biasing the results to show greater learning in "psychopaths" when working for a reward. Because these types of influences have not been addressed in research reports, their effects are as yet unknown.

A few comments need to be made about the comprehensiveness of the learning deficiency theory. Some important gaps in the theory were noted. Specifically, the commonly enumerated psychopathic characteristics of manipulative behavior and an incapacity to love (initially listed by Cleckley in 1941) are not easily explicated by Eysenck's formulations. Additionally, although Eysenck developed an explanation of why a punishing stimulus should elicit a learning deficit in psychopaths [based on Eysenck's conception of conscience as a conditioned reflex poorly learned by psychopaths (Eysenck, 1977)], the theory lacks an explanation of why psychopaths may in fact excel in their ability to learn when rewarding stimuli are used (given a noncomplex task and the motivation to attend).

In fairness to Eysenck, however, his theory seems to have been designed only to explain antisocial behavior by elucidating why psychopaths do not condition with fear to aversive stimuli in the same manner as normal individuals. To this end, the theory has received substantial verification.

SUMMARIZING THE REVIEW OF EYSENCK'S THEORY OF PSYCHOPATHY

The conditionability deficiency theory of psychopathy was found to be a rather complex conceptualization of the disorder's descriptive and causative factors. Eysenck described psychopaths as people located within a specific space within a multidimensional model of personality defined by high extraversion, high neuroticism, and high psychoticism (the last two terms being defined idiosyncratically). That view was well supported by research using criminal populations and Eysenck's psychometric instruments. The dimension of neuroticism as descriptive of psychopaths specifically, however, was found to be consistently contraindicated when appropriate physiological (versus questionable psychometric) indexes were employed. Support for the hypothesis of a low cortical arousal in psychopaths seemed strong. As will be described in Chapters 4 and 6, however, that finding has been interpreted in multiple ways, Eysenck's being only one. Eysenck's conclusion about the conditionability deficit in psychopaths appeared well verified as long as one remained within spheres of instrumental and, to a lesser degree, classical conditioning utilizing aversive (as opposed to rewarding) stimuli. Completely in contradiction to Eysenck's theory were the findings that psychopaths learn as well, if not better than nonpsychopaths given certain circumstances. Overall, while the theory has promoted much research, the contraindications and omissions make the theory's continued utility questionable.

CHAPTER 4

Quay's Theory—The Psychopath as a Pathological Stimulation Seeker

One year after Eysenck published the first systematized version of his theory, Herbert C. Quay promoted a related conception of psychopathy with a short article in the *American Journal of Psychiatry* based on evidence similar to that employed by Eysenck. In that 1965 publication, Quay described the psychopathic disorder as a manifestation of "an extreme of stimulation-seeking behavior" (p. 180). As Quay explained:

> It is the impulsivity and the lack of even minimal tolerance for sameness which appear to be primary and distinctive features of the disorder. In accounting for these and related features of the disorder . . . attempt an explanation of psychopathic behavior in terms of the concepts of need for various sensory stimulation, adaptation to sensory inputs, and the relationship of these to affect and motivation.

(p. 180)

There were two facets to Quay's theory. The first was that psychopaths are characterized by a primary abnormality in their physiological reaction to sensory input which causes a higher degree of optimal (i.e., most satisfying) stimulation. (The reader should consult the article by Wachs, 1977, for a full explanation of the optimal stimulation hypothesis.) For psychopaths, this physiological abnormality was hypothesized to stem from a relatively low basal reactivity level or especially rapid adaptation to stimuli.

Quay's second postulate stated that the psychopaths' assumed higher optimal level of stimulation leads to an extremely high degree of motivation to increase sensory stimulation so as to compensate for

47

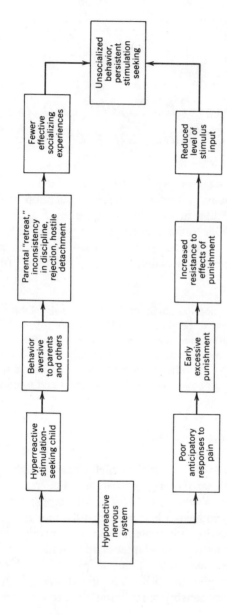

FIGURE 2. Schematic representation of Quay's interactional conception of the development of psychopathy. (Source: "Psychopathic behavior: Reflections on its nature, origins, and treatment" by H. C. Quay. In I. Užgiris & F. Weizmann (Eds.), The structuring of experience. New York: Plenum Press, 1977. Copyright 1977 by Plenum Press, New York. Reprinted by permission.)

their underarousal due to their physiological abnormality. In essence, Quay viewed "much of the impulsivity of the psychopath, his need to create excitement and adventure, his thrill-seeking behavior, and his inability to tolerate routine and boredom as a manifestation of an inordinate need for increases or changes in their pattern of stimulation" (Quay, 1965, p. 181).

As was further elucidated, psychopaths frequently find themselves experiencing a kind of stimulus deprivation, a constant state of ennui, due to their difficulty in attaining or maintaining optimal levels of stimulation due to their extremely high threshold. "Since this condition [i.e., sensory deprivation] is affectively unpleasant he is motivated to change this affective state by the seeking of stimulation" (Quay, p. 182). Summarizing Quay's 1965 theory, the psychopath was viewed as a pathological stimulation seeker due to physiological abnormalities.

Quay elaborated on his theory in a 1977 publication to include environmental factors in the development of adult psychopathy. As portrayed in Figure 2, Quay's newer formulation again stated that the psychopath starts life with an inborn hyporeactive nervous system, the effects of which were viewed as twofold. In one direction, psychopathic children's resultant sensation-seeking behavior becomes aversive to parents who react with hostility, rejection, and inconsistent discipline. These negative reactions cause the children to increase their deviancy, thus increasing the parents' frustration, thereby again increasing their own inconsistency and the children's deviancy. The conclusion is a seemingly endless vicious cycle of interpersonal interaction patterns. The presumed eventual retreat of the parents from their children was perceived as decreasing the potentially positive socialization experiences the children might have had. The outcome is poorly socialized, sensation-seeking individuals.

From the second direction, these children are simultaneously experiencing poor anticipation of physical pain due to their underreactive nervous system (a concept in keeping with the evidence reviewed previously concerning Eysenck's concept of neuroticism). "Since punishment [by the parents] must be at a high level to produce avoidance, the child very likely receives early, excessive (by most standards) punishment for much of his behavior" (Quay, 1977, p.

378). Because of habituation (i.e., the steady decline of physiological or behavioral responses when one is confronted with a repetitive stimulus), however, the child's ability to resist the effects of punishment increases. The parents withdraw from a child who seems beyond their control. The ultimate effect, similar to that of the first theorized series of events, is undersocialized, sensation-seeking children on their way toward becoming adult psychopaths.

In neither the 1965 nor the 1977 article did Quay fully define what he meant by stimulation. My reading of both articles led to the following formulations: (1) stimulation is the impingement on the individual of novel or sufficiently intense environmentally induced sensations of any form (auditory, visual, gustatory, olfactory, tactile, or kinetic), or simply the increase in general emotional arousal levels in response to that stimulation. Hence (2) the seeking of stimulation represents a motivational state geared toward increasing the intensity and/or variability of impinging environmental stimuli or the heightening of emotional excitement.

Quay used the concept of stimulation-seeking behavior to explicate psychopaths' impulsivity, inability to delay gratification, penchant for creating excitement for the moment without regard for later consequences, and their general intolerance for routine and boredom. Interestingly, Quay offered two types of treatment plans for psychopaths based on his 1965 theoretical notions, both designed to compensate for the psychopath's supposed physiological abnormality. The first suggestion was the employment of drugs to increase psychopaths' basal reactivity or decrease their rapidity of adaptation to stimuli. The second treatment plan was to use strong, unconditioned stimuli to condition avoidance reactions in psychopaths, and use strong, unconditioned stimuli coupled with reinforcement varied both temporally and qualitatively to condition appropriate approach reactions from persons exhibiting the psychopathic disorder.

RESEARCH SUPPORT AND CONTRAINDICATIONS

Quay's 1965 theory will be examined initially in this section. After that review, the added features of his 1977 theory will be evaluated.

Two realms of research have been employed in the attempt to verify Quay's 1965 theory. The first of these concerns the demonstration that psychopaths behave in ways that are more sensation seeking than does the average person. The second research area involves the psychopath's abnormal physiological reaction to usual levels of stimulation.

Stimulation-Seeking Behavior of Psychopaths

What evidence exists that psychopaths exhibit a pathological degree of stimulation-seeking behavior? Investigations have explored that question from two directions. The first has been through the employment of psychometric instruments designed to quantify the degree to which one seeks a variety of sensations and excitement. The second research methodology has been through the actual varying of a stimulus type and intensity by the experimenter and observing the reactions of psychopathic and nonpsychopathic subjects. Results from both of these procedures are described below.

In an enlightening article, Schiff (1977) reviewed most, if not all, of the psychometric measures of stimulation seeking. These included the Change Seeker Index (Garlington & Shimota, 1964), the Sensation-Seeking Scale (Zuckerman, Kolin, Price, & Zoob, 1964), the Stimulus-Variation Seeking Scale (Penney & Reinehr, 1966), McKechnie's Environmental Response Inventory (McKechnie, 1972, in Schiff, 1977), and a measure of arousal seeking tendency by Mehrabian and Russell (1973). All of those indexes were based on the optimal level of stimulation hypothesis. Schiff was not able to find significant correlations among those scales contrary to the results obtained by McCarroll, Mitchell, Carpenter, and Anderson (1967), who reported significant relationships between the Sensation-Seeking Scale and the Change Seeker Index, and the former compared to the Stimulus-Variation Seeking Scale.

Unlike the other scales, the Sensation-Seeking Scale (SSS) has gone through a series of revisions since its 1964 publication to its most recent form IV (Zuckerman, 1975). Zuckerman's extensive research has caused the SSS to become the most widely used and best validated of all these scales. [See Zuckerman, 1974, 1978, 1979, and

Zuckerman, Bone, Neary, Mangelsdorff, and Brustman, 1972, for summaries of the development and substantial validation of the SSS scales. Briefly, SSS scores have been found to be related to social behaviors, occupations, physiological factors, and genetic inheritance (Zuckerman, 1979).] Form IV of the SSS is segmented into four subscales based initially on factor analysis of form III (Zuckerman, 1971): (1) the Thrill- and Adventure-Seeking Scale (TAS), (2) the Experience-Seeking Scale (ES), (3) the Disinhibition Scale (Dis), and (4) the Boredom Susceptibility Scale (BS). The four dimensions are not orthogonal, though they seem to represent differentiable modes of seeking sensation and arousal. Each factor was found to be reliable in its item content across the sexes except for BS which was more clearly defined for males than for females in Zuckerman's study. As described by Zuckerman (1978):

> The Thrill- and Adventure-Seeking Scale (TAS) consists of items expressing a desire to engage in outdoor sports or other activities involving elements of speed and danger. Most of the activities are socially acceptable.

> The Experience-Seeking Scale (ES) seems to assess the search for experiences through the mind and the senses rather than the autonomic arousal of danger. It includes traveling, unusual dress and behaviour, use of mind-affecting drugs, associating with unconventional people, and enjoyment of modern music and art. There is also a nonconforming life style and a disregard for "irrational" authority.

> The Disinhibition Scale (Dis) consists of positive attitudes towards variety in sexual partners, social drinking, "wild parties" and gambling.

> The Boredom Susceptibility (BS) items indicate a dislike for repetition of experience, routine work, predictable, dull or boring people, and restlessness when the environment is unchanging.

> *(p. 167)*

Even though the SSS was devised utilizing undergraduate college students, all of the factors seem to come into play in studies of psychopathy. According to Zuckerman, the Disinhibition factor is the most relevant to psychopathic behavior. Indeed, that impression was supported in a study reported by Blackburn (1978). Using groups of primary psychopaths, secondary psychopaths, and nonpsychopaths (defined using an empirically derived MMPI typology), Blackburn found that his primary and secondary psychopathic groups each scored significantly higher on all four factors and the overall general score than did the nonpsychopaths. In keeping with Zuckerman's viewpoint, the primary psychopaths were particularly differentiated from the other groups by their scores on factor Dis, significantly different from even the secondary psychopaths' scores.

Similar results were obtained by Emmons and Webb (1974), who defined their subject groups (of prisoners) using composite scores from the MMPI and the Activity Preference Questionnaire (APQ) (Lykken & Katzenmeyer, 1968). In that investigation, psychopaths scored higher than nonpsychopaths on three subscales of the SSS (ES, Dis, BS), although not on the general factor score. (Because the subject groups were delineated using psychometric measures, this investigation could be viewed as simply a reliability study of the SSS.) Some empirical outcomes based on the use of various forms of the SSS seem consistent with the view that psychopaths score higher than nonpsychopaths (e.g., Cox, 1978, using university students and self-report measures of socialization; Farley & Cox, 1971, employing high school students; Farley & Sewell, 1976, utilizing delinquents versus nondelinquents), though the results are equivocal (Abudabbeh, 1974, using correctional camp inmates and the MMPI for group definition; Shostak & McIntyre, 1978, utilizing three separate sets of subjects, delinquents, adult offenders, and college students, and a questionnaire by Quay and Peterson, 1964). The reader may note that of those studies cited, the ones which employed adult offenders, probably the most appropriate type of subject for psychopathy research of those listed, did not find psychopaths to score higher than nonpsychopaths on the SSS.

Do psychopaths demonstrate an increased need for stimulation in ways other than self-report inventories? The answer seems to be a resounding yes. Quay (1965) cited an early investigation by Fairweather (1953) which explored the learning rates of psychopaths under three different conditions: certain reward, uncertain reward, and no reward. The results indicated that the subjects learned best when reward was uncertain. Quay interpreted this outcome as supporting his theory; the uncertainty of reward was preferred because the variability of stimulation heightened arousal. This, according to Quay, in turn facilitated the psychopaths' learning. (Quay's description of Fairweather's unpublished study did not mention if any non-psychopathic comparison group was used, thereby leaving open the possibility that any type of subject would have behaved similarly. Such might be the case, for instance, in the use of slot machines where the excitement comes in part from the uncertainty inherent to the situation.)

A study of learning rates and the desire for stimulation was performed by Hare (1966b) using psychopathic and nonpsychopathic criminals (defined using Cleckley's criteria of psychopathy) as well as normal noncriminals (i.e., students). With the rationale that most subjects would prefer to receive an unavoidable shock immediately rather than after a 10-second delay (based on Cook & Barnes, 1964), Hare gave his subjects a choice on each of six trials between immediate or delayed electric shock. The delayed shock was viewed as more distressing and hence subjectively more painful than the immediate shock (a perspective supported by Melzick & Wall, 1965). In keeping with Quay's theory, psychopathic criminals preferred the immediate shock 5.5 percent of the time while the other groups chose that alternative 87.5 percent and 78.9 percent of the time respectively. One could conclude that the psychopaths desired the increased stimulation even though it was seemingly aversive.

More recently, Shostak and McIntyre (1978) found limited evidence in support of the stimulation-seeking theory. The researchers utilized delinquents, adult offenders, and college students in a design that differentiated them into psychopathic, neurotic, subcultural, and normal groups based on test scores from a questionnaire developed by Quay and Peterson (1964). Although Shostak and McIntyre could not substantiate differences among their groups on the Sensation-Seeking Scale, the employment of a behavioral task involving visual stimuli resulted in the unsocialized psychopathic group showing the greatest tendency to increase their sensory input. Shallenberger (1976) demonstrated similar results using auditory stimuli of a "highly emotional nature"; psychopathic subjects showed an increased rate of habitutation to the emotional stimuli.

Cox, a student of Hare, took this type of research in a slightly different direction. In an investigation of the physiological and behavioral effects of reduced stimulation, Cox (1978) utilized male university students divided into five groups based on psychometric scores: (1) high on a measure of socialization and low on an index of sensation seeking, (2) low in both socialization and sensation seeking, (3) high on both measures, (4) low in socialization, high in sensation seeking, and (5) about the median on both scales. Group four was the crucial group, as low socialization and high sensation-seeking inclinations are linked to antisocial behavior (and, at least in theory, psychopathy, though one could debate how representative even students low in socialization and high in sensation seeking are of psychopaths).

Cox exposed the subjects to 70 minutes of sensory isolation in an acoustically shielded room. Interestingly, the low socialization, high sensation-seeking (group four) students showed physiological and behavioral patterns particularly similar to those theorized for psychopaths. During isolation, they became drowsy and appeared to use reverie and perceptual distortion as sources of stimulation. The subjects were disturbed by the physical restraints imposed by the recording devices, which was interpreted by Cox as representing a desire to obtain physical stimulation. Despite the students' apparent discomfort, they demonstrated autonomic stability throughout the experimental period, a finding which was anticipated to be characteristic of a group of people who resemble psychopaths in their degree of socialization and sensation-seeking tendencies.

Similar behavioral manifestations of stimulation seeking during experiments have been described before. Orris (1969) performed an investigation of the psychopath's vigilance at a simple visual monitoring task. Delinquents were employed, being divided into groups labeled psychopathic, neurotic, and subcultural according to results from a personality questionnaire by Quay and Peterson (1964). The results from Orris' study showed the expected deficit in the psychopaths' performances relative to those of the other groups. A possible explanation suggested by Orris was that the psychopaths' excessive self-stimulating behaviors (singing, looking around, talking), designed to alleviate their boredom, served to interfere with their vigilance abilities. Likewise, besides finding that their "antisocial" children (not properly labeled psychopaths due at least to their age) attended more to novel stimuli and habituated more quickly than their "neurotic" children, DeMyer-Gapin and Scott (1977) found that the antisocial subjects self-stimulated more through such actions as talking, making up stories, and moving around.

In summary, research verification that persons labeled psychopaths act in ways that appear to be sensation seeking has been found rather consistently. The accumulated evidence supporting Quay's major theoretical statement has been derived from experiments which directly test for stimulation-seeking behaviors in psychopaths as well as research which found such results more coincidentally.

Physiological Basis for Pathological Stimulation Seeking

In this section, the evidence for a physiological basis for pathological stimulation seeking in psychopaths will be explored. Quay's basic contention that psychopaths suffer underarousal due to either hyporeactivity and/or especially rapid adaptation to stimuli will be emphasized.

That psychopaths are characterized by an abnormally minor reaction to stimuli was supported in research reviewed for Eysenck's theory showing psychopaths to be cognitively underaroused and emotionally stable even under physically stressful conditions (e.g., electric shock). The reader should note, however, a potential impropriety in comparing those research outcomes with Quay's physiological postulates. Quay (1965, 1977) did not specify to what extent the psychopath's hyporeactivity and rapid adaptation to stimuli were cognitive or affective. In other words, is the rapid adaptation to stimuli emotional and autonomic in nature or purely descriptive of the psychopath's brain and central nervous system? How should one operationalize arousal and adaptive quickness, using autonomic arousal measures (such as GSR) or cortical arousal measures (such as the two-flash threshold test)? When researchers have referred to Quay's theory, they have invariably cited autonomic studies to argue their points. The cortical investigations employed by Eysenck are not mentioned. Considering Quay has never taken issue with the autonomic arousal interpretation of his theory, that perspective shall be assumed appropriate here.

A frequently cited autonomic study performed by Lykken (1957) was an avoidance conditioning experiment in which psychopaths (defined according to Cleckley's criteria) evidenced both less sensitivity to noxious stimuli (i.e., hyporeactivity) and a more rapid recovery to basal galvanic skin response (GSR) after onset of the stimulation. This finding supports Quay's theory in substantiating both a lower basal reactivity and a more rapid adaptation (i.e., more rapid habituation) to sensory input in psychopaths.

Is it possible to choose between lower basal reactivity and more rapid habituation as the more appropriately labeled physiological substrate to excessive stimulation seeking? A study by Fox and Lippert (1963) has been used to answer that question. These researchers compared the amount of spontaneous GSR changes between a group of 10 male psychopathic offenders (i.e., male inmates of a detention center, each with the diagnosis of sociopathic personality disorder) and an equal number of offenders (from the same detention center) diagnosed as inadequate personalities. As hypothesized, the psychopaths exhibited significantly less spontaneous activity. Based on the Mundy-Castle and McKiever (1953) finding that a decreased frequency of spontaneous GSR responses was related to an increased rate of habituation, Fox and Lippert (1963) concluded that their psychopathic group habituated to stimuli quicker than their nonpsychopathic group. A similar difference was not found between the groups' basal reactivity levels. After reviewing this research, Quay (1965) suggested that "the problem is one of rapid adaptation rather than diminished basal reactivity" (p. 182). In other words, the conclusion was made that psychopaths do not react less than other people, simply that they habituate to stimuli quicker.

But is that conclusion correct? Blackburn (1978) examined more recent empirical outcomes that strongly suggested that Quay's conclusion was not well supported. For instance, a variety of cardiac reactivity investigations (Blankstein, 1969, as in Blackburn, 1978; Fenz, 1971, using a distinction between primary and secondary psychopathy; Hare & Craigen, 1974, using prison inmates and a strict interpretation of Cleckley's criteria; Hare & Quinn, 1971, using prison inmates and a strict interpretation of Cleckley's criteria) have all failed to find differences among subject groups in their rates of habituation of the cardiac-orienting response (i.e., a characteristic cardiac rate change which occurs on the presentation of a novel stimulus). One investigation by Hare (1968), in fact, found psychopaths (defined using Cleckley's criteria with prison inmates) to be slower than nonpsychopaths in cardiac-orienting habituation. (Hare's two groups were similar in their electrodermal habituation rates).

Similar results were obtained by Blackburn (1978) in an experiment which employed primary and secondary psychopaths as well as a nonpsychopathic group (defined on the basis of an empirically derived MMPI typology developed by Blackburn, 1975) in a study of their relative autonomic activity. Subjects' GSR, heart rate, and systolic blood pressure were monitored while the participants were (1) at rest, (2) listening to a repetitive tone, and (3) immersing one hand in iced water (the cold pressor test). Contrary to Quay's hypothesis and Fox and Lippert's (1963) study described previously, primary psychopaths in Blackburn's investigation displayed more spontaneous fluctuations in skin conductance when at rest than other subjects (though the results were not consistently significant). Again, drawing on the results of Mundy-Castle and McKiever (1953), one could conclude that primary psychopaths showed a decreased rate of habituation compared to the other groups. Likewise, psychopaths at rest displayed significantly more cardiac deceleration, thereby facilitating more sensory input stimulation to the cortex (Lacey & Lacey, 1974) than nonpsychopaths. No differences among the groups were found in their rates of autonomic habituation. Blackburn's conclusion stated that "the peripheral autonomic data lent little support to Quay's proposal that psychopaths are . . . rapid habituators" (p. 159). (Although Blackburn did not mention the topics, his concentration on primary psychopaths and his unique method of defining his subject groups may have influenced his results in ways that caused different outcomes from previous research findings.)

Blackburn also reviewed research showing Quay's alternative suggestion that psychopaths are hyporeactive to be, at best, equivocally supported. Quay's theorized outcomes have been found employing GSR measures with delinquent adolescents (using nonaversive stimuli) by Borkovec (1970, using a behavioral checklist developed by Quay, 1964) and Siddle, Nicol, and Foggitt (1973, using a general deliquent sample), but Hare (1968, using prison inmates with a strict interpretation of Cleckley's criteria) could not demonstrate those results when employing adult psychopaths. Similarly, Zuckerman (1975, as cited by Blackburn, 1978) reported that students high on the Sensation-Seeking Scale (a sample of people, certainly not all of whom were psychopaths, though they shared this one characteristic) were in fact more reactive than low scorers. These latter negative findings suggest a diminished reactivity may not underlie the adult psychopath's increased need for stimulation. In summary, Blackburn portrayed both of Quay's hypotheses concerning specific physiological mechanisms as poorly supported.

A review by Quay (1977) is optimistic in its conclusion when it relates that "on the basis of available evidence, it is difficult to choose between lowered basal reactivity and more rapid adaptation" (p. 373). Additionally, "the neurochemical mechanisms for . . . underractivity cannot be fully explicated at this time" (p. 378). At best, no strongly supportive statement about Quay's theorized physiological substrata to excessive stimulation seeking can be made.

Even with this doubt concerning Quay's contentions, Blackburn still promoted the idea of an anatomical base to the psychopath's pathological stimulation seeking, a concept with which Blackburn did not take issue. Drawing on narrowly selected research investigating the psychopath's cortical reactivity, Blackburn suggested that "it may be possible to relate stimulus seeking to the apparently greater cortical reactivity of psychopaths" (p. 162) by utilizing the concept of an optimal level of information rather than Quay's optimal level of arousal. (The reader should note Blackburn's change from autonomic to cortical realms of investigation.) Blackburn's hypothesis, however, seems unwarranted due to the preponderance of evidence demonstrating that psychopaths exhibit a lower, rather than greater than average degree of cortical reactivity (see Hare, 1970, or the review of Eysenck's theory in Chapter 3). In conclusion, the contention that the psychopath's pathological stimulation seeking stems from a physiological abnormality has been difficult to substantiate, even with a variety of postulated anatomical substrata from which to choose.

The 1977 Revision

Quay's newer theoretical formulation essentially added two features to his 1965 theory: (1) that the parents' reaction to an excessively stimulation-seeking child is rejection, inconsistent discipline, and retreat and (2) that the children's inborn physiological abnormality causes a poor ability to anticipate painful consequences of their actions. The first feature is of particular note due to its environmental, rather than biological nature. After 1977, Quay no longer described psychopathy as a syndrome based solely in physiological causes.

What empirical support is there for these new contentions? No direct experimental evidence exists which delineates how parents typically react to a stimulation-seeking child as the degree to which children seek sensation has been impossible to manipulate experimentally. Instead evidence for Quay's postulates has been accumulated from studies which depend on retrospective reports from psychopaths and their parents, and observations of the parent–child relationships in cases where the child appears to be headed toward psychopathy. [Of relevance to the second type of investigation is that the children observed in those studies were labeled psychopathic. With the latest set of diagnostic criteria (American Psychiatric Association, 1980), however, such children would now be more properly classified as suffering conduct disorders rather than antisocial personality disorders, at least until they reach age 18.]

The findings of almost all of the research are consistently supportive of Quay's theory. McCord and McCord (1964), after an extensive review of the empirical literature, concluded that "the vast majority of psychopaths have been rejected in childhood" (p. 82). Similarly, more recent studies have indicated that psychopaths

(1) have equally negative attitudes toward both parents (Megargee & Golden, 1973); (2) report their parents to have been rejecting, inconsistent in discipline, nonreinforcing, and hostilely detached (Hezel, 1968); [and] (3) participate minimally in family interaction and decision making (Hetherington, Stowie, & Ridberg, 1971).

(Quay, 1977, p. 377)

That psychopaths experience or at least report unsatisfying and sometimes overtly poor relationships with their parents seems clear.

Does the child's presumed inborn physiological abnormality cause a diminished ability to anticipate punishment? Investigations of cortical arousal designed to examine this question were summarized in the critique of Eysenck's theory with the conclusion of a somewhat qualified yes. Hare (1970) reviewed a multitude of autonomic research with essentially the same conclusion. (See the critique of Hare's theory in Chapter 5.) Both the cortical and autonomic investigations, however, were typically performed using adult psychopaths rather than children with apparent nervous system abnormalities. Definitive studies with children seem to be lacking.

In summary, the added features of Quay's 1977 theory appear to be strongly supported by the investigations to date. Coupled with Quay's earlier formulations, the theory gives the impression of a rather complete, relatively well-founded explication of psychopathy. The theory's only major empirical weakness lies in the lack of consistent autonomic differences between psychopaths and nonpsychopaths.

The effect of the various methods of defining subject groups in the previously cited research on their inconsistent outcomes is uncertain. From the investigations reviewed, however, one may see a connection between studies employing Quay's questionnaire method of classifying subjects and support for his autonomic hypothesis. Investigations using strict interpretations of Cleckley's criteria of psychopathy (i.e., Hare's studies) consistently fail to support Quay's postulates. One might conclude that Quay's questionnaire somehow selects people with physiological abnormalities while Hare's methodology does not.

CRITICISMS FROM OTHER RESEARCHERS

Quay's theory has not received much direct criticism. To the contrary, several theorists have presented perspectives similar to that proposed by Quay. For example, Petrie (1967) offered a theoretical description of psychopathy which does not differ substantially from Quay's. Eysenck continued postulating and researching overlapping theoretical topics such as the psychopath's reaction to stimuli. Likewise, Hare (1970) described the psychopath's actions as heavily influenced by biological factors (as delineated in Chapter 5). All of those theorists cite research which, in addition to supporting their own viewpoints, helps verify Quay's theory.

After granting the plausibility of the sensation-seeking explanation of psychopaths' behavior, Smith (1978) pointed out the fact that a variety of stimuli, all with their own intensities and sensory modalities (e.g., auditory, visual), have been used to test the theory. The assortment of empirical operationalizations of "stimulation" was perceived by Smith as representing unclarity in the term itself. Such inexplicitness has made the comparison of separate research findings difficult due to differing means of defining stimulation. Additionally, the employment of differing means of stimuli from study to study allows for the accounting of findings which contradict the theory as based on insufficiently strong, or too intense stimulus materials. With stimulation that is too weak or too strong, all subjects can be expected to behave in similar ways, wiping out any potentially supportive result. Negative results, therefore, can only lead to ambiguous conclusions without the addition of substantially more research. This issue, however, was not viewed as particularly damaging to Quay's theory even by Smith. His final statement on the topic expressed that the subject of varying stimulus parameters "serve[s] as a reminder that theory is easier to posit than confirm" (p. 50).

ADDITIONAL COMMENTS

The essence of Quay's theory appears to remain relatively unscathed after the attacks of empirical work designed to test it. Even so, the stimulation-seeking theory seems to be lacking as a comprehensive theory of psychopathy.

Using Quay's formulations alone, it is unclear why psychopaths are unable to experience guilt or form meaningful interpersonal relationships, lack moral sense, possess superficial charm, and show specific loss of insight. Explications involving factors of parental practices, probably one of the most common explanations of moral development (i.e., superego development to the psychoanalysts), seem possible based on the emotional detachment that occurs between parent and child. Counter to that argument, though, Quay's postulates stipulate that excessive punishment is exercised by the parents before detachment happens. Such punishment should, in theory, cause an excessively strong moral system, not what we find in the psychopath.

These post hoc explanations do not lead to a satisfactory conclusion. Eysenck bypassed this issue by including the whole topic of sensation seeking as simply one aspect of what it means to be an extravert, that, in turn, being only one aspect of psychopathy.

The issue of conceptual clarity and explicitness arose twice. First noted was the ambiguity concerning the affective versus cognitive nature of the theorized physiological substrate of sensation seeking. Second noted was Smith's criticism of the notion of stimulation seeking as too broad for consistent empirical test.

Additionally, there appears to be an inaccuracy in perceiving psychopaths as stimulated by novelty. If that were so, one might expect that psychopaths would be involved in a variety of activities to increase their experience of novelty. Psychopaths who become involved in criminal activity would probably commit a variety of different crimes due to their varied behaviors. My personal experience with incarcerated psychopathic offenders (with lengthy lists of convictions) coupled with anecdotal evidence (e.g., Larsen, 1980), however, has led me to believe that at least a significant proportion of such offenders demonstrate recurrent convictions for the same crime, rather than a set of continually novel types of crimes. (An individual's specific favorite crime appears to vary greatly from person to person.) If that impression is correct, it would seem to argue against the concept that psychopaths are naturally motivated to seek particularly novel stimulation.

In summary, Quay's theory was perceived as a relatively well supported, though somewhat incomplete representation of the psychopathic disorder. Although the theory's terminology was found to be sufficiently defined to allow for empirical test, the concepts were viewed as lacking appropriate clarity and potential accuracy.

SUMMARIZING THE REVIEW OF QUAY'S THEORY OF PSYCHOPATHY

The sensation-seeking theory of psychopathy was found to be well supported by empirical investigations of psychopaths' overt psychometric and experimentally bound behaviors. Research studying the

hypothesized physiological substrata of pathological stimulation seeking were not as impressive in their outcomes. Any statement affirming
the theorized autonomic based to excessive sensory needs would seem
unwarranted. The environmental revisions made the theory substantially more comprehensive, though the theory was still viewed as
incomplete and inexplicit.

CHAPTER 5

Hare's Theory—Psychopathy as Biologically Based Response Perseveration

The reader may have noticed that Robert D. Hare's research has been cited frequently in this book. Indeed, he appears to be the most prolific researcher to date of the psychopath's physiology. That fact alone could explain why a theory of psychopathy based on his empirical investigations is included here. Additionally, however, Hare's (1970) theory represents the most explicitly detailed biological theory of psychopathy today.

Hare, drawing support from a literature review by McCleary (1966), delineated a perspective on psychopathy which he termed response perseveration. A description of that theory follows.

Psychopaths were viewed as suffering lesions (i.e., contusions) in the limbic system of the brain which affect the psychopaths' ability to inhibit or disrupt ongoing behavior. One effect of these lesions would be to make it difficult for psychopaths to learn to inhibit an action that is known to lead to punishment.

That inhibitory deficiency was presumed by Hare to cause the perseveration of the most dominant response in any given situation. That is, without apparent fearing, or at least attempting to avoid the punishing consequences of their actions, psychopaths will continually act with their most preferred responses irrelevant of the consequences.

Hare employed this theory to explain why psychopaths seem unable to learn from punishment and appear controlled by their immediate needs with no thought for the future. The theory could probably also be used to explicate the psychopath's irresponsibility, inability to form meaningful relationships, egocentricity, and apparent immorality.

RESEARCH SUPPORT AND CONTRAINDICATIONS

There are three facets to Hare's response perseveration theory of psychopathy: (1) psychopaths have lesions in the limbic area of their brains, (2) such lesions cause the loss of inhibitory mechanisms, and (3) such a loss brings about the perseveration of the situationally dominant behavior. Each of these issues is discussed in the following sections.

Brain Lesions in Psychopaths

Do psychopaths typically demonstrate the existence of cerebral damage? This has been a difficult question to answer. Much of the relevant empirical work has involved the electroencephalograph (EEG), a systematic recording of the rhythmical and transient fluctuations of the electrical activity of the brain.

Early EEG research reviewed by Hare (1970) tended to confirm that psychopaths have atypical wave patterns. For instance, Ellingson (1954) reviewed 13 EEG studies employing a total of 1500 (inadequately defined) psychopaths in which between 31 and 58 percent of the subjects showed some sort of EEG abnormality. The most frequent type of abnormality was widespread slow-wave activity, found in a variety of brain areas. Similar outcomes were found by Knott, Platt, Ashby, and Gottlieb (1953, employing "carefully screened patients diagnosed primary behavior disorder or psychopathic personalities"), and Ehrlich and Keogh (1956, using patients diagnosed as psychopathic personalities); from 49 to 80 percent of psychopathic subjects demonstrated EEG abnormalities, usually widespread slow-wave activity. (The reader should note that the subject classification procedures utilized in early research such as those cited are open to suspicion according to today's standards).

These early findings led some investigators to suggest that psychopathy is caused by cortical immaturity; that because the psychopath's brain is similar to that of children (who typically show widespread slow-wave activity), it is not surprising that the psychopath acts in ways similar to children. This "maturational retardation hypothesis," as it has been called, was used to explain the psychopath's egocentricity, impulsivity, and inability to delay gratification. Hare (1970), however, correctly pointed out that the hypothesis does not explicate why cortical immaturity produces psychopathy, why many psychopathic characteristics differ from those of the average child, nor why approximately 15 percent of the general population show similar EEG abnormalities without demonstrating any behavioral deviance. Hare concluded that psychopathy could be explained by the cortical immaturity hypothesis only if coupled with other as yet unspecified organic or environmental factors.

Reviewing more recent EEG studies of cerebral lesions, Syndulko (1978) concluded that although psychopaths tended to show a higher incidence of EEG abnormalities than normal controls, they did not exceed the incidence noted among other psychiatric groups. In Syndulko's review, six investigations clearly supported Hare's hypothesis while another four were found to have mixed or contradictory results.

In the attempt to differentiate psychopaths from other groups using electrocortical methods, researchers have concentrated their efforts on extremely aggressive, impulsive, and dangerous psychopaths with the rationale that persons with such atypical behavior would be most likely to exhibit abnormal brain-wave patterns. Hill (1952), studying particularly aggressive psychopaths (classified according to the diagnostic impression of the researcher and a colleague), found that approximately 14 percent showed abnormal slow-wave activity centered in the temporal lobes of their brains (the cerebral area which contains much of the limbic system). The incidence of peculiar temporal lobe activity was substantially greater for psychopaths than it was for nonpsychiatric subjects (2 percent) and schizophrenics (4.8 percent). Moreover, there was a tendency within the psychopathic group for a greater frequency of temporal slow-wave activity in subjects who demonstrated a higher degree of overt aggression. Similar results were reported in the review by Ellingson (1954) and the study by Stafford-Clark, Pond, and Lovett Doust (1951, using persons considered extremely aggressive). Finally, Kurland, Yeager, and Arthur (1963) explored the incidence of EEG positive spikes (a particular type of abnormal electrical burst in the temporal area of the brain) in highly aggressive psychopaths (delineated according to the Joint Armed Forces Nomenclature and Method of Recording Psychiatric Conditions, a system with many similarities to that employed by the American Psychiatric Association at that time) with the conclusion that positive-spike activity may be as high as 40 to 50 percent in that population, significantly higher than what was found using controls.

A note of caution is necessary. To consider the research cited as supportive of Hare's theory, one must assume that the EEG can accurately imply the existence of cerebral damage.

> This possibility, though plausible, must be tempered by the knowledge that an EEG abnormality does not necessarily mean that there is a corresponding brain abnormality; nor, for that matter, does a normal EEG always indicate the absence of a brain disorder.
>
> *(Hare, 1970, p. 33)*

In summary, the EEG research has been somewhat supportive to Hare's theory. Syndulko (1978) generally agreed when he answered the question about EEG abnormalities in psychopaths with a "maybe," qualified by his concerns for different studies' methodological problems and deficiencies.

The Loss of Inhibitory Mechanisms Due to Brain Lesions

Unlike the previous section, the issue discussed here concerning the effects of limbic brain lesions on behavioral inhibitory mechanisms can be addressed in definitive terms. The crucial factor here is that this question can be investigated experimentally using lower animals instead of humans. McCleary (1966) reviewed such animal research with the conclusion that lesions within the limbic area cause a loss of the ability to inhibit ongoing behavior patterns.

Experimenters interested in brain physiology have known for some time that certain areas within the limbic system exert a great deal of influence over an animal's ability to alter its behavior given changing circumstances (i.e., ability to inhibit ongoing, previously effective behavior) (Kaada, 1951; Kabat, 1936; Mettler, 1942). No specific region within the limbic system seems to be crucial to that ability, however. Lesions in the septum (e.g., Lubar, 1964, using cats), hippocampus (e.g., Teitelbaum & Milner, 1963, using rats), amygdala (e.g., Bacon & Stanley, 1963, using dogs), stria terminalis (e.g., Ursin, 1965, using cats), the anterior caudate (e.g., Fox, Kimble, & Lickey, 1964, using cats), and the insular cortex (e.g., Paré & Dumas, 1965, using rats) seem to share the same effect on passive avoidance learning (i.e., behavioral inhibition). No matter what specific regions are involved, the conclusion seems clear that lesions within the limbic system can cause a loss of the ability in lower animals to inhibit punished behavior. The argument seems plausible that the same is true for humans.

Diminished Capacity to Inhibit and the Tendency for Response Perseveration

The final issue raised by Hare's theory of psychopathy involves the relationship between the loss of inhibitory abilities and the perseveration of situationally dominant responses. At one time, researchers believed that the behavioral deficit caused by limbic damage (specifically septal lesions in the rat) involved the suppression of a specific fear reaction known as the crouch reflex (e.g., Kenyon & Krieckhaus, 1965; Krieckhaus, Simmons, Thomas, & Kenyon, 1964). According to McCleary's (1966) review, however, the deficit is more general than previously surmised.

McCleary related details of a study in Ursin, McCleary, and Linck (1966) which explicates some of the intricacies of lesion-caused response perseveration. The experiment used a runway with a starting box at the center and two goal boxes, one at each end of the runway. Individual rats, some with lesions and some normal controls, were trained to go to one goal box to obtain food. Subsequently, they were shocked while eating.

When placed back into the starting box to see if they would return to the food or in some manner avoid doing so, the two groups reacted differently. Without exception, normal animals actively avoided the food by running toward the opposite goal box from the food. Rats with septal damage, however, showed mixed reactions. One of the ten such animals ran toward the opposite end. Four of them simply remained in the starting box. Half of the rats, however, continued to run toward the food and recent area of punishment. In a situation where punishment could be expected (as the normal rats correctly anticipated), rats with limbic damage tended to continue acting in ways that appeared to be their most preferred, or most dominant response, give the situational availability of food. Response perseveration was demonstrated by those brain damaged animals.

Similar results were obtained in a study by Schwartzbaum, Kellicutt, Spieth, and Thompson (1964). Septally lesioned rats showed the tendency to overrespond in a pattern which could not be understood as a simple form of hyperactivity when faced with a non-reinforced stimulus in a discrimination task. Increased responding was not found with the presentation of the rewarded stimulus (when compared to the response rate of normal rats). Moreover, the researchers were able to demonstrate that the perservation characteristic of animals with a septal lesion continues during extinction (the cessation of an action on the removal of its reinforcement) even when each animal's baseline level of responding was taken into consideration. Of importance, the overresponding associated with septal lesions was found to wane with continued postoperative practice at the task. McCleary (1966) derived that last conclusion from a host of research.

Zucker and McCleary (1964) extended this type of investigation by using cats and a task requiring the animals to reverse their behavior to obtain food. The cats first learned in which of two positions they could find food that was hidden from them. Then the position of the food was altered. The cats' reactions to the reversal test depended on whether they had an effective cranial lesion (effective being measured by a demonstrated behavioral deficit on an earlier task). Normal cats tended to stop responding briefly after discovering the originally correct position was devoid of food. Animals with effective lesions, however, continued to respond to the incorrect side over and over, despite the absence of reinforcement. (Interestingly, cats that had lesions but did not show the earlier behavioral deficit performed as well as the normal subjects in learning the reversal.) The second time the researchers ran a reversal trial, the perseverative deficit began to diminish such that it was no longer significantly different between the groups. Of importance in evaluating this study, the reader should note that the lesioned subjects acquired the initial habit as easily as the normal controls, suggesting that the difficulty in reversal did not stem from a general learning deficit.

At the end of McCleary's (1966) review, he drew some intriguing conclusions. As McCleary stated:

> It now seems that what is disinhibited by the septal lesion is a response which, first of all, has a high probability of occurrence (or high habit-strength) in the particular test situation, if such a response exists under a given set of experimental circumstances. As we already have seen, factors which increase habit-strength, such as an increased number of previous reinforcements or an elevation of appetitive drive level, increase the perseverative deficit. Furthermore, under experimental conditions in which septal perseveration is quite apparent, the contrasting "normal" reaction of the control animals cannot be viewed simply as one of "response inhibition"—if such a behavioral state can even be imagined. Rather, the control subjects start emitting substitute or competing responses (sitting, exploring) while the septally damaged animal persists in performing the *previously* adaptive response.
>
> *(p. 259)*

One final empirical example should serve to make McCleary's perspective very clear. Liss (1965, as described by McCleary, 1966) placed lesioned rats into a situation where they could avoid a shock through either active or passive means depending on an alternating schedule on different days. The animal's ability to reverse its behavior was observed. In keeping with McCleary's conclusion, the lesioned rats which showed the greatest perseveration when required to alter their behavior from active to passive avoidance also demonstrated the greatest difficulty reversing from the passive to the active. "As Liss pointed out, the important point here is that his operated subjects had difficulty suppressing a currently ongoing response even when it was the 'passive' one of withholding an active response" (McCleary, p. 260).

So what does all this mean for Hare's theory of psychopathy? In brief, it appears that lesions in the limbic region of the brain can (though do not always) cause a loss of inhibitory mechanisms which in turn leads to the perseveration of the situationally most dominant response. How long that perseveration lasts is not clear, as a comparison between the aforementioned studies by Schwartzenbaum et al. (1964) and Zucker and McCleary (1964) demonstrates.

CRITICISMS FROM OTHER RESEARCHERS

The criticisms of Hare's theory seem to center on the question of whether or not psychopaths characteristically suffer brain damage. Researchers do not seem to challenge the hypothesized effects of such damage.

Gale (1975, as described by Smith, 1978) for instance, stated that the EEG research which purportedly demonstrated brain abnormalities in psychopaths has been ambiguous, correlational (as opposed to causally modeled), and more clearly against rather than in favor of the contention that psychopaths suffer brain lesions. By way of example, the research just reviewed found from 31 to 80 percent of their psychopathic subjects exhibited abnormal EEG patterns. Therefore, if one assumes that abnormal EEGs necessarily imply brain damage (which they do not), one can conclude that from 20 to 69 percent of psychopaths do not show symptoms of brain damage. Gale also discussed the relatively consistent finding of EEG abnormalities in habitually violent subjects, though he questioned whether those individuals are psychopaths within the usual definition of the term. The conclusion drawn by Gale was that psychopaths are not characterized by an abnormal EEG or the theorized correlate of cerebral lesions.

Syndulko's (1978) review of EEG studies of psychopathy was not as negative. His conclusion was that

> the studies reporting little or no differences between sociopaths and controls . . . are not overconvincing methodologically and certainly cannot be considered any more definitive than those studies showing differences. . . . When one considers that research efforts have been directed at this problem for almost 40 years, the issue of EEG abnormality incidence in sociopaths begins to appear rather uninformative. . . .

Are there EEG "abnormalities" in sociopaths? The answer is still "maybe," and probably will continue to be "maybe" as long as we ask the same question and try to answer it in the same way.

(pp. 149–150)

Syndulko went on to describe other methodologies for cerebral lesion research, though he suggested that results from investigations using those other procedures have not yielded consistent positive findings either. In essence, Syndulko's conclusion about brain damage in psychopaths was a definite maybe.

ADDITIONAL COMMENTS

The question about whether psychopaths typically suffer cerebral lesions seems to be the crucial one for Hare's theory. Granted such brain damage, at least within the limbic region, the empirical support for the theory generally appears strong (given non-human subjects).

One item from the research concerning response perseveration needs to be discussed, however. As the reader may remember, once lesioned animals were allowed to practice at a task, signs of response perseveration rapidly disappeared. If Hare is to employ animal research to support his theory, he needs to be able to incorporate this learning component of response perseveration. As it stands, the theory does not seem to imply, nor would it seem likely that psychopaths can quickly overcome their physiologically-based deficit, though of course some learning would be expected.

From Hare's (1970) discussion of his theory, he did not appear to intend the response perseveration concept to explain all of the manifestations of psychopathy. Indeed, it does not seem to do so. For example, one could be hard pressed to use Hare's theory to explicate the psychopath's superficial charm, untruthfulness and insincerity, and apparent inability to experience guilt. In summary, as with all of the theories previously reviewed, Hare's theory was perceived as lacking comprehensiveness.

SUMMARIZING THE REVIEW OF HARE'S THEORY
OF PSYCHOPATHY

The response perseveration theory of psychopathy was found to be well supported if one granted that psychopaths typically have cerebral lesions. No strong conclusion could be drawn concerning that issue. Only one type of relevant empirical finding emerged that did not seem in agreement with Hare's formulations—that of the duration of the psychopath's perseverative deficit. As similar to the other theories reviewed, the response perseveration theory was seen as lacking comprehensiveness in explaining psychopathy in its entirety.

CHAPTER 6

The Integrative Theory—Psychopathy as the Persistent Challenge for Environmental Control

Certain research findings reviewed previously have been consistently replicated. As they were often uniquely relevant to a specific theory, recapitulation of those findings from each of the critiques should summarize our current understanding of psychopathy. Such a list follows.

Research on Gough's theory led to the conclusion that psychopaths are deficient in role-playing ability. In essence, the psychopath has a diminished capacity to anticipate others' reactions and perceptions.

The review of Eysenck's theory revealed three consistent empirical outcomes. First, the psychopath tends to be cortically underaroused (and concordantly extraverted), though the specific mechanisms of underarousal were not delineated. Second, psychopaths show a diminished capacity to learn when confronted with punishing stimuli as compared to the conditionability of normal subjects. Third, contrary to Eysenck's contentions, psychopaths tend to show relatively little emotional reactivity to stimuli.

Quay's original theoretical formulation led to evidence that psychopaths show strong tendencies to seek stimulation. Tests of Quay's revision have led to findings that the parents of psychopaths seem to reject and inconsistently discipline their children. Also consistent with Quay's view was research showing that psychopaths have an enhanced resistance to punishment, presumably making aversive stimuli less salient to them than to others.

Finally, Hare's theory brought us into the realm of the biological determinants of the psychopath's behavior. If one grants that psychopaths suffer cerebral abnormalities (a topic which has been studied with the production of inconsistent findings), then we can also infer from the reviewed research that psychopaths may exhibit a diminished capacity to inhibit ongoing behavior patterns. Given the specific brain damage, psychopaths are expected to perseverate in their response pattern even when punishing consequences are present.

None of these findings contradicts any of the others. Even when the theories are viewed as a group, however, they are not fully comprehensive in the explication of psychopathy. For instance, the four theories do not describe why approximately three of every four psychopaths are male. Likewise, the theories lack an explanation of why psychopaths' behavior is frequently seen as manipulative (i.e., involving shrewd and often fraudulent means of influencing others so as to obtain a desired end) (e.g., Smith, 1978). A role-playing deficit does not explain it, nor does poor conditionability, pathological stimulation seeking, or response perseveration. As a whole, the theories of Gough, Eysenck, Quay, and Hare offer us explanations of most facets of the psychopathic personality. Even though each theory seems to address a separate aspect of the psychopathic disorder, however, we appear to lack a complete explication.

The remainder of this chapter presents a theory of psychopathy which integrates the strong points from each of the four theories along with other consistent empirical results into a coherent explanation of psychopathy. In so doing, explanations of the preponderance of male (versus female) psychopaths, of the psychopath's manipulative tendencies, and of each theory's areas of omissions will be specified, thereby making our understanding of the psychopath more complete.

INTEGRATIVE THEORY

In the author's experience working with psychopathic clients, a few major psychological themes seemed to repeat themselves during psychotherapy sessions. These themes rarely evolved with other clients.

For instance, the concept of control, of being able to regulate one's own rewards, has been a recurrent topic of discussion. General comments such as "I really need to be my own boss" and "If people would just leave me alone to run my own life, I would be fine" have been common. More exemplary of the point was a conversation concerning one client's personal life and his relationship with two women:

> I used to control these women. . . . They wouldn't go places unless I said so. . . . Now that's been wiped out. Ain't nothing I can do. . . . They're ripping me up. They're tearing me up.

Later that same session, when speaking about how he anticipated handling interactions with others on his release from prison, the client stated:

> Like when I get out, like [I'm] just going somewhere else where nobody knows me. [I'm] just having nothing to do with folks in Alabama, my folks, nobody; just, you know, become a drifter. . . . [I'll] put a backpack on and hit the highway. I'm really thinking about that.

Is there a more efficient way to take control of the (short-term) rewards in one's life than to abandon all responsibilities except to "number one"? The client seemed to believe that by becoming a drifter, he would keep other people from interfering in his life. From a simplistic perspective, he was probably correct.

Another prevalent theme was that of challenge. Though the psychopathic clients clearly labeled their actions this way, they seemed often to act with the motivation of simply seeing if they could "get away with something." For example, a few clients admitted petty thievery. Ironically, they rarely kept what they stole. Rather, they often gave away the items or sold them for nominal fees.

While working with one psychopathic client, I happened on the individual's delineation of what was fun to him. This is what he said:

> Fun is taking the money I have and start hanging out at a country club and pick up some rich lady and play her for a while. You know, you act like you're rich and all that, but all the while you have her spending all the money. I've done that. To slide a check across the counter, knowing it was bad, you see, sliding it across that counter and matching wits with the teller and see if she was going to cash that check; that's enjoyable, at the time. Now, before it's not enjoyable because you're

anticipating and you say, "Oh, shit, I don't know about this." But once you get there and decide that's what you're going to do you slide it over. When she cashes it, it's a thrill. . . . To walk into a bank and take out a loan in somebody else's name, that's fun. . . . I think that nearly all the things I like to do have to do with matching wits with somebody, an adversary thing. [Therapist: And once you know you won, or can win?] Then there's no fun in it, no enjoyment in it because I already know I've done it, or could do it. [Therapist: Just knowing you can do it?] I have to know that I'm going to do it. . . . I have to have that man tell me, well, this is December 30, man. January 10, I'm going to make you the shop foreman. Okay (slaps hands in a sliding motion), I won't be back no more. Just that when I feel like that's it, I'm gone. . . . Maybe I just have to prove to myself that I'm better than the next guy . . . smarter anyway.

There seemed little doubt when in psychotherapy with this client that he was motivated by things he perceived as challenging. As he became able to receive a sought-after reward (e.g., the aforementioned foreman position), he no longer cared about it. In fact, rewards appeared to have little to do with his behavior. During his young life, he had walked away from job promotions and had given away many of the items he stole.

Sometimes, he saw challenges where other people do not, where the possible reward for "winning" was remote. Consider the following conversation:

You know, if you only speak up when you know you're right, then a lot of times you can make someone believe you're right even if you're not. [Therapist: Which is also a challenge?] Yes, sir!

Convincing other people that he was right when he knew he was lying was enjoyable to him. It was a challenge. In behavioral terms, he was probably reinforced purely because he enjoyed the challenge of the situation.

A similar statement was made by a different client in describing his enjoyment of illegal activities:

I enjoy the rewards, you know, for the things I've done. I'd have to say that. . . . There's a certain sense of satisfaction knowing the efforts (monetary, intelligence, whatever) spent trying to prevent something like that. You know, me against the cops, whatever. Something like that. I suppose there's some satisfaction in there basically. [Therapist: I'm not sure what you mean, satisfaction in terms of what? What is satisfying?] Beating the people who are trying to prevent you from getting this at their own game.

Again, the client appeared to find satisfaction and reward in overcoming a perceived challenge. "Beating people at their own game" seemed of great importance.

What does this say about psychopaths? What is it about control and challenge that is so reinforcing to psychopaths? I asked myself these questions periodically when working with psychopathic clients.

No answers could be found, however, in any existing theory. Gough's role-playing deficiency theory did not help as it does not relate to the issue of challenge. Neither did Eysenck's theory of deficient learning capabilities seem relevant. Quay's sensation-seeking theory suggested that control and challenge could be stimulating to psychopaths, but the theory did not address why that form of stimulation would be so prominent in psychopaths' lives. At times, even seeing how "the challenge" could be stimulating was difficult, such as in the previously discussed example involving lies. Finally, Hare's concept of response perseveration would be helpful if we postulated the behaviors the psychopath finds most preferable (i.e., dominant in a variety of situations) are those which involve control and challenge. If that were true, we could anticipate that psychopaths would enact those behaviors often, and virtually irrelevant of the consequences. Even with that postulate, however, we would lack an understanding of why psychopaths initially prefer those types of behaviors.

After reviewing the research literature, I concluded that the answer sought was enmeshed within various theories and research findings but never addressed directly. Through an integration of the empirically-supported aspects of the four reviewed theories along with additional relevant research results, a theory of psychopathy was developed which addresses the topics of control and challenge. That theory is described in this chapter. (See Figure 3 for an encapsulated representation of the theory.) The initial portions of the theory are

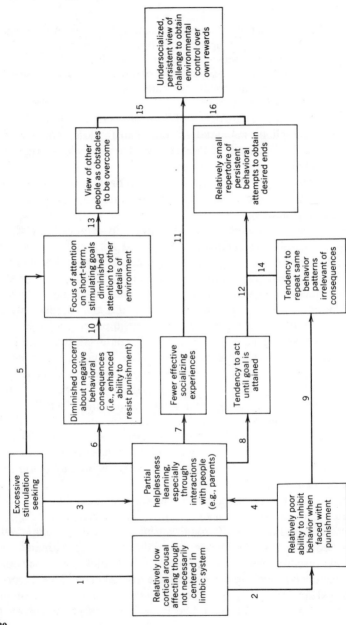

FIGURE 3. Schematic representation of Doren's integrative conception of the development of psychopathy.

largely etiological foundations for the latter, more empirically verifiable postulates. Some of the utility of the earlier sections, therefore, lies in their synthesis of research findings to form a reasonable, logical transition to postulates more testable with adult psychopaths.

The psychopath is hypothesized to be born with a relatively low degree of cortical arousal. This is not to say that they typically suffer brain damage (as Hare's theory suggests). Rather, the person who later becomes psychopathic is born functioning on the lower end of the continuum of cortical arousal, the lower end of a normal distribution. His genetic endowment is not necessarily defective, simply lacking in vitality. Of course, someone born with brain damage could also experience low cortical arousal and thereby be overtly indistinguishable from the undamaged, low cortical aroused child. The point is that, for whatever reason, the child who is later to become a psychopath must experience an early extended period of cortical underarousal compared to that which would be optimal. (Hare and Schalling described a low cortical arousal model of psychopathy in 1978.)

An analogy to this condition can be made to the causes of mental retardation in newborns. One can be mentally retarded because of cerebral damage which severely interferes with one's ability to learn. Additionally, one can be mentally retarded simply by having been born with a relatively low degree of intelligence (i.e., on the lower end of the normal intelligence distribution). Granted, people suffering substantial brain damage are more likely to be mentally retarded than not, due to their brain's loss of effective functioning. That fact explains why mentally retarded populations show a greater proportion of brain damaged people than do normal populations. However, that fact does not negate that one can be born without cerebral damage and still be appropriately labeled mentally retarded. The same situation may exist in regard to cortical arousal in psychopaths.

The innately determined cortical underarousal that is characteristic of the developing psychopath is similar to that which is typical of children labeled hyperactive. A variety of theories have been formulated to explain hyperactivity including at least one stating that the hyperactive child has a physiologically based need for greater sensory stimulation and decreased ability to inhibit motor activity

(Satterfield, 1978). Satterfield contends that the ability to inhibit motor activity and one's level of cortical arousal covary. That contention is of importance in view of Satterfield's theorized relationship between hyperactivity and psychopathy: hyperactivity is a precursor to psychopathy. That view is supported by the work showing that many hyperactive children become children with conduct disorders who in turn represent the group of children who most often become adult psychopaths (American Psychiatric Association, 1980). This author also considers the two syndromes to be related, at least to the extent that they both start with cortical underarousal. Specific experiences (environmental factors delineated below) are necessary to make a hyperactive child into an adult psychopath, but adult psychopaths are expected to have displayed some of the symptoms of child (Attentional Deficit Disorder) hyperactivity.

Lower levels of cortical arousal are theorized to affect the child's limbic system negatively. Even without brain damage, a deficiency in brain stimulation causes a decreased cerebral ability to function effectively and efficiently. The limbic system is delineated here as particularly susceptible only because it is the region which affects behaviors that other people are most likely to notice. As mentioned in the review of Hare's theory, the limbic system tends to regulate our emotions and influence our ability to learn. Since much of our outward behavior is affected by our emotions and learning ability, it seems reasonable to assume that the limbic system is crucial to our ability to function in society. Postulated is that children born with inadequate cortical arousal, however, do not have effective use of their limbic system (as evidenced by the hyperactive child's difficulty in attending, learning, and motor control). Hence they start life at a disadvantage.

There are asserted to be two direct behavioral effects of this biological deficiency (labeled arrows 1 and 2 in Figure 3). The first is the excessive attempt to gain a satisfactory amount of sensory stimulation in compensation for that which is naturally lacking (arrow 1). The second effect is the decreased capability to arrest ongoing actions or general motor activity when confronted with a new set of behavioral contingencies and consequences (arrow 2). As both of these effects have been described in detail within the critiques of other theories (Quay's and Hare's respectively), no further discussion will be made of these issues except to emphasize one point which becomes crucial later. Even though psychopaths' decreased ability to arrest ongoing actions will affect their overt behavior, that process does not imply that they fail to learn behavioral contingencies (i.e., to make cognitive associations). In other words, a learning/performance distinction is critical to evaluate the effects of biologically based deficiencies appropriately.

The effects of stimulation seeking and poor inhibitory control combine to influence the next step in the process of becoming a psychopath (arrows 3 and 4). That next stage, partial helplessness conditioning, does not invariably occur, however, even after the preceding steps. This environmental factor is nevertheless crucial in the development of psychopathy.

In brief, partial helplessness learning is a conditioning procedure where one is both rewarded and punished for the same behavior, one type of disciplinary measure at a time in a random order of occurrences (or at least an order which is difficult to predict.) Sometimes one obtains what one sought and sometimes one gets punished for trying. One is "helpless" because one does not control the schedule of rewards. One is only partially helpless because one can still obtain the reward, albeit only periodically (through the persistent repetition of specific actions).

Partial helplessness conditioning represents one of the two inperative factors for the development of psychopathy. An inborn low level of cortical arousal is the other. These two factors together are necessary and sufficient, neither one being sufficient alone. Even though partial helplessness first occurs after the existence of low cortical arousal, the conditioning process is not directly caused by the biological factor.

How the parents react to a child who is both stimulation seeking and difficult to train through usual punishments is the crucial issue. Quay (1977) suggested that parents often begin to employ excessive punishment in the attempt to control such a child. Interspersed with that increased punishment, however, would also be times where the child obtains the reward he or she seeks because the parents succumb to the child's incessant demands. Quay referred to this pattern of reward and punishment as inconsistent discipline.

I agree with Quay's analysis, as far as it went. The effects of "inconsistent discipline" as they have been described by Quay, however, are not sufficiently inclusive. The only effect Quay mentioned is that the child experiences a lesser degree of socialization than would otherwise be usual. My contention is that much more occurs than a lack of appropriate conditioning. The child also learns some special, peculiar lessons through the process of partial helplessness conditioning.

When in a situation where the same behavior can elicit both reward and punishment from the environment on an irregular basis, children can rarely predict whether an action will bring positive or aversive results. Not doing anything, though, almost guarantees a lack of reward. Hence children under these conditions learn to act when they want something. The actions will be sensation seeking and show little regard for consequences, both in keeping with the children's low cortical arousal and poor inhibitory capabilities. Periodically the children are reinforced by getting what is sought. That periodic reward, known in the literature as partial reinforcement, is an excellent teacher. Inconsistent discipline by the parents (or anyone else) thereby teaches children (1) that they do not control the outcomes of their behavior at any specific time, but (2) persistence in acting may eventually bring about that which is desired.

There are a few points that need emphasis here. First, the term inconsistent discipline should not be construed as implying only the parental reactions to undesired behavior. The process of socialization being referred to includes rewarding and punishing reactions of adults to children's behaviors which are either wanted or unwanted. Inconsistent disciplining of children is the central issue, whether it is designed to increase or decrease the frequency of specific behaviors.

A second issue is how much inconsistent discipline is enough to lead to partial helplessness. After all, virtually all children experience some degree of inconsistency in their upbringing. Based on some research and some conjecture, the contention is that the inconsistency must be frequent, of a relatively long duration, and involving some severe parental reactions (e.g., significant physical "punishment"). In other words, one of the more salient factors in the children's socialization, from the children's perspective, must be the lack of consistent behavioral consequences. As with any socialization procedure, the effects of partial helplessness conditioning on children will be strong to the degree that this socialization process is predominant in their lives.

The third issue pertains to the type of parent who would administer this type of disciplining. Although it is beyond the scope of this book to describe the parents of psychopaths, some comments are of relevance here. One can speculate that, on the average, certain types of parents are more likely to be very inconsistent in their disciplining than other types. For instance, parents who are psychopathic, alcoholic, psychotic, or absent much of the time might fit our intuition. Indeed, many of the parents of psychopaths fit these descriptions (Hare, 1970).

What does partial helplessness learning mean for these children? Three effects are of key importance. The first one (arrow 6), the outcome parents find particularly difficult to handle, is that children show a lessened concern about the negative consequences of their behavior. If children perceive an inability to predict reward and punishment from their behavior, and a benefit from withstanding some punishment in order to receive a reward, then punishment loses its usual capabilities for behavioral control. Instead children become focused on how to get what they want in the quickest manner possible, without concern for the punishment that may be likely along the way. (They would not withdraw from situations where some helplessness exists because they have learned that reward is possible only through action, as described in greater detail below). In essence, children develop an enhanced ability to withstand punishment and resist its ability to alter their behavior.

Similarly, children will show a tendency to continue acting, doing something, until the desired end is obtained (arrow 8). Through the previously described partial reinforcement learning process, the children have been taught to persevere in their actions, through any punishment, until the reward is received. By way of example, consider the boy who throws a temper tantrum over a desired toy in a store window. Initially the mother denies his request, stating that he has not been a good boy. The child persists, however, making himself difficult to handle. Among the many comments made by the mother is "We'll see later!" The child has obtained a ray of hope (reinforcement for his whining), so he continues to pester his mother. This time she gives him an excessively hard spanking, partially from her desire to discipline the child and partially from her own frustration. Still the child persists, this time because persistence the last time he was at the store got him some extra cookies. Finally, with exasperation, she buys the toy for her son with the rationale that she would do so only this once. Unfortunately, she has just made her situation even more difficult next time. She has again reinforced the child's learning that if he perseveres through punishment (negative evaluations, spanking), then he eventually will get what he wants. The process would be similar given any case of inconsistent discipline occurring during a single incident (as in the example) or among events divided by time. Each new occurrence reinforces the learning from times previous. The final lesson is that through the maintenance of overt action, the child will obtain his goal at the possible cost of punishment along the way.

The third effect of partial helplessness learning (besides diminished concern about negative consequences and the tenacious inclination to act until a reward is obtained) is a diminished degree of appropriate socialization, a concept in keeping with Quay's (1977) theory (arrow 7). Because the children's interactions with their parents (or adults in general) elicit frustration and inconsistent actions on their part, the children do not experience the same degree of socialization to society's expectations as other children. They fail to learn to appreciate emotional closeness, that being associated with frustration and inconsistency. They fail to understand the value of long-term goals. Additionally, the children not only fail to learn society's mores, but they often learn other rules instead, such as to take what they want and ignore their effects on others.

From this stage on, there are three major avenues of influence leading to the full development of psychopathy, each stemming from one of the three effects of partial helplessness conditioning. The first of these (represented by arrows 5, 10, 13, and 15) explains how psychopaths come to their peculiar view of people and the environment. The second arrow (arrow 11) describes the major source of poor socialization which leads to an undersocialized individual. The final avenue (arrows 9, 12, 14 and 16) explains how developing psychopaths learn to seek rewards, given their low cortical arousal and early conditioning experiences. The combined influence of these three avenues culminates the etiology of psychopathy. Each direction of influence is discussed in detail next.

The first avenue leads to the psychopaths' peculiar view of people and the environment. The process begins with psychopaths' diminished interest in negative consequences of their behavior. From this factor, coupled with the influence of the need for stimulation, adult psychopaths' perception of others can be derived in the manner described.

Minimized attention to negative behavioral consequences leads psychopaths to concentrate almost solely on the obtainment of rein-forcement, even at the cost of punishing consequences. The reinforce-ment they seek is sensation and physiological excitement due to their ever present need for stimulation. Additionally, that reinforcement would be the fulfillment of immediate desires rather than long-term plans for two reasons: (1) their learned perception that the future (i.e., consequences of their behavior) is largely unpredictable and (2) their relatively immediate physiological need for stimulation. The effect of minimized attention to negative behavioral consequences, therefore, would be a focusing of attention on short-term goals of stimulation (arrow 10).

Other details in the environment, those considered extraneous to their immediate needs, would be largely ignored by the developing psychopath. Their interests would become substantially focused on how their immediate environment could influence the satisfaction of their wants. This characteristic of the developing psychopath is what has been termed egocentricity, the tendency to view the environment and particularly other people's actions almost solely from a perspective of one's own interests.

That egocentricity, coupled with the propensity to give short-term stimulating goals highest priority, brings about the psychopaths' abnormal perspective on other people (arrow 13). Unlike the usual individual who interacts with at least some people with concern, love, and as an equal, psychopaths come to view others as objects to be manipulated for the purpose of obtaining what the psychopaths want.

Due to their focused attention, people are ignored as inconsequential details of the environment; or, when related to the psychopaths' wants, perceived as of potential importance to their satisfying their immediate yearnings. As the former, people are seen as of no importance whatsoever. In the latter condition, they become either objects of satisfaction (such as a sexual partner) or, more usually, obstacles interfering with the psychopaths' wishes (such as someone with opposing authority or desires).

When seen as obstacles, people represent environmental impediments to the satisfaction of the psychopaths' desires. Based on their previously learned capability to ignore potential punishment and their continual tendency to act when frustrated, the psychopaths will usually act in response to what they see as a challenge to their ability to satisfy their desires. They have learned through partial helplessness conditioning not to back down when confronted with an obstacle to the satisfaction of their wants. Similarly, they have been conditioned to view others as obstacles to be surmounted because that approach has served in the satisfaction of desires before (during partial helplessness conditioning). In essence, psychopaths view people within their field of attention as objects which challenge the psychopaths' obtainment and control of the environmental rewards they seek.

For definitional purposes, the perception of people as objects can be described in multiple ways: (1) a demonstrated minimal concern about the welfare of others even when there is no aversive outcome to that concern, (2) an attitude about others which suggests people are no more than tools to be manipulated toward one's own ends, or (3) the expectation that people will act in stereotypical ways. These affective, attitudinal, and cognitive definitions all suggest a psychopathic emotional detachment from others.

Psychopaths could no more come to love another person than they could love any environmental object. They do not view the two in significantly different ways. From this line of reasoning, the fact that psychopaths do not show guilt after injuring other people is more expected than surprising.

Lacking strong emotional ties to other people, however, does not explain why psychopaths are so often antisocial in their behavior. One can certainly be asocial without necessarily acting in ways contrary to society's laws and mores.

The second avenue of influence explicates the antisocial nature of psychopaths' actions. Not only do developing psychopaths learn to view people as objects and obstacles, but they also fail to experience effective socialization through their interactions with parents and other adults (arrow 7). While receiving a deficient level of effective socializing experiences, developing psychopaths do not simply remain uneducated in ways to seek what they want. Rather, they spend those formative years learning actions society wishes they never did, ways to satisfy their desires that are often illegal and harmful to others. Coupled with the propensity toward the satisfaction of immediate stimulation goals, psychopaths rarely demonstrate the socialized characteristic termed the delay of gratification. The result is individuals who not only lack proper training, but who have learned many behaviors which are inappropriate, destructive, and short sighted (arrow 11).

Of importance, the developing psychopaths experience some enjoyment from their destructive actions, this enjoyment being based on two causal factors. The first is the frustration they often feel stemming from the unpredictable punishment they blame on others. Destructive behavior can be their way of fighting back. The second factor reinforcing destructive actions is the sensory stimulation and emotional excitement that they bring. Such behavior often causes a great deal of immediate stimulation and extended attention and reactions from others, both of which psychopaths will enjoy.

The last avenue of influence describes how psychopaths have learned to approach the problem of getting what they want. The preceding argument already concluded that psychopaths demonstrate a relatively poor ability to inhibit behavior patterns when faced with punishment because of their impaired limbic system. In keeping with the evidence reviewed for Hare's response perseveration theory, that lack of inhibitory capacity is viewed as causing psychopaths to repeat the same set of behaviors over and over again, virtually irrelevant of the consequences of their actions (arrow 9). The implication that psychopaths fail to learn the contingencies of their behavior (as Eysenck stated) is only partly true. If psychopaths attend to behavioral outcomes, they sometimes learn even more rapidly than normal individuals because of their tendency to focus on a small set of environmental features. (That postulate is supported by the results of research using rewards reviewed in Chapter 3.) As psychopaths concentrate a great deal of effort toward that which interests them, they will not show a learning deficiency if they attend to all of the relevant environmental cues.

The catch to that argument, of course, is that psychopaths must first attend to all of the important details of their environment. Usually, because of their characteristically tunneled attention, they fail to learn of the pertinent environmental cues and hence fail to differentiate one situation from another accurately. For example, they might react to the request of a police officer in essentially the same way they have learned to dismiss requests from fellow employees at work or drinking buddies at the local gin mill. Or psychopaths may interact with their wives in the same manner they have treated prostitutes much of their life.

The psychopaths may be reinforced for approaching many situations with the same small set of behaviors. Sometimes, the actions serve to accomplish what they want. That occasional success represents a partial reinforcement learning pattern, one of the most effective conditioning procedures known. As far as the failures are concerned, one must remember that psychopaths have been conditioned to expect reward only on an occasional basis. As long as they are rewarded a sufficient number of times in between the periods of punishment, psychopaths will fail to discriminate among the variety of superficially similar situations and therefore perform a multitude of self-defeating, self-destructive, and socially harmful behaviors. Based on what is known about conditioning, psychopaths are expected to generalize the application of their limited set of behaviors to more and more situations as they are continually reinforced (on a short-term basis) for doing so.

As mentioned previously, one of the major effects of psychopaths' early partial helplessness conditioning is to persevere in action until their desired end is obtained (arrow 8). Rather than give up in desperation when apparently defeated, psychopaths will tend to persist by doing something to keep the possibility of reward alive.

They have been conditioned to do so. They have learned to respond to the perceived challenge. The tendency to act when frustrated, however, does not tell us what form those actions will take. After all, persistence toward the accomplishment of a goal can be a highly favorable characteristic.

Unfortunately, psychopaths' perseverance does not usually lead them toward societally approved pursuits. One must remember that psychopaths are most interested in short-term, physiologically stimulating goals. The persistence they demonstrate is rarely toward any long-term end. Moreover, their antisocial, egocentric morality does not incline them to act in ways society would find beneficial. Finally, their persistence can only be coupled with the knowledge of effective actions available to them (arrows 12 and 14). Even though psychopaths are conditioned to act when frustrated, the repertoire of behaviors they draw on is substantially smaller than that for normal individuals who have learned to discriminate among similar situations differing only in some critical way. Hence the psychopaths' determination to succeed in obtaining a desired goal is marred by their short-sightedness, immorality, and limited repertoire of behaviors from which to choose. (These characteristics explain the frequently heard remarks concerning psychopaths that usually begin with "If they would only exert all that effort toward something constructive. . . .")

At the end of the complete etiological process, the three avenues of influence combine to form undersocialized individuals who persist in performing a limited number of behaviors to obtain short-term goals (arrows 11, 15, and 16). Their way of perceiving the world is egocentric and substantially lacking in detail, implying that they view the world in simplistic terms (exemplified by comments such as "If everyone would just leave me alone, I would be fine"). The blame for their failures is usually placed by them onto other people in keeping with their perspective that the behavioral contingencies to which they are subjected are unpredictable and governed by others. If psychopaths cannot fully govern what happens after they act, how can they be responsible for the result?

They strive to control their capability to obtain short-term stimulation and excitement. The challenge of gaining such control over their environment and the perception of control become stimulating in and of themselves through being associated with intermittent rewards in a process called secondary conditioning. [Perceived environmental control is defined as the expectation that one can effectively regulate situational factors of reward and punishment. Perceived challenge is defined as any of the following: (1) movement toward a goal considered difficult to reach, (2) action against a person or object with the explicit purpose of demonstrating an ability to manipulate the person or object, (3) movement in response to other people's comments specifically to demonstrate the inaccuracy of those comments (such as "You can't"), or (4) behavior designed to cause specific actions from others, actions they would not otherwise make. The first possible definition of challenge may not often apply to psychopaths due to their desire for short-term goals of stimulation, rather than long-term goals which require concentrated effort over a long period of time for their attainment.] Psychopaths stop needing successful outcomes to reinforce their enjoyment of a challenge and the experience of environmental control. Those experiences become rewarding by themselves. As secondary reinforcers, the products of secondary conditioning, the perception of environmental challenge and control become self-perpetuating goals for the psychopath.

The etiology of those goals can actually be traced to psychopaths' longstanding excessive stimulation needs and early partial helplessness training. Psychopaths have learned that rewards of stimulation are generally won only after battles with punishment. Hence they concentrate their efforts on overcoming environmental obstacles to their stimulation (i.e., they respond to perceived people-oriented challenges) and the wrestling of control over their behavioral contingencies.

The "challenge" or "control" theory just discussed includes an integration of each of the previously reviewed theories. That being the case, it retains virtually all of the explanatory power of each theory. Gough's role-playing deficiency theory is incorporated where the control theory states that partial helplessness conditioning causes fewer effective socialization experiences (arrow 7) and the eventual view of other people as objects (arrows 6, 10, and 13). Developing psychopaths fail to comprehend others' viewpoints (i.e., are deficient role players) because they have learned that other people's actions are largely unpredictable.

Eysenck's learning deficiency theory can be thought of as represented by the theorized low cortical arousal, diminished concern about negative behavioral consequences, and the resultant peculiar view of other people as objects. Of importance, however, is that Eysenck's theorized *direct* relationships between low cortical arousal and a learning deficit and between a learning deficit and a poorly developed conscience are not seen as accurate portrayals of the psychopath's development (see Figure 3).

Quay's (1965) stimulation-seeking theory is directly represented by the postulated low cortical arousal leading to excessive stimulation seeking followed by a focus of attention on short-term, stimulating goals (arrows 1 and 5). Note that Quay's concept of autonomic underarousal has been altered to cortical underarousal. The 1977 revision of Quay's theory is also incorporated and somewhat embellished with the addition of partial helplessness learning, diminished concern about negative behavioral consequences, and fewer effective socialization experiences (arrows 3, 6, and 7).

Finally, Hare's response perseveration theory has been borrowed rather explicitly, with the single change that brain damage is no longer postulated to be necessary for cortical underarousal. In the integrated theory, low cortical arousal and limbic system inefficiency are viewed as causing a deficiency in the ability to inhibit ongoing behavior patterns, implying a tendency to repeat that same action even when punished (arrows 2 and 9).

The integration of four theories into one, particularly with the addition of some other critical factors (e.g., the tendency to act until a goal is attained), serves to increase the comprehensiveness and utility of this theory of psychopathy. As described below, virtually all of the commonly enumerated characteristics of psychopathy can be explicated using the control theory.

For instance, psychopaths are said to exhibit an inability to learn from experience, especially punishing outcomes. The control theory explains this conditioning deficit in three interacting ways. First, psychopaths experience partial helplessness that teaches them not to pay attention to the less than immediate outcomes of their behavior. That diminished attention often causes them to fail to comprehend what factor or factors of their environment link their behavior to punishment. (Although their diminished attention to detail affects their learning of behavioral associations with rewards, the effect is not as great with rewards due to psychopaths' sustained interest in gaining rewards versus avoiding punishments.) Similarly, they are not likely to retrace their steps to discover where they went wrong because they have already learned that punishment is something to be expected as part of the process of obtaining rewards. Hence, psychopaths do not alter their behavior when punished. From an observer's perspective, psychopaths have not learned from the consequences of their actions. Whether or not psychopaths can demonstrate a verbal understanding of the relationship between their actions and contingent punishment is expected to vary depending on their motivation to attend to the relevant factors. A second factor causing an apparent learning deficit is that psychopaths are born with a relative deficit in the ability to inhibit their behavior when confronted with negative consequences. That inborn deficit interferes with the psychopaths' ability to demonstrate what they have learned, leading outsiders to believe that psychopaths do not learn at all. Additionally, the response perseveration caused by the inhibitory deficit actually interferes with psychopaths' ability to learn new behaviors, thereby limiting their ability to learn from punishing consequences.

Finally, psychopaths' conditioned emphasis on the issue of control leads them not to enact "appropriate" behavior in a variety of circumstances because they would view that as relinquishing whatever control they possess. To act in conforming ways is construed by psychopaths as giving others control over the psychopaths' behavior. Hence from a psychopaths' perspective they do not suffer a learning deficit, but simply an unwillingness to demonstrate what they have learned so as to avoid giving other people control.

A second attribute commonly ascribed to the psychopath is a lack of a sense of responsibility. Again the issue of control applies, this time coupled with the influence of the psychopath's perception of others as objects of challenge, early partial helplessness learning, and excessive stimulation seeking. First, psychopaths are unwilling to act in responsible ways because that would mean they have relinquished control of their actions to the forces which dictate what constitutes responsible behavior (i.e., society and specific people). Second, their peculiar view of others serves to excuse them from feeling responsible to them. Psychopaths see other individuals as adversaries for control of rewards, thereby alleviating themselves of any responsibility to others. Additionally, because of partial helplessness conditioning, they have learned to view the world from a very egocentric perspective. As seems obvious, egocentrism does not lend itself to strong feelings of responsibility to others due to the excessive concern about oneself. Finally, coupled with each of these factors, which simply fail to induce a sense of responsibility, is one factor which leads in an alternative direction, the excessive desire for stimulation. Without compelling reasons to act responsibly, psychopaths' constant egocentric push for short-term stimulation frequently leads them to act in ways which specifically demonstrate irresponsibility toward others.

Psychopaths have also been characterized by their inability to form meaningful interpersonal relationships and an incapacity to experience guilt. A variety of factors could be enumerated here in explanation of such characteristics, but the separate factors' final product is probably of greatest importance. As described, psychopaths come to view other people as objects within the environment. If not within their immediate environment, individuals are of no concern at all. If within psychopaths' immediate setting, other people are seen in ways that are not conducive to emotional intimacy (i.e., as challenges to be overcome or as objects of sensation). Under these conditions, psychopaths could not be expected to form close emotional ties with anyone. Similarly, they could not be expected to feel guilty when they beat an adversary to gain rewards. Obtaining control over rewards by overcoming other people is what psychopaths' lives are all about. The fact that they will not feel guilty about being successful in the activity they enjoy most is not surprising.

The postulated explanations of many other characteristics are straightforward. The impulsivity of psychopaths stems from their concentration on short-term stimulation coupled with their relative inability to inhibit behaviors in the face of punishment. The manipulation that so typifies psychopaths represents their attempts to control, a result of the entire theorized learning process (which explains the prominence in their lives of attempts to manipulate others). Their antisocial nature is based on an incomplete and inappropriate socialization process coupled with the desire for short-term sensation and the tenacity to keep trying something until they know they can win control or have already done so. Similarly, their failure to follow any life plan stems from their emphasis on immediate sensation coupled with the view of the future as unpredictable.

The lack of insight demonstrated by psychopaths stems from their strong propensity to blame failures in their lives on other people. That tendency in turn results from their partial helplessness conditioning. Others are viewed as possessing control. Hence they must be to blame when desired events do not come to be. With such a convenient, ever-present excuse, psychopaths rarely feel a need to question their own motives and perceptions.

Finally we come to psychopaths' apparent lack of anxiety and depression (remembering that these attributes are true of primary, but not secondary psychopaths). For these attributes, we need to digress to explore the foundations of nervousness and dejection. Put simplistically, anxiety is typified by a strong concern or fear about what the future will bring (either because of one's own choices or the effects of events outside one's control). Without such concern, one has little cause to feel anxious. Similarly, depression can be based on guilt, inhibited anger, a feeling of complete helplessness, self-blame for perceived failure, or a loss of someone or something with which one had an emotional attachment. If one does not experience guilt, finds no reason to inhibit anger, does not feel completely helpless, blames others for any failures, and lacks emotional ties, then one has no cause to feel depressed.

Psychopaths meet all of these conditions. They do not concern themselves with anything but the immediate future. Hence the only nervousness they will experience is when they believe they may lose control of the satisfaction of their immediate desires such as when initially frustrated during an incarceration. Even under those circumstances, psychopaths would not be expected to experience feelings of remorse, merely transient anxiety.

The situation is the same with depression. Psychopaths experience little depression because they (without significant outside constraints) have no basis on which to do so. They do not feel guilt, completely helpless, self-blame, strong emotional ties, or the inhibition of the expression of anger. In reference to the experience of complete helplessness, psychopaths' tendency to act when frustrated may serve to enhance their feeling of control in getting what they want. Without that persistence in action, psychopaths could experience strong feelings of helplessness, and hence substantial depression. One can think of psychopaths as coping with the threat of depression by acting in ways they believe are useful. (The relationship between learned helplessness, a theorized cause of depression, and partial helplessness, a theorized factor in psychopathy, will be discussed later in this chapter.) Since psychopaths virtually always have some actions available that serve to enhance their feelings of control over rewards, they rarely experience complete helplessness or depression.

One research finding about psychopaths is of importance in this enumeration of their characteristics. Some researchers have contended that psychopaths are generally of above average intelligence (e.g., Wechsler, 1958). Reviews of the literature (e.g., Hare, 1970) however, can only conclude that psychopaths have at least average global intelligence. Even so, the question arises of how a group of people with low cortical arousal (and sometimes brain damage) can at least approximate the average intelligence of general society. No answer to this question can be found in any of the postulates previously discussed. I suggest that a sampling bias may be involved, however. Mentally retarded persons are specifically excluded from the appropriate diagnosis of antisocial personality disorder (i.e., psychopathy) in the most recent diagnostic manual of mental disorders (American Psychiatric Association, 1980; see Chapter 1). Studies which use other criteria, such as paper and pencil questionnaires (e.g., personality inventories such as the MMPI or that developed by Quay and Peterson, 1964), will often exclude individuals with severe comprehension difficulties, including the mentally retarded and illiterate. Hence psychopaths with such difficulties may not have been included in investigations of psychopaths' intelligence. Subject classification techniques dependent on a professional staff's evaluations may be biased in the direction of considering antisocial, mentally retarded individuals as mentally retarded rather than psychopathic due to the possibility of explaining antisocial behavior with retardation and not vice versa. For all of these reasons, psychopathic populations may have been unwittingly trimmed of their least intelligent members when research samples are drawn. That process would serve to raise the overall average; therefore, we should not be surprised that psychopaths score at least average in studies of intelligence. Admittedly, however, this argument is weakened by studies using matched control groups in which the mentally retarded have also been eliminated.

The issue of the sex distribution of psychopaths has yet to be discussed. As the reader may remember, approximately three of four psychopaths are male (American Psychiatric Association, 1980). Related to that statistic is the additional finding that childhood hyperactivity seems to be four to nine times more prevalent in boys than girls (Omenn, 1973). A genetic factor which differentially affects males more often than females has been suggested in explanation of that finding with hyperactivity (Omenn, 1973). Considering that both psychopaths and hyperactive children have been hypothesized to suffer similarly deficient innate levels of cortical arousal, the speculation that the prevalence of male psychopaths is at least somewhat due to the same genetic factors as theorized for hyperactivity seems reasonable. Although the specific genetic mechanism at work in causing the excess of psychopathic males is presently undetermined, there is some evidence that the androgens and their effect on neurotransmitters such as monoamine-oxidase (MAO) may be involved (Wheeler, 1973; Zuckerman, 1978). The existence of such mechanisms would also lead to the hypothesis that psychopathy should follow some patterns of heredity transmission (realizing, of course, that critical learning patterns must also occur for the full development of the syndrome). That hypothesis will be supported in the review of research in the next section.

One last topic should be mentioned here: the general causes of behavior. Since Freud's time it has been commonly assumed that behavior is multiply determined. Most actions are caused by more than one preceding personality and/or environmental characteristic.

Previous theories of psychopathy, however, represent attempts to explain the whole disorder through only one line of causal relationships, implying that the disorder stems from a single circumstance. [Quay's revised theory may appear to be an exception by using two lines of influence (see Figure 2). The single factor of underarousal, however, was still theorized as causing both lines.]

The control theory described in this chapter does not view psychopathy in the same simplistic manner. Both genetic and learning features are seen as necessary for the development of psychopathy without either factor causing the other. Neither aspect is sufficient alone. Additionally, virtually every commonly listed characteristic of the psychopath is seen as the result of two or more factors combining their influence toward the same end. Certainly some parsimony is surrendered in a theory which views behavior in this complex manner. Such a perspective, however, seems far more in keeping with psychology's general assumption about multiple determinism than the perspectives taken in other theories of psychopathy.

In summary, the control theory of psychopathy states that two major components are necessary for the development of the disorder: low cortical arousal and partial helplessness conditioning. Although not fully independent, there is no direct link between the two. Once both of those conditions exist, a series of learning experiences combine to produce poorly socialized persons who persist in viewing people as challenges to be overcome to attain the psychopaths' own immediate rewards.

RESEARCH SUPPORT AND CONTRAINDICATIONS

Much of the control theory of psychopathy was borrowed from the works previously reviewed in this book. Therefore, the research support for much of the theory does not need to be reiterated here. The following critical concepts, however, still need to be discussed: (1) low cortical arousal, related to that found in hyperactive children, can occur without brain damage; (2) there is a hereditary component to psychopathy; (3) underarousal can affect limbic system functioning; (4) partial helplessness conditioning directly causes the theorized

outcomes of a diminished concern about negative behavioral consequences and an increased tendency to act when frustrated; (5) psychopaths demonstrate poor attention to aspects of the environment; (6)
psychopaths view people as objects and obstacles to be overcome; (7)
psychopaths demonstrate a limited behavioral repertoire; and (8)
psychopaths are preoccupied with the issues of challenge and control.

Psychopathy, Hyperactivity, and Underarousal without Brain Damage

There are two issues involved in the comparison between
psychopathy and hyperactivity. The first is whether hyperactive
children demonstrate low cortical arousal similar to the psychopath's.
The second involves the degree to which that cortical underarousal
can occur without demonstrable cerebral lesions.

The reader may remember from the review of Hare's theory that
psychopaths as a group typically show a greater frequency of
abnormal EEG patterns than is usual in normal populations, though a
substantial proportion of psychopaths (20 to 69 percent) fail to show
any brain wave abnormality. The fact that a large number of
psychopaths do not demonstrate abnormal EEGs helps substantiate
my claim that a person does not need to suffer brain damage to
become psychopathic. When such an electrocortical abnormality has
been located, it has often been described as excessive slow wave
activity.

Of importance, hyperactive children have also demonstrated an
increased frequency of abnormal EEGs, though again only a portion
of all such children show these patterns (Capute, Neidermeyer, &
Richardson, 1968; Hughes, 1971). Similarly, excessive slow wave
activity is the most common EEG abnormality reported for
hyperactive children (Satterfield, 1978). Based on EEG studies, at
least some psychopaths and hyperactive children share a similar
cerebral flaw.

Satterfield (1978) reviewed empirical findings which also suggest
that adult psychopaths and hyperactive children are similar in their
early symptomatology (e.g., Robins, 1966); excessive probability of
psychopathic, alcoholic, or hysterical (biological) parents (e.g.,
Cantwell, 1972; Morrison & Stewart, 1973; reaction to stimulant

medication (e.g., Conners & Eisenberg, 1963; Hill, 1947); as well as the low central nervous system arousal levels (e.g., Satterfield & Dawson, 1971). Satterfield concluded from his review that "one psychiatric disorder of children, the hyperactive child syndrome, may be a precursor of juvenile delinquency and adult psychopathy" (p. 329).

Based on Satterfield's comparison as well as the results of EEG studies, one can conclude that child hyperactivity and adult psychopathy are related syndromes. Psychopaths' characteristic low cortical arousal is therefore perceived as an underlying factor common to both disorders.

Does that underarousal occur without demonstrable cerebral lesions? Unfortunately, this question has not been empirically addressed for psychopaths. No study was found which attempted to test the relationship between EEG abnormalities (an imperfect measure of brain damage) in psychopaths with behavioral measures of cortical underarousal such as the two-flash threshold test (described in the critique of Eysenck's theory in Chapter 3). Although such a study would help clarify the issue of whether or not cortical underarousal can exist without cerebral damage, I recognize that such research might not be conclusive due to the difficulty inherent in interpreting EEGs. As pointed out by Kiloh and Osselton (1966), an EEG abnormality does not necessarily mean that there is a corresponding brain abnormality, nor does a normal EEG always indicate the absence of brain damage. Of importance, Luria's (1973) theoretical work strongly supports the concept of underarousal without demonstrable cerebral lesions based on research with an alternative methodology to EEGs. A definitive answer to this question, however, cannot be offered at this time due to the lack of research addressing the issue.

In conclusion to the discussion of cortical arousal similarities between psychopaths and hyperactive children, the evidence tends to support the hypothesized relationship between the two disorders. Whether or not the characteristic underarousal can occur without brain damage remains an open question. For both of these issues, the research that was found supported the postulates within the control theory.

The Hereditary Component of Psychopathy

Of the four theories of Gough, Eysenck, Quay, and Hare, only Gough's did not include biological components in an explanation of psychopathy. Eysenck specifically postulated that most of the reason for psychopathy was genetic, that the cause of high extraversion, neuroticism, and psychoticism was hereditary. Similarly, Quay suggested that the cause of a hyporeactive nervous system was at least in part genetic. While Hare recognized the potential contribution of heredity, he did not specify by what means the theorized brain lesions develop.

The concept that heredity causes psychopathy has been with us since the days when Pinel and Pritchard postulated an inborn defect to explain "moral insanity" (McCord & McCord, 1964). An early study by Partridge (1928) was designed to verify a "direct line" of genetic influence through a meticulous tracing of the lineage of 50 psychopathic personalities. Of the 50, 24 were found to have had recent ancestors who exhibited psychopathic characteristics. Other studies found similarly high incidences of epilepsy, alcoholism, and "maladjusted personalities" among the ancestors of psychopathic subjects (Gottlieb, Ashley, & Knott, 1946; Powdermaker, Levis, & Touraine, 1937). From today's perspective, however, those early investigations were seriously flawed in that "psychopathic" subjects were defined using vague terms (erratic, eccentric, and antisocial). Based on this evidence alone, the conclusion that psychopathy must be substantially genetically caused seems unwarranted.

Genetic studies have also been performed by proponents of the "constitutional school" such as Hooton, Kretschmer, Lombroso, Sheldon, and Spranger. The constitutional school argued that a relationship exists between physique and personality, that one's physical build reflects the same genetic factors which influence one's personality and behavior. Hence one could study structural anatomy to discover the correlates of specific personality traits. With such an argument, the constitutionalists assumed a genetic base for personality and for any disorder thereof, including psychopathy. According to McCord and McCord (1964), however, the constitutional perspective never became popular because of empirically contradictory results. For instance, Hooton concluded that the criminal was physically inferior to the normal man while Sheldon held that the delinquent was physically superior to the average boy (more muscular and athletic). Those researchers' work, therefore, has not been accepted as strong support for a genetic influence on personality.

The investigations by Glueck and Glueck (1956) also seem to have related bodily constitution to delinquency causation. The Gluecks compared the body types of 500 juvenile delinquents with 500 nondelinquents. Results showed that the delinquents were generally superior to the nondelinquents in gross body size and homogeneity of build. Unlike other constitutionalists, the Gluecks did not postulate the existence of a relationship between physique and heredity. Physique was not viewed as the dominant cause of delinquency. Instead, bodily constitution was portrayed as one factor among many dynamic factors which influence behavior. Although the Gluecks' work may therefore be enlightening in delineating the many causes of delinquency, no conclusion from their studies should be drawn concerning the genetic component of psychopathy. To emphasize the point, the reader should note that the Gluecks studied delinquents, not specifically psychopaths.

From this review, McCord and McCord (1964) concluded that

heredity cannot yet be excluded as a causal factor [of psychopathy]. With more adequate delineation, with more rigidly controlled experiments, and with more sensitive measurement, a hereditary link may possibly be established. Given our knowledge, however, the extravagant claims of the geneticists must be questioned.

(p. 61)

The cautionary wording of that conclusion seemed warranted in 1964. By the mid-1980s however, a different perspective has emerged.

Eysenck (1975) reviewed a variety of relatively recent studies which revealed that at least 50 percent of the total variance of personality characteristics can be attributed to genetic factors. For instance, data concerning neuroticism and extraversion gathered by Shields (1962) were reanalyzed by Jinks and Fulker (1970) using recently developed biometric genetical methods which allow for an estimate of the degree of variability that can be accounted for by genetic influence. From that investigation, neuroticism was determined to have a heritability index of 0.54, meaning that more than half of the variation among people in neuroticism is associated with genetic factors. A similar finding was made with extraversion, for which 67 percent of the variability was approximated as associated with heredity and heredity–environment interactions (such interactions representing the variance beyond pure heredity and pure environmental influences). Eysenck concluded from studies such as these "that there is strong evidence to suggest that individual differences in the personality variables which have been shown to be associated with psychopathic behavior are determined to a large extent by genetic causes" (Eysenck & Eysenck, 1978, p. 212).

Although other researchers (e.g., Cloninger, Reich, and Guze, 1978) have considered those percentages too high based on various research methodological considerations, most recent investigators agree that there is some hereditary component to psychopathy. For example, Christiansen (1974), who performed an extensive study of Danish twins born within a 40-year period, concluded that some genetic influence seemed to exist for the transmission of criminality. Hutchings and Mednick (1975) concurred with the results of their study using criminals. Investigations by Schulsinger (1972) and Crowe (1974) dealt more directly with the issue of genetic transmission of psychopathy in their twin and adoption studies of psychopathy. Both of those investigations supported a heredity component to psychopathy. Mednick and Hutchings (1978) described their own and others' longitudinal twin studies with the conclusion that "there seems to be a genetic factor in the aetiology of criminality and psychopathy" (p. 248). Finally, from an extensive critique of studies dealing with the causes of psychopathy, Gregory (1974) deduced that the evidence of genetic influence suggests congenital determinants are involved in the development of psychopathy. Although many criticisms can be forwarded about the methodology of most twin and adoption studies, the consistency of the findings in the studies just discussed suggests support for a genetic factor in psychopathy.

One other indication of genetic influence in the etiology of psychopathy can be described: the prevalence of male psychopaths.

The preponderance of male hyperactive children and the relationship between hyperactivity and psychopathy have already been discussed. Satterfield (1978) concluded that the genetic (versus environmental) factors which influence the predominance of male children who suffer cortical underarousal leading to hyperactivity are the same factors which cause the disproportionate number of male psychopaths.

Cloninger, Reich, and Guze (1978) also studied the question of the genetic transmission of psychopathy by using the relationship of sex to the disorder. By using a multifactorial model to approximate relationships among variables, the investigators concluded that "the sex difference in the prevalence of sociopathy appears to be due to sex-related cultural and biological factors causing a threshold for sociopathy to be more deviant in women than in men" (p. 230). Both the environment and heredity were perceived as important.

In conclusion, empirical evidence suggests that heredity does play a role in the development of psychopathy, though it cannot be considered the only factor. This conclusion is in keeping with the control theory which states that both a biological condition of low cortical arousal and an environmental condition of partial helplessness conditioning are necessary for the development of a psychopath.

Cortical Underarousal and Limbic System Functioning

The control theory of psychopathy includes the hypothesis that a generally low level of cortical arousal would cause a lessening of the effective and efficient functioning of the limbic system. No studies were found which addressed this issue, however. Hence no statement can be offered about the empirical support or contraindication of the postulated relationship between cerebral arousal level and optimal limbic system functioning. Only Luria's (1973) theoretical work was found which related to this issue, with strong support for the hypothesis.

Partial Helplessness Conditioning and Its Effect

Three direct effects from partial helplessness conditioning are hypothesized in the control theory: (1) a lessening of the developing psychopath's degree of concern about negative behavioral consequences, (2) a lessening of the frequency and effectiveness of appropriate socialization experiences, and (3) an increase in the tendency to act when frustrated. The second effect was considered in the critique of Quay's revised theory (see Figure 2) and therefore will not be discussed again. Empirical evidence for effects 1 and 3 follows.

Partial Helplessness versus Learned Helplessness Conditioning

Before relating the support for effects of partial helplessness learning in the psychopath, however, a few issues concerning the conditioning process itself need to be discussed. The first such issue is how partial helplessness conditioning is distinguished from the more well-known process termed learned helplessness. Additionally, the discussion will outline the theoretical relationship between psychopathy and depression. Second, an examination of evidence which demonstrates that psychopaths have been subjected to partial helplessness will be made. Third, one highly speculative outcome from partial helplessness learning will be mentioned.

Learned helplessness is a result of learning that the reinforcement one receives is independent of one's behavior (Seligman, 1975). This type of (classical) conditioning involves the expectation that one is not capable of causing desired outcomes (i.e., if generalized to a variety of situations, something analogous to what has been termed external locus of control).

Researchers have studied learned helplessness by presenting situations to subjects in which their responses cannot free them from aversive stimuli such as shock or noise (e.g., Hiroto & Seligman, 1975). Afterward, when placed in new situations where they could escape with the correct behavior, the subjects typically fail to attempt to perform the necessary actions. Although learned helplessness was initially demonstrated using animals (Seligman, 1975), the appropriateness of the concept's application to humans has been well established (DeVellis, DeVellis, & McCauley, 1978; Garber & Hollon, 1980; Hiroto & Seligman, 1975; Maier & Seligman, 1976; Price, Tryon, & Raps, 1978; Roth & Kubal, 1975).

Learned helplessness has been associated with depression for two reasons. First, depressed people have been found to describe themselves as helpless in skilled situations not viewed as universally uncontrollable (e.g., Garber & Hollon, 1980). Second, the effects of learned helplessness found in the laboratory closely resemble characteristics of depression. As Seligman (1975) stated:

> Six symptoms of learned depression have emerged: each of them has parallels in depression:
>
> (1) Lowered initiation of voluntary responses—animals and men who have experienced uncontrollability show reduced initiation of voluntary responses.
>
> (2) Negative cognitive set—helpless animals and men have difficulty learning that responses produce outcomes.
>
> (3) Time Course—helplessness dissipates in time when induced by a single session of uncontrollable shock; after multiple sessions, helplessness persists.
>
> (4) Lowered aggression—helpless animals and men initiate fewer aggressive and competitive responses, and their dominance status may diminish.
>
> (5) Loss of appetite—helpless animals eat less, lose weight, and are sexually and socially deficient.
>
> (6) Physiological changes—helpless rats show norepinephrine depletion and helpless cats may be cholinergically over-active.
>
> *(p. 82)*

Seligman described the relationship of each of these symptoms to human depression through the use of empirical results, case examples, and current theory. That a relationship between learned helplessness and at least some form of depression seems clear.

How are learned helplessness and partial helplessness related? Learned helplessness is the condition where one perceives his behavior as independent of desired reinforcement. The belief is that no matter what one does, it will not bring about wanted results. Partial helplessness implies that one's actions are seen as independent of desired reinforcement to the extent that specific outcomes cannot be predicted at any given time. Over the long run, however, one still retains the expectation that eventually one's goals will be attained, specifically through persistent actions.

There are therefore two major distinctions between the two

conditioning procedures, one cognitive and the other behavioral. First, partial helplessness conditioning leaves one with the expectation of eventual goal satisfaction whereas learned helplessness does not. Hence psychopaths have been conditioned through their early experiences to expect that their actions will sometimes result in desired consequences. The depressed, on the other hand, have no such expectation. Second, psychopaths will continue to act until a reward is obtained because of their early partial helplessness conditioning while depressed people will typically not show psychopaths' tenacity due to the learned expectancy of complete helplessness.

Psychopaths can even be thought of as avoiding the experience of depression through their persistent perception of viable behavioral alternatives, at least according to anecdotal evidence. Tuovinen (1974) wrote a theoretical article on psychopathy based on case studies from his clinical work. One conclusion he drew from those studies was that the behavior of the psychopath represents a defense and compensation against either depression or psychotic disintegration. Vaillant (1975) derived a similar conclusion from his case histories of psychopaths, stating that psychopaths avoid the experience of depression through "intense and persistent" (p. 181) actions.

In summary, partial helplessness differs from learned helplessness in ways that make psychopaths relatively impervious to the experience of depression. Their continual hope of obtaining what they desire assures that they are not likely to feel depressed.

Psychopaths' Experience of Partial Helplessness as Children

This section describes the evidence concerning psychopaths' experience of partial helplessness as children. Some of the research involving psychopaths' poor parent–child relationships and inconsistent discipline was reviewed in the critique of Quay's theory (Chapter 4). That research led to a supportive conclusion on this issue. An extensive study by Glueck and Glueck (1950) came to the conclusion that delinquents often come from families who demonstrate substantial incohesiveness and erratic discipline (i.e., parents being both extremely punitive and lax). Though the Gluecks' investigation did not employ psychopaths specifically, their study may still be considered supportive of the postulate herein because the sample may be thought of as including a number of developing psychopaths, not yet old enough for the adult diagnostic label.

A review by Gregory (1974) of a multitude of empirical results concurred with the control theory's postulate, finding that parents of psychopaths typically administered inadequate and inconsistent discipline to their children. Gregory went so far as to state that inadequate discipline was a contributing influence in the development of the disorder, along with congenital factors and the specific learning of antisocial behavior by imitating the antisocial acts by the parents. Based on the available research, it seems likely that many psychopaths have experienced partial helplessness conditioning during their early years.

Partial Helplessness and the Psychopath's Self-Concept

An interesting, speculative digression can be made here concerning the effect of partial helplessness conditioning on the self-concept of psychopaths. Given the experience of recurrent situations leading to the belief that one cannot directly cause desired ends, then a negative evaluation of self-efficacy would be expected [as is typical of those who experience learned helplessness (e.g., Garber & Hollon, 1980)]. However, if one virtually always perceives other people as the basis for one's failures, then there would be no reason to make a negative self-evaluation. Interestingly, both the perspective of immediate ineffectiveness and the viewpoint that other people are the cause of one's failures coexist in the psychopath, leading to what appear to be contradictory outcomes (i.e., a negative self-evaluation and no negative self-evaluation, respectively). One possible explanation is that a variety of inconsistencies are present in the self-evaluations of psychopaths, perspectives that make sense by themselves but seem incongruous when put together.

The one empirical investigation which tests this hypothesis of inconsistency supports it. Tamayo and Raymond (1977) used psychometric measures to examine the self-concept of psychopaths (classified using the MMPI and behavioral history data) and found several such inconsistencies. For instance, psychopaths demonstrated an average overall level of self-esteem. They portrayed themselves as having a sense of personal worth and feelings of adequacy comparable to those of the average person. When comparing themselves to others, however, psychopaths appeared to degrade their personal capabilities, describing themselves as inadequate in interpersonal settings and morally worthless.

My speculation is that these characteristics are caused by partial helplessness conditioning. The inconsistent and contradictory manner in which psychopaths perceived themselves seems congruent with the previously stated expectations about the effects of partial helplessness.

Etiological Effects of Partial Helplessness Conditioning

Thus far, the discussion concerning partial helplessness conditioning has centered on general issues and related concepts. The following discussion describes the research evidence for two of the outcomes from such conditioning as specified by the control theory: (1) a lessening of concern about negative behavioral consequences, and (2) an increase in the tendency to act when frustrated.

One line of supportive evidence for the first theorized outcome comes from a study by Patterson (1975) which investigated patterns of interactions between parents and particularly aggressive children. Although both parents and their children contributed to the overall system of interaction, Patterson discovered that the parental use of social reinforcers and social punishers in an inconsistent or noncontingent manner often created situations in which the children were less likely to be controlled by either. Phrased differently, partial helplessness conditioning by the parents caused the children to ignore the social consequences of their behavior.

A second type of support is the set of studies which have found deficiencies in psychopaths' ability to avoid punishment. As reviewed in the critique of Eysenck's theory (Chapter 3), much research has demonstrated that psychopaths tend to fail to alter their behavior when confronted with punishing consequences compared to the responses of nonpsychopaths (e.g., Bachand, 1978; Hare, 1965b; Lykken, 1957; Nygard, 1975; Schachter & Latané, 1964; Schmauk, 1968, in Hare, 1970; Schoenherr, 1964, in Hare, 1970). Similarly, psychopaths have been found to show less concern and smaller physiological arousal than nonpsychopaths when anticipating certain shock (Cook & Barnes, 1964; Hare, 1966a, 1966b). Although one can infer that psychopaths do poorly on these tasks because they do not attend adequately to them, the fact remains that they demonstrate a lesser concern about the negative consequences of their behavior.

In contrast, psychopaths have not demonstrated performance deficits compared to nonpsychopaths when presented with rewarding stimuli (e.g., Bernard & Eisenman, 1967; Hutchinson, 1977; Martinez, 1976; Matthey, 1974; Schmauk, 1968, in Hare, 1970) except when those stimuli or the conditions for reinforcement are particularly complex (e.g., Painting, 1961; Siegel, 1978). Apparently psychopaths are willing to attend to rewarding stimuli as much as average individuals, at least up to the point where complexity interferes. (One speculation concerning why complexity interferes with the psychopath's performance is that complicated behavioral contingencies are difficult to comprehend and their consequences difficult to predict. Those characteristics are similar to features of partial helplessness conditioning. Hence psychopaths are more likely to stop attending to complex stimuli and contingencies that they associate with unpredictability than are nonpsychopaths who have no such association. The stimulating effect of novelty may only partially counteract this tendency.)

Putting together the two lines of evidence, we find that (1) certain patterns of interaction between parents and children similar to partial helplessness conditioning procedures cause a lessening of the effect of punishment (and, in complex situations, reward) on the child, and (2) adult psychopaths show a relative tendency not to alter their behavior in the face of punishment which they do not typically demonstrate when attempting to obtain a reward. Based on these statements alone, it would be a logical leap to conclude that partial helplessness learning leads to a diminished concern about negative consequences of behavior. These empirically based statements, however, are at least consistent with such a perspective.

Anecdotal evidence leads to a similar conclusion. Ross (1969), when working with institutionalized adolescent offenders, noted that children who have been exposed to inconsistent reward and punishment tend to fail to develop negative emotional states when they are confronted with apparently frustrating and/or punishing situations. The temporal association between aversive stimulation and the hope or expectation of reward was suggested as preventing the experience of negative emotional states. Ross' model sounds very much in accord with the concept of partial helplessness conditioning and its theorized effect. Again, although this evidence does not demonstrate the theorized relationship between partial helplessness learning and a lowered interest in negative consequences to behavior, Ross' statements are consistent with the theorized perspective. Overall the evidence relating to the theorized relationship is uniformly consistent with the control theory.

Ross' work also has relevance in the demonstration that partial helplessness learning leads to the inclination to act when frustrated, the second theorized effect of such conditioning. Ross stated, as an adjunct to his model, that the child exposed to inconsistent or mixed training could be expected to show persistent behavior in the face of nonreward or punishment, an addendum which relates well to the control theory.

Ross and Doody (1973) set out to support that concept empirically. The researchers employed 18 psychopaths and 18 nonpsychopaths in a motor task experiment. Each subject was initially trained to which of five levers was the "correct" one with the utilization of continuous reinforcement; that is, they were reinforced each time they chose a correct lever and not reinforced or punished when they selected an incorrect lever. After the training period, subjects were placed into one of three conditions; (1) continuous reinforcement, (2) partial reinforcement (rewarded on an intermittent schedule of correct responses), or (3) intermittent punishment (the loss of already earned rewards). All subjects were then tested for persistence, operationally defined as resistance to intermittently punished extinction (i.e., the loss of reward caused by continued responding in the absence of reinforcement).

The results supported Ross' hypothesis in that psychopaths demonstrated more persistence in the face of punishment and nonreward (the last test condition) than did nonpsychopaths. Although this study is limited by the simple instrumental task, the investigation supports the concept of a psychopathic tendency to persist behaving when punished to do so.

Siegel's (1978) research can be interpreted with a similarly supportive conclusion. The reader may remember from the critique of Eysenck's theory that Siegel studied the effect on psychopaths of varying probabilities of punishment. Siegel concluded that psychopaths suffer a decrement in the ability to learn to avoid punishment, particularly as that punishment becomes more and more uncertain. A reinterpretation of Siegel's results suggests that psychopaths demonstrate a tendency to persevere through occasional punishment in their attempts to obtain reward, particularly when the punishment is effectively unpredictable. Features of Siegel's research design, unpredictable punishment and periodic reward, can be considered comparable to the process of partial helplessness conditioning. Therefore, the finding that psychopaths tend to perseverate in responding within this setting supports the contention that partial helplessness learning causes an increased tendency to act when frustrated (i.e., by suffering punishment and lack of reward).

Case history data support this perspective as well. Henderson (1972) wrote an analysis of therapy with three adolescents he labeled psychopathic. In that analysis, psychopaths were described as having a "doing character," implying a proclivity toward action. For instance, Henderson stated of one client that "it seemed as though doing something . . . was still the only adaptive mechanism that he knew how to use under the stress of internal tension" (p. 315). Additionally, Henderson related that "a sense of helplessness seemed to be one of the main affective feelings in the personality of my three sociopaths as I got to know them better" (p. 316). To exemplify, Henderson quoted one of his clients as saying "I never felt like my parents paid any attention to anything I said or did, so I just had to keep on doing more and more violent things . . . to get them to notice" (p. 316). From the perspective of the control theory, one could say that Henderson's clients commonly reacted to the feelings of helplessness with action. That perspective concurs with the research results discussed.

In summary, especially convincing and consistent empirical findings in support of the concept that partial helplessness conditioning leads to an increased tendency to act when frustrated are lacking. The research that was found, however, was in accord with the theorized relationship.

Psychopathy and Poor Attention to Environmental Cues

The empirical evidence supporting the control theory to be reviewed in this section is all derived from investigations of marginally related issues. No one has studied attentional deficits in the psychopath directly, possibly because previous theories of psychopathy have not addressed the topic. Even so, a substantial degree of evidence suggests that psychopaths are lax in their attention to environmental cues.

There will be four research topics discussed in this section, each relating to the issue of psychopaths' attention to features of their environment: (1) instrumental conditioning with aversive stimuli, (2) learning in response to rewards, (3) reactions to complex stimuli, and (4) generally distracting behaviors during periods calling for concentration.

Poor Attention and Aversive Instrumental Conditioning

Much potentially supportive evidence comes from studies on psychopathic learning deficiencies which employed shock as an aversive stimulus. The utility of these studies in supporting the concept of poor attention, however, is diminished by the multiple ways to interpret their outcomes.

For instance, Eysenck postulated that these studies support a genetic factor which causes a lessened ability to condition to punishment. Quay interpreted these studies as supporting his postulate that early excessive punishment by parents leads to an increased resistance to later punishment. These biological and environmental hypotheses are not shared by the control theory.

The control theory states that psychopaths tend to condition poorly to punishment because they are inclined to ignore it. Aversive stimuli do not typically get much attention. Hence the psychopath is relatively poor at anticipating and avoiding such stimuli.

Is there support for this perspective? An early review by Stern and McDonald (1965) related that psychopaths tended to become drowsy in experimental situations using shock in which other subjects become anxious and stressed. The researchers attributed that finding to a psychopathic autonomic underarousal, making the psychopaths less emotionally aroused at the prospect of physical pain. A possible interpretation consistent with the control theory is that the psychopathic subjects demonstrated less anxiety because they had already learned substantially to ignore aversive stimuli. The psychopaths may simply have been given the prospective shock little attention.

Hare (1968) drew a similar conclusion from his study of the orienting response in psychopaths (defined using Cleckley's criteria). Based on an investigation which found that psychopaths showed smaller orienting responses to a novel stimulus than did nonpsychopaths, Hare stated the tentative conclusion that the psychopath is somewhat less attentive and sensitive to environmental stimulation alterations than is the nonpsychopath. One must pay attention to a stimulus before one can react to it. (The reader should note that the fact that psychopaths reacted less than nonpsychopaths in response to a novel stimulus does not contraindicate the concept of psychopathic stimulation seeking. The passive listening to a repetitive tone which ultimately changes to a different, novel tone can hardly be considered stimulating.)

Interpretations similar to Hare's can be made with virtually all of the research with psychopaths using shock in an instrumental conditioning paradigm (e.g., Bachand, 1978; Lykken, 1957; Nygard, 1975; Schachter & Latané, 1964; Schmauk, 1968, in Hare, 1970; Schoenherr, 1964, in Hare, 1970). The potential shock may have commanded less attention from the psychopaths than from the nonpsychopaths. Hence the former group took longer to learn to alter their behavior because of it.

Poor Attention and Rewards

Those findings, however, can be explained by the control theory with the view that psychopaths have been conditioned to ignore punishment through their early experience of partial helplessness. The concept of differential attention to environmental cues is simply an alternate way to explain why psychopaths show a performance deficit when confronted with punishment. In fact, to say that psychopaths lack attention to aversive stimuli, the postulate discussed in this section, is to say that they relatively ignore it, the latter being a conclusion drawn concerning partial helplessness conditioning.

Therefore, demonstrations of other attentional deficits, ones not specifically centered around punishing stimuli, are needed. When reviewing the work employing rewarding stimuli, however, those deficits are not found. Studies have shown that psychopaths perform as well as, if not better than, nonpsychopaths when working for a reward, especially a monetary one (e.g., Hutchinson, 1977; Martinez, 1976; Schmauk, 1968, in Hare, 1970).

Bernard and Eisenman (1967) found that their incarcerated female psychopaths (classified according to MMPI elevations on scales Pd and Ma) learned a verbal task better than did a group of nurses when the subjects' reward was praise from a male experimenter. The fact that the incarcerated subjects rarely had the opportunity to interact with a male while the nurses did implies that the experimenter's praise may have been a more meaningful and salient reward to the psychopaths than for the nurses. That extra degree of salience may have compensated for the attentional deficit the psychopaths would have otherwise demonstrated.

The same type of argument could be made in explanation of the outcomes of studies using monetary rewards and nonincarcerated control groups. The psychopaths, virtually always incarcerated individuals, may have focused their attention on the reward because it was particularly meaningful to them.

I recognize that this argument can explain almost any empirical result which conflicts with the control theory. The determination of psychopaths' attention level to specific environmental stimuli, however, is not directly testable. It must be inferred from performance, something which can be affected by a multitude of factors. Although the argument concerning compensation for the psychopath's attentional deficit through salient reward may be reasonable, it is not particularly useful. To avoid this problematic argument, the remainder of this review concentrates on research which did not specifically investigate the effects of reward and punishment.

Poor Attention and Psychopaths' Reactions to Complexity

One such type of research involves the difficulty psychopaths demonstrate when confronted with complex stimuli or reward contingencies. Psychopaths often perform poorer than nonpsychopaths when they need to decipher a complex relationship between behavior and outcome.

In Painting's (1961) study, psychopathic criminals (classified behaviorally and psychometrically), neurotic criminals (classified behaviorally and psychometrically), and normal college students were required to predict which of two lights would be lit during each of 200 trials (as described in Chapter 3). In response to a random lighting pattern, psychopaths showed a tendency to repeat the correct response from the preceding trial, a tendency Painting viewed as rigid and stereotyped. (The inclination to keep going back to where reward was last found is something that would be expected of someone who both concentrates on reward to the exclusion of punishment and demonstrates a limited behavioral repertoire.)The second lighting pattern, involving a 75 percent probability that the last correct response would be incorrect on the present trial, resulted in the finding that psychopaths performed somewhat better than either of the two groups of nonpsychopaths in predicting accurately.

Psychopaths, however, showed a substantial deterioration in their performance compared to other subjects when confronted with the third and most complicated lighting sequence. During that sequence, the correct response was opposite the correct response two trials earlier. Nonpsychopaths had some difficulty with that pattern, but not nearly as much as the psychopaths who appeared to be deficient in the ability to relate past events with present behavioral contingencies. Painting offered the explanation that the psychopathic subjects lacked the motivation to attend to complicated contingency situations. Another conclusion, similar to Painting's, is that psychopaths have an attentional deficit, making it more difficult for them to discover recurrent patterns in situations which require a high degree of concentration.

Another way to approach the issue of a psychopathic attentional deficit in the face of complexity is to investigate how well psychopaths are able to describe and predict other people's behavior. The concept here is that situations involving people are inherently more complex than situations lacking human involvement. Hence human behavior should be more difficult for the psychopath to comprehend.

The "person perception" literature provides two studies which address this topic. Moss (1975) and Smith (1976) both discovered that nonpsychopaths were more adept than psychopaths in predicting other people's reactions. Coupled with that outcome was the finding that psychopaths and nonpsychopaths did not differ in the ability to employ complex concepts in describing stimuli that were devoid of human or social content. When the human element was present, however, psychopaths showed a relative deficiency in their ability to utilize information given to them (Moss, 1975). Putting these results together, a reasonable conclusion is that psychopaths are deficient in their ability to perceive and/or comprehend social cues which are considered complex stimuli, the understanding of which requires some attention. These results, therefore, were consistent with, and supportive of the control theory's postulate that psychopaths suffer a deficit in their ability to attend to situational stimuli.

Poor Attention and Distracting Self-Stimulation

Finally, similar support can be found in the research literature on stimulation seeking. As mentioned in Chapter 4 concerning Quay's theory, two studies have found that antisocial subjects show poor attentive abilities during experiments. An investigation by Orris (1969), which showed an expected learning deficit in psychopaths, also demonstrated that those subjects tended to pay little attention to the presented stimuli. Instead the subjects self-stimulated a great deal through behaviors such as singing, talking and looking around. DeMyer-Gapin and Scott (1977) recorded the same finding with "antisocial" children (subjects who would probably be classified today as suffering a conduct disorder). In both cases, the subjects demonstrated an attentional deficit.

In summary of the complete topic of attentional deficits in psychopaths, there is no direct evidence that psychopaths are deficient in their ability to attend to environmental cues. Indirect evidence, however, suggests that concept is a reasonable portrayal of psychopaths, at least up to, though not necessarily including their attending to stimuli which represent a forthcoming reward. The peculiarity of psychopaths' reaction to reward can be explicated by the concept that particularly salient stimuli can compensate for psychopaths' attentional shortcomings. That latter concept should be tested with especially salient, nonrewarding stimuli, however, before one generalizes the concept beyond the effect of rewards.

People as Objects and Obstacles to Be Overcome

As this review proceeds with delineating empirical findings relevant to the control theory, less and less research evidence can be described under each successive rubric. Previous research on psychopathy rarely pertains to the control theory as the hypotheses have not been postulated before.

So it is with the topic of the psychopath's perception of other people as objects and obstacles to be overcome. No directly supporting or contraindicating study was found. The only investigations that were at all pertinent were also tangential.

For instance, one would expect that if psychopaths view other people as objects (i.e., as things to be manipulated for their own benefit), then psychopaths would likely be more Machiavellian than would nonpsychopaths in their approach to interpersonal interactions. Smith and Griffith (1978) studied the relationship between psychometric indicators of psychopathy and Machiavellianism among college students. (This approach can be considered appropriate only to the extent that one regards psychopathy as correctly represented by a continuum.) The research found a statistically significant correlation of 0.25 between the measures of psychopathy and Machiavellianism. This finding is in keeping with the control theory, though it is not considered particularly strong support.

The same is true of a study by Rotenberg (1974). He investigated the concepts of "affective role taking" versus "cognitive role taking" as they apply to delinquency (not specifically psychopaths). Rotenberg found that delinquents were not deficient in cognitive role-taking skills although they were significantly lower than nondelinquents in affective role-taking abilities. If one interprets these results to mean that delinquents are relatively emotionally detached from others, though still possessing an intellectual understanding of others' behavior, and if one assumes that delinquents share these qualities with psychopaths, then one can conclude that Rotenberg's findings support the contention that psychopaths view other people as objects. Because these qualifications are necessary, however, this study does not represent strong support for the control theory.

The reader may remember the previously described study of psychopaths' self-concept by Tamayo and Raymond (1977) which demonstrated that psychopaths tend to view themselves (in relation to others) in negative terms. Such a negative sense of self-esteem has been shown to be related to a low degree to acceptance of others in a variety of early studies (Beger, 1952; Omwake, 1954; Phillips, 1951; Stock, 1949; Swinn, 1961). If one assumes that a low degree of acceptance of others can imply a tendency to view others in impersonal ways, then these studies are supportive of the view that psychopaths see others as objects in their environment. That conditional statement, coupled with the fact that none of those early investigations employed psychopaths as subjects, makes the degree of support afforded the control theory by these studies minimal.

Finally, a theoretical article was found that is more to the point. While discussing behavioral descriptions of psychological disorders, Ullmann and Krasner (1969) stated that "other people do not become effective secondary reinforcing stimuli for [the psychopath]" (p. 455). In other words, the psychopath has not learned to perceive associations with other people as rewarding. Similarly, Ullmann and Krasner describe the psychopath as "not paying attention to the other person's welfare: he is less likely to avoid lying to the other person and to worry about the ultimate aversive consequences for the other person" (p. 455). In essence, psychopaths do not find people reinforcing and they do not concern themselves about their effects on others. One would expect that interactions with such people would be rather impersonal and often manipulative. Ullmann and Krasner's view of psychopaths seems consistent with the perspective taken herein.

In summary, no direct or strong evidence was found relating to the issue of how psychopaths perceive other people. The tangential evidence that was found was supportive to the control theory.

Psychopathy and a Limited Behavioral Repertoire

No research addressing the topic of a limited behavioral repertoire in psychopaths was found. Hence no statement based in empiricism can be made concerning the support or contraindication for that theorized characteristic. Of interest, Hare (1978) has stated that most of the factors that help to inhibit antisocial and aggressive behavior in normal persons—empathy, fear of punishment, etc—are more or less missing in the psychopath. As a result, he has a larger repertory of actual behaviors than does the normal person.

(p. 58)

Although it seems obvious that psychopaths are often more willing to exhibit antisocial behaviors than are nonpsychopaths, I believe that Hare erred when he made his conclusion. Psychopaths typically do not show the same ability to express affect, or to express that affect assertively as the average person. Similarly, I believe that most "normal persons" have the behavioral ability to act in antisocial ways but simply choose not to do so. That lack of willingness in the normal person should not be confused with a lack of ability as would be implied from a smaller "repertory of actual behaviors."

Psychopathy and the Preoccupation with Control and Challenge

"The attribution to self of success and the attribution to external factors of failure provides for the continuation of control attempts" (Kelley, 1971, p. 23). With those words, Kelley described his notion of "effective control." His postulate was that it is important for individuals to be able to exercise control over their environment so as to maintain self-esteem and avoid cognitive dissonance.

The control theory concurs with Kelley's perspective. The psychopath is not described as the only type of individual for whom environmental control is important. To the contrary, a desire for such control is considered simply a part of what it means to be human. Psychopaths, however, are perceived as being excessively concerned with environmental control and of being preoccupied with the desire to regulate their own rewards.

In this section, four research topics will be discussed in support of the theorized perspective on control. The first will be evidence for the relevance of environmental control in all of our lives. The second line of support will be drawn from the research on learned helplessness. Third will be a discussion of the psychopath's preoccupation with the issue of control. Finally, the concept of challenge will be considered, particularly from the psychopaths' perspective.

General Issue of Environmental Control

The concept that individuals strive for mastery and control over their environment is not new. Such a concept has played a central role in a variety of theoretical works (e.g., deCharms, 1968; Kelley, 1971; Kelly, 1955; White, 1959; Woodworth, 1958). Early empirical work studying environmental control (operationalized as the ability to predict and be certain about behavioral outcomes) concluded that people prefer predictability and certainty over unpredictability and uncertainty, even when that predictability does not affect the probability of reward (Prokasy, 1956; Wyckoff, 1952). Subjects in those studies found the predictability of the environment desirable in and of itself.

More recent research has concurred. Fisher and Pritchard (1978) studied the relationship between intrinsic motivation and both extrinsic rewards and personal control. The researchers concluded that personal control is a more important determinant of intrinsic motivation than is extrinsic reward.

Wortman (1975) was able to demonstrate that people will perceive themselves to be in control even when they cause a chance event. In her study, subjects were shown two differently colored marbles which were then placed in a can such that the marbles could not be seen. Subjects were told they could win one of two consumer items they were shown, depending on which marble was drawn from the can. Three separate conditions were run. One third of the subjects were told that the experimenter would pick the marble for them and the prize each marble would represent. Another third could pick their own marble (blindly from the can), but they were not informed which marble determined which prize until after the marble was selected. The remaining subjects were able to choose their own marble (blindly) and were informed beforehand of the relationship between marble color and the prize won.

The results indicated that subjects who caused their own chance outcome of marble selection and knew beforehand what they hoped to obtain attributed to themselves more control over the outcome, more choice about which prize they received, and more responsibility for their outcomes than subjects in the other conditions. A second experiment by Wortman replicated that result. Apparently people see themselves in control even when the events are random as long as they had "a hand" in causing the event to occur.

The perception of control has been shown to be a critical variable in the alleviation of, or adaptation to stress. For instance, Pervin (1963) found that when given a choice, the subjects preferred to self-administer an aversive stimulus rather than have the experimenter do it. Corah and Buffa (1970) concluded that such a choice is virtually equivalent to giving the subjects a sense of control over the threatening stimulus. That choice variable was viewed as reducing the aversive quality of the stimulus, and therefore explained subjects' resultant reduction in physiological arousal in response to the stimulus. Less severe reactions to aversive stimuli under conditions of perceived, though not necessarily veridical control, versus perceived noncontrol has been a consistent finding (Geer, Davison, & Gatchel, 1970; Gilbert & Mangelsdorff, 1979; Glass, Reim, & Singer, 1971; Glass, Singer, Leonard, Krantz, Cohen, & Cummings, 1973).

In summary, empirical results have repeatedly shown that the issue of perceived control is important to us all. Interestingly, as the last set of cited studies indicate, control need not be veridical but must be perceived as such.

Environmental Control and Learned Helplessness Conditioning

If perceived control can alleviate or minimize physical stress, can we assume that such a perception will also compensate for, or prevent the feeling of helplessness? Empirical results suggest the answer is yes. In fact, the perception of control and the experience of learned helplessness seem to have a strong negatively correlated relationship.

At one time, learned helplessness was thought to result from the impact of "no control," that is, from noncontingent outcomes related to one's behavior (e.g., Roth & Kubal, 1975; Seligman, 1975). Since then, researches have discovered that uncontrollable outcomes may not be necessary, and are certainly not sufficient to yield the performance decrements associated with learned helplessness conditioning. Rather the essential component seems to be the individual's expectation that the particular situation is potentially able to be affected by some people, but that he or she specifically cannot respond in the necessary ways to obtain desired results (Confer, 1978;

Garber & Hollon, 1980). In essence, learned helplessness results from a reduction in perceived control coupled with ineffective attempts to restore control (Baum, Aiello, & Calesnick, 1978).

Crucial to the control theory's postulates is whether learned helplessness can be reversed or prevented through an increase in the perception of control. Some research suggests that this is so. Tennen and Eller (1977) reported one way of reversing the effect of learned helplessness, a way which can be reasonably interpreted as facilitating an increase in perceived control. After their subjects had some exposure to noncontingent reinforcement, the researchers told the subjects that they were facing a difficult task. The effect of such information was a reversal of the effect of learned helplessness training, to the extent that the subjects' performances were facilitated. Apparently "when available cues indicate that uncontrollability might be situation specific, individuals seem to redouble their efforts on a subsequent task" (Tennen & Eller, 1977, p. 269). When individuals attribute their failure to an external cause, they show an increased tendency to persist in behaviors designed to gain reward, apparently because they believe they are still capable of doing so. (The relationship found between the attribution of a failure to an external cause and the subsequent persistent behavior designed to gain the reinforcement is in concordance with the theorized relationship between partial helplessness conditioning and the tendency to persist in action when frustrated.)

Marotta (1978) discovered one method for the prevention, or as she phrased it, the immunization against learned helplessness. In a study employing inescapable noise as the uncontrollable aversive stimulus, Marotta varied the subject's amount of prior exposure to control versus no control experiences in a separate task. Results indicated the existence of a negative linear relationship between the amount of prior exposure to control and the resultant "immunization" which prevented impaired performance, with self-reported helplessness.

In summary, the perception of control over the environment in the attempt to obtain reinforcement seems highly interrelated with the experience of learned helplessness. As psychopaths have experienced partial helplessness conditioning, a process which both acknowledges and denies environmental control, they have been partially immunized against feelings of helplessness. Persistent behavior is therefore designed to gain reinforcement and the perception of control (in keeping with Tennen and Eller, 1977).

Psychopaths' Preoccupation with Environmental Control

Unfortunately there are no empirical tests of that assumption or of the general relationship between psychopathy and perceived control. In fact, only two case studies using "psychopathic" adolescents could be found that were at all pertinent.

In reference to three disordered youth, Henderson (1972) related that

> It became clear that as long as they could regard people as objects which they could control, maneuver, manage, shift at whim, magically and without regard for rules, they felt relatively secure in dealing with other people, or at least they could maintain their status quo.

> *(p. 318)*

As long as Henderson's adolescents felt in control of other people's behavior, they felt at ease.

A similar situation was described by Schmideberg (1978). She related the case of a young male with a history of violence, fire setting, killing and maiming of a variety of animals, and a variety of psychiatric evaluations diagnosing the youth as psychopathic. At one point, Schmideberg stated that "Juan got into an argument with the uncle and struck him. He came for his treatment very excited, saying, 'I have good news for you. I hit my uncle. I am grown up now and nobody can control me any more'" (p. 23). Juan's statements about being under no one's control and being boss suggest that he viewed the world as a constant battle for control and that this concept was often on his mind. (Although there is a possibility that some of Juan's attitudes are based in cultural values and roles, his violent behavioral history suggests that Juan had not adopted many of his cultural mores and attitudes in a variety of other areas, diminishing the strength of the cultural explanation of his perceptions.)

These two case reports, like any anecdotal data, do not represent strong evidence for the theoretical contention that psychopaths are preoccupied with the issue of environmental control. Nevertheless, being the only relevant writings found, it is of importance to note that they are consistent with the control theory.

Psychopaths' Preoccupation with Perceived Challenge

Only a slightly greater number of writings relate to the issue of a psychopathic preoccupation with perceived challenge. Although most of the supportive evidence is anecdotal, two relevant empirical investigations were found.

Widom (1974) studied the interpersonal conflict and cooperation of psychopaths through the use of the Prisoner's Dilemma game. Briefly, the Prisoner's Dilemma game is a two-person, non-zero sum game in which mutual cooperation benefits both participants, one-sided cooperation is punished, and mutual competition leads to large losses by both parties. In this case, the game was employed as a vehicle for studying the behavior of psychopaths in an interpersonal conflict situation.

Subjects included primary psychopaths, secondary psychopaths, and normal subjects (classified using Cleckley's criteria). The pairings between the different types of subjects were varied. Similarly, Widom varied the subjects' ability to communicate with each other, having one communication condition and one no-communication condition. Before subjects made their own selection on each trial, they predicted their partner's response. In that way, Widom obtained a measure of each subject's intentions. All payoffs occurred immediately after each trial. At the end of the experiment, subjects were questioned about their perceived interpersonal roles in the game.

Results indicated that primary and secondary psychopaths did not differ from controls in how they played the game. The psychopaths cooperated as often, tolerated the boredom of 60 trials as well, and predicted future retaliation as well as the control subjects. The subject groups perceived their interpersonal roles, however, in substantially different ways. Both primary and secondary psychopaths viewed themselves and the other individual as competitors and opponents. On the other hand, control subjects most frequently saw themselves and the other person as collaborators, accomplices, cooperators, and partners. This perceptual difference suggests that psychopaths are much more likely to perceive competition and challenge in situations other people do not.

Vada's (1977) research investigated the relationship between the perceived source of control (termed locus of control) and manipulative attitudes and behavior in imprisoned psychopaths (classified according to the MMPI). Two hypotheses were tested: (1) psychopaths' locus of control is a function of the ability to manipulate individuals in the environment and (2) psychopaths would score higher on attitudinal and behavioral measures of manipulation.

Results from Vada's study did not support either hypothesis. The psychopaths did not differ from normal incarcerated subjects (based on the MMPI) on either attitudinal or behavioral measures of manipulation. A potentially crucial error by Vada in his subject selection procedure, however, may have been to blame. Research has found that the MMPI can differentiate psychopathic criminals from nonpsychopathic criminals in only a gross way (Craddick, 1962; Hare, 1970; Silver, 1963). The inefficient and potentially inaccurate subject selection procedure employed by Vada may have canceled out findings which otherwise would have been relevant to the control theory.

Theoretical writings have generally supported the control theory's perspective concerning the issue of challenge. For instance, Schuster (1976) summarized case history data by stating that "for the psychopathic youth everyone is out there trying to 'get over' and it is better to be exploiter rather than victim" (p. 131).

Alfred Adler (1976) described criminals, a group which shares some (though not necessarily some of the crucial) characteristics with psychopaths, in the following way:

> We all struggle to rise from an inferior position to a superior position, from below to above. . . . We should not be surprised, therefore, when we discover exactly the same tendency among criminals. . . . What distinguishes them is not the fact that they are striving in this fashion, it is the direction their striving takes. . . .
>
> To deprive others—this is his idea of superiority.

(p. 131, 136)

Adler's description of a striving toward depriving others sounds like the challenge to obtain what others have. Based on Adler's postulates, that striving for superiority is a central issue in all of our lives and that criminal striving is toward depriving others, we may assume that the challenge to deprive others is central in the life of a criminal. Although it can be argued that some criminals do not deprive others (e.g., those who commit "victimless" crimes), and that criminals and psychopaths do not share this personality dimension, Adler's statements can be considered consistent with the control theory.

Lykken (1957) and Hare (1968) both explained psychopaths' lack of anxiety in response to shock by noting that psychopaths probably view experimental situations as more of a challenge than a threat. Finally, Smith (1978) stated the following about psychopaths:

> Indeed, the entire raison d'être of certain psychopaths seems predicated on reading the wishes, wills, weaknesses of others, then dangling the appropriate variety of carrot until the other succumbs.

(p. 62)

In conclusion, although there is not yet much research evidence to support the concept, various researchers and theoreticians do seem to agree that psychopaths demonstrate an exaggerated inclination toward the perception of environmental challenge. This tendency appears especially strong when other people are involved.

In summary of the overall review of research support and contraindications for the control theory, most theorized relationships were substantiated empirically when relevant studies could be found. Unfortunately, many concepts described by the control theory have not yet been researched, at least with psychopaths. When direct tests of theorized relationships were lacking, indirect tests were found to be consistent with the theory.

ADDITIONAL COMMENTS

One of the major differences between the control theory and the theories reviewed previously is the control theory's complexity. None of the other theories approach the detail incorporated within the control theory. As described next, that characteristic can be considered a weakness, though that weakness is compensated for by the comprehensiveness that only such a detailed theory can claim.

The evaluation of the control theory will follow the guidelines outlined by Hall and Lindzey (1970) described in Chapter 1. They delineated six criteria of a "good" theory.

The first criterion was that a theory should lead to the collection or observation of relevant empirical relationships not yet observed. As enumerated in the research review just completed, there are a multitude of relationships specified in the control theory that have yet to be empirically investigated. Various relationships described in the theory have not been postulated previously.

The second criterion employed to evaluate a theory is its utility. Hall and Lindzey specified three aspects to a theory's utility: (1) verifiability, (2) comprehensiveness, and (3) heuristic influence. Each of these aspects will be discussed separately.

A theory is verifiable to the extent that predictions can be generated from it which are then confirmed when empirically tested. At this stage in the life of the control theory, the capacity to generate testable hypotheses is crucial. The determination of the research support for any of those predictions will have to wait until the appropriate investigations are performed.

The multitude of postulated relationships in the control theory suggests that a great variety of predictions can be developed from the theory. Not all of these will be easily tested, however. The early etiological sections of the theory will not easily lend themselves to empirical verification (e.g., that psychopaths experience partial helplessness conditioning). Most tests of hypotheses stemming from those theorized etiological relationships will be at best suggestive. Unfortunately, such is the plight of any psychological theory which specifies the existence of etiological factors during early childhood (i.e., partial helplessness conditioning) and at birth (i.e., low cortical arousal).

Theorized relationships from later processes, however, seem to suggest numerous predictions for which data could be collected for verification. For instance, the concept that psychopaths tend to act when frustrated could be tested using predetermined frustrations of reward acquisition with various behavioral recourses available. In such a setting, psychopaths would be expected to persist in their overt attempts to gain the reward, especially if the behaviors available to them had brought them success earlier. Similarly, the concept that psychopaths view other people as objects and obstacles to be overcome suggests that the psychopath should be found to be more competitive than the average person, in degree and/or frequency. Competitiveness can be tested using various methodologies.

The verifiability of the control theory is therefore seen as substantial, at least beyond the early etiological features of the theory. There appears to be a great capacity for the generation of testable predictions.

An even stronger characteristic of the theory is its comprehensiveness. Compared to the four reviewed theories of psychopathy, the control theory incorporates more relevant research and explains more facets of the disorder. No major behavioral manifestation of psychopathy was ignored. Additionally, genetic and environmental factors were intimately embodied in the theory.

The heuristic influence of the control theory cannot yet be determined. Only time will tell the extent to which the arousal of disbelief or resistance in researchers will generate related empirical investigations.

Overall, the theory seems to have much potential to be useful. The realization of the utility remains to be seen.

The third evaluative criterion for theory is the incorporation of known empirical findings into a logical and reasonable framework. The determination of how well the control theory measured up in this regard is partially up to the reader. The theory incorporated a great variety of research through the integration of strong points from four separate theories. The degree to which the theory is logical and reasonable, however, can only be determined via other people's inspection of what the theory states.

Parsimony is the fourth criterion of evaluation employed here. At first glance, the control theory may seem poor in this area. The theory's series of postulates is anything but simple. That characteristic, however, should not be considered sufficient reason for condemnation. Parsimony as an evaluative criterion specifically applies to the comparison of two theories which forecast the same events. In that case, the theory which is more parsimonious is to be preferred. When one theory is significantly more comprehensive than another, predicting and specifying more relationships than the other, then the theory with greater comprehensiveness is more useful (assuming the other criteria are equally met).

Compared to the four reviewed theories, the control theory is more comprehensive and less parsimonious. This combination suggests that the control theory may prove more useful than any of the other theories.

The fifth criterion is concept clarity and explicitness. That issue relates to the theory's testability. As described below, the control theory is generally found to be sufficient, though occasionally lacking in meeting this criterion.

On the one hand, the theory mostly deals with observables, phenomena which can be watched and measured. Stimulation seeking, enhanced ability to resist altering behavior in response to punishment, the inclination toward action when frustrated, and the persistent behavioral emphasis on environmental control all fit into this category.

On the other hand, explicit definitions for some concepts are lacking. Perceived challenge, for example, was defined from a variety of perspectives: (1) movement toward a goal considered difficult to reach, (2) action against a person or object with the explicit purpose of demonstrating superiority, (3) movement in response to other people's comments specifically to demonstrate the inaccuracy of those comments (such as "You can't"), or (4) behavior designed to cause specific actions from others, actions they would not otherwise make. As explained earlier in this chapter, the challenge for psychopaths does not generally include movement toward long-term goals, though the application of the concept does include any of the other three perspectives. Although this definitional array may be clearly stated, that very multiplicity of definitions diminishes the consistent utility of the concept for empirical endeavors. The concept of the perception of people as objects of pleasure or obstacles to be overcome shares this shortcoming.

The final evaluative criterion is the capacity of the theory to focus our attention on crucial aspects of the phenomenon so to avoid the abyss of complexity we all know to exist. The control theory, like the other theories reviewed, meets this criterion through a step by step explanation of psychopathy's crucial elements. The integrative theory of psychopathy delineates a greater number of critical aspects than the other theories do so as to be more comprehensive in the explanation of the phenomenon.

In conclusion, the control theory of psychopathy appears to rate at least as well on the six criteria of theory evaluation as the theories reviewed in Chapters 2, 3, 4, and 5. The major strength of the integrative theory is its increased comprehensiveness, and therefore potential utility, over the other theories. Some relative weaknesses, such as the verifiability of etiologically early postulates and the multiple definitions of certain concepts, were found.

SUMMARY OF THE REVIEW OF THE CONTROL THEORY OF PSYCHOPATHY

The control theory stated that two factors are necessary and sufficient for the development of psychopathy: low cortical arousal and partial helplessness conditioning. Most of the research that was found supported this conceptualization of the syndrome. Many of the theorized relationships, however, have not yet been empirically investigated in sufficient detail to allow for conclusions of support to be drawn. Evaluation of the theory using Hall and Lindzey's (1970) six criteria led to the finding that the control theory ranks well among the theories of psychopathy in its formal attributes. The final evaluation of the theory, of course, remains in the hands of researchers and clinicians who will test and employ its postulates.

PART TWO

Treatment Issues

CHAPTER 7

Preliminary Issues in the Treatment of Psychopathy

This chapter discusses two topics which must be addressed as preliminary to successful therapy procedures with psychopaths: (1) the issue of accurate historical information and (2) differentially assessing psychopathy early in therapy.

ISSUE OF ACCURATE HISTORICAL INFORMATION

As any experienced clinician recognizes, one cannot always accept the biographical information given by a client as accurate, for a variety of reasons. The client may be too embarrassed to acknowledge something from his past. His memory may be distorted or absent concerning certain events. Within certain settings or when it concerns certain illegal behavior, the client may be afraid to admit to certain wrongdoing. In some cases, such as with a psychopath, the client may also simply enjoy telling lies.

A client's lies can take on incredible proportions when your client is a psychopathic "con-man." Imagine the information you might get when attempting to assess the man described in the following newspaper article. (Parenthetical comments were not part of the original article, from the front page of the *Tallahassee Democrat*, July 24, 1981, but have been added to highlight the person's psychopathic characteristics.)

The story of Norman Gregory Howard is the story of the ultimate sting: a con of the FBI.

Conceivably, he could cost the U.S. Treasury $100 million.

A few years ago the FBI considered Howard a prize underworld informant. With top priority from Director William Webster, the bureau assigned him a version of "Mission Impossible." (The title suggests quite a "challenging" situation.)

Howard's job: Crack a Mafia-run ring that bribed public officials for construction projects.

"I don't want any money," Howard, an ex-con, told FBI agents. (Note the criminal history.) "I want a presidential pardon." (Testing the limits of his power in the situation, even though those limits are essentially irrelevant given his apparent intentions not to fulfill his part of the bargain, as described in the following.)

To infiltrate the mob, Howard posed as an insurance salesman and collected hundreds of thousands of dollars in fees.

Now the FBI can't find him. It can't find the money either. And recently the Justice Department admitted liability for a fraudulent sale that Howard made in Florida. It cost the government $560,000.

Howard is a charming, disarming, distinguished man of 55. (I doubt Cleckley would have described most 55-year-old psychopaths any differently.) He has graying temples, a balding head and a trace of a mustache. He exudes sincerity and confidence. (The description is again noted.) Once he was a cop in Chicago, a good cop. That was from 1954 to 1960.

He was also a good insurance salesman in his spare time. He found it more profitable and he turned in his badge.

He got in trouble in 1970. The Indiana insurance commissioner fined him $10,000 for selling useless auto insurance. (The first time they caught him, but the following account seems to suggest he had been involved in such schemes for years before this.)

"He should have gotten one to 10 years in state prison," says Morris Cochran, a Better Business Bureau manager in Gary. "Instead, he claimed he had heart trouble and had to fly to Switzerland for surgery." (A useful lie?)

In 1974 Howard got himself into trouble again. This time he swindled three Chicago-area banks out of $1.3 million, using fake loan credentials. (The "confidence man" way of life continues.)

Facing 47 years in prison, Howard said he had information, good information, which he would give to U.S. Attorney Richard Hanning in exchange for a lenient sentence. (Psychopaths usually attempt to interact with the highest person in charge when they need to deal with any person in authority.) It worked.

Howard got a few months in jail and saw a psychiatrist. (One has to wonder what information this professional obtained during the assessment.)

For the easy treatment, Howard helped bust up a construction racket. Then, to enhance his new career as an informant, he threw in Philip Kitzer, one of the nation's premiere swindlers.

Gary, Ind., FBI agents Jim Wedick and Jack Brennan, posing as Howard's business partners, nailed Kitzer for fraud.

"Howard seemed to enjoy working with the FBI and pulling a con on the man the media called the world's greatest con man," says prosecutor Hanning. "He seemed to enjoy conning the con man." (The ultimate challenge?)

Howard's panache in the underworld impressed two Chicago FBI agents, Leroy Himelbauch and George Spinelli.

On Friday the 13th in January, 1978, the agents took Howard to lunch at The Palmer House, a posh hotel. Howard, attired in a fine silk suit, spoke of the Mafia.

Howard told the agents what they wanted to hear. (This is one of the "games" for control discussed in Chapter 9.) The mob was moving into the construction industry. It paid off union leaders, bribed public officials and collected big insurance money for unfinished jobs. (One must assume, given his audience, that the story Howard weaved was intricate, making it seem more believable. This process is discussed in Chapters 9 and 10.)

Howard's plan: Let him pose as an insurance salesman to set up the sale of performance bonds. Developers buy these bonds to protect themselves against delays in building. Mafia-connected outfits have a hard time getting them. Howard promised to hand over financial records to prove the Mafia link.

All Howard wanted, he professed, was a pardon from the president. (Again, he attempts to bargain with the person with the most authority; the greater the authority, the greater the challenge.)

FBI Director Webster approved the undercover sting. But no one promised Howard a pardon. (Imagine how charming and sincere Howard must have appeared to gain the FBI's belief that this "con man" could be trusted without any promise from the FBI of getting the only "payment" for which he asked.)

The FBI needed a legitimate cover. The bureau came up with a patriot, Carl Barton, president of the prestigious New Hampshire Insurance Co.

On March 2, 1978, agents introduced Howard to the insurance executive as a one-time policeman and experienced informant. They didn't identify him as an ex-con. Barton's only concern: He didn't want his company to be liable for insurance contracts.

The FBI agreed. No one bothered to put it in writing because of "Justice Department red tape," agent Spinelli explained later. (How trusted Howard must have been! Given that the FBI is not ignorant of "con men," Howard must have played his part especially well.) . . .

Thinking Howard was just another newly hired salesman, an unknowing executive gave him 50 power-of-attorney forms on March 23, 1978. The forms authorized Howard to write "any and all bonds"—the paper equivalent of millions of dollars in bond fees.

Said agent Spinelli later: "At that particular time I did not know what a person could do with a power of attorney. I was totally unaware of what could happen."

What happened began the first night of his employment. Howard wrote a bond—without telling the FBI—and collected $18,000 in a paper bag from New Jersey contractor Rudolph Orlandini. (The psychopath's real intention shows itself at his first perceived opportunity.)

Thus begun the ultimate con—the sting of the FBI. The $18,000 hasn't been seen since.

Howard proved to be a tremendous salesman. (Could this have been based in his charming, sincere nature, or maybe some "bargain" rates he was giving the buyers, or both?) A week after Howard began, an uninformed executive marveled:

"He told me he is picking up 25 accounts in NYC this week!"

During his brief "employment," Howard collected somewhere between $300,000 and several million dollars in bond fees, court records indicate. But no one but Howard knows for sure.

The insurance company suspected something might be haywire April 4, 1978, when it learned that Howard was writing bonds on his own. Politely but firmly, the company attorney told him to stop.

He didn't stop. (Verbal reprimands typically have no effect on psychopaths' behavior.) More letters followed, including several to the FBI.

Howard told the FBI he wasn't writing bonds (an obvious lie from the company's perspective). The FBI chose to believe him instead of the insurance company. (Again, Howard's ability to charm others shows itself.)

On April 20, 1978, Barton, the patriotic insurance executive, flew to Chicago for a secret meeting with agent Spinelli.

More worried than ever, Barton asked in exasperation why Howard was continuing to write bonds. He didn't want his company responsible.

Spinelli tried to calm him, saying he didn't believe Howard had done anything wrong.

"Our man is good," the agent assured the insurance executive. "A straight arrow. You've got nothing to worry about."

"I'm not convinced you've got him on a short leash," Barton replied. (Typically the psychopath can fool only some people, but often is able to find "new believers" as the old set come to learn the truth, a process described in detail in Chapter 9).

"It's a short leash, all right. We've got enough on him to put him away for life." (The perception that long-term, versus short-term, negative consequences to psychopaths' behavior will deter them from those behaviors is usually mistaken, as it was here.)

This shocked Barton. He didn't know Howard had a criminal record. . . .

The insurance company didn't buy the FBI's explanation. (A lesson to remember: Behaviors speak louder than rationalizations.) On its own, it cut off Howard. Barton revoked Howard's powers of attorney even though the FBI insisted Howard was, yes, a straight arrow.

Finally, the Chicago FBI office began to get nervous. Agents raided Howard's office on North Michigan Avenue, confiscating the few remaining power-of-attorney forms.

The date was June 1, 1978. . . .

By September, 1978, the FBI knew IT had been stung, not the Mafia.

Its Operation Frontland, targeted in five states, hadn't caught a single crook. Not even Howard.

The FBI's immediate problem: Get Howard "out of circulation, in from the cold," an FBI insider said.

There was a way. Howard had written a phony performance bond several years earlier on a Burger King in West Palm Beach. A grand jury indicted him in October, 1978. He pleaded guilty on Feb. 20, 1979. A judge put him away for a year at the federal prison at Eglin Air Force Base. (The most common place to find psychopaths involved in some kind of therapy is in prison.)

He got out two months early for good behavior, March 7, 1980.

By then more than a dozen companies sued New Hampshire Insurance and the FBI because the company wouldn't honor the bonds. The Justice Department agreed to defend the suits in court.

Gerald James, a county attorney from Fort Pierce, filed one of them. He was an innocent victim.

He had financed a condominium, purchasing a $1.7-million performance bond. He paid Howard a $39,000 fee. When construction stopped, New Hampshire wouldn't pay. James sued.

After three years of litigation, James won a $560,000 settlement out of court this month (July, 1981).

Still unresolved are 10 similar lawsuits. Those suits claim the government is liable for $100 million. . . .

The FBI is now talking about another Howard scam. This one occurred in Atlanta a couple of months after his parole for good behavior.

Suddenly, dozens of car owners complained that Howard sold them useless auto insurance, just like a decade earlier in Indiana. (Old patterns of partially reinforced behavior tend to repeat themselves.)

Georgia Deputy Insurance Commissioner Jerry Holbrook tried to close him down. "He's the slickest confidence man I've ever met," Holbrook said. (Dishonesty does not imply stupidity.) "I checked my wallet the first time I met him."

The Dekalb County Police Department took notice too. Officer D.A. Hardeman tried to arrest him at his $90,000 home in Decatur Feb. 3, 1981.

"He's not here," his wife, Cynthia, said. "He's in Chicago." (The psychopath is usually able, through charm or intimidation, to get other people to support his actions.)

Hardeman looked around anyway. He found Howard hiding in an upstairs closet. . . .

Although Howard had violated his probation by moving to Atlanta, County Magistrate James Kirkland let him loose on a $2,000 bond.

The judge didn't know anything about the FBI sting. . . .

On April 28, 1981, a Georgia grand jury indicted Howard on 12 counts of selling phony insurance. He could get 120 years. But this time the Georgia cops couldn't find him. Howard had skipped town, fleeing Georgia.

That made him a federal fugitive. So it is now up to his former employer, the Federal Bureau of Investigation, to find him.

At 12:32 *a.m.*, May 22, 1981, Howard telephoned Holbrook, the Georgia deputy insurance commissioner. . . .

The FBI traced the call to Buffalo, Mich. Within 30 minutes, agents found a mouthpiece dangling from a pay phone outside a church.

No one has heard from Howard since he last spoke to a Georgia district attorney six months ago (meaning he abandoned his "supportive" wife).

Howard said he had some information, good information, that would help break up a huge insurance scheme.

He even volunteered to work undercover to break the case. In exchange, of course, for his own lenient treatment. (In trying this scheme again, he seems to demonstrate that he was not cognizant of the consequences of his previous actions on people's perception of him.)

In most cases, the lies and intricate stories will not be as complicated as in this example. However, once a clinician has come to suspect that the client is psychopathic, then it is probably a safe idea to believe little of the reported history until it is verified by outside sources. After all, many psychopaths simply enjoy lying for the sake of seeing what they can get past other people.

For example, one incarcerated client had a chart full of contradictions. In some filed reports, the client was born in 1940; in others 1945. The chart contained reports of his having been married while other writings indicated he had never married. The client consistently gave reports that he had served in the military in Vietnam, including places and dates, until it was proven he had never been there. He persistently stated that he was a member of an infamous motorcycle gang even though there were strong indications that this was simply one way he attempted to intimidate (i.e., control) others. One filed report based on his statements indicated his father had died many years before while other reports showed his father still to be alive.

Probably his most successful lie, for about two weeks, was when he informed the staff where he was incarcerated that he had received a telephone call from his sister telling him that his mother had died. He feigned grieving until one of the staff spoke to his healthy mother and confronted him about it. Even then, he initially claimed that the staff person was lying! Eventually he acknowledged this lie when the evidence that his mother was alive and that his sister had not had contact with him in years was about to become overwhelming. When asked for his reasons for this and other lies, he offered many statements that were later determined also to be lies.

How can this problem be handled? Clearly one cannot take the word of a psychopath about his history without being misled. The answer involves some extra work.

The clinician, or the clinician's co-worker, must do two things: (1) check all available records for contradictions and (2) contact people and obtain records from outside of the therapy setting. These steps are invaluable when doing therapy with a psychopath because they allow you to have some knowledge of the client's lies and half-truths as they occur. (The therapeutic value of this knowledge is discussed in Chapters 9 and 10.)

The issue becomes complicated when the clinician does not realize that the client is psychopathic and likely to be offering misinformation. Are you always supposed to be checking outside sources, just in case?

While that can be useful if you have the time, most of us do not function with that kind of luxury. Therefore, the assessment that a client is psychopathic must often be made without verifiable historical information, at least tentatively.

DIFFERENTIALLY ASSESSING PSYCHOPATHY EARLY IN THERAPY

How should one make such an assessment? What signs should be considered indicators? Are there other conditions that present themselves in ways similar to psychopathy, but need to be treated very differently? This section discusses answers to these questions.

The first place many clinicians turn in their attempt to assess psychopathy is the Diagnostic and Statistical Manual for Mental Disorders, Volume III (DSM-III) (American Psychiatric Association, 1980), under the category of Antisocial Personality Disorder. I warn against drawing a conclusion about the presence of psychopathy based solely on a client's meeting the criteria for antisocial personality disorder, however. The reason is that the criteria for the diagnosis of antisocial personality disorder seem to be too broad compared to the descriptors of psychopathy. Hare (1981), for instance, reported two of his studies that found that although approximately 77 percent of inmates in various Canadian penal institutions meet the criteria for antisocial personality disorder, only about 30 percent of the total set of inmates seem to be psychopaths based on Cleckley-type criteria. The finding that less than half of the incarcerated people meeting the criteria for the antisocial personality disorder are psychopaths indicates that DSM-III criteria are too inclusive to serve as our indicators of psychopathy.

Hare has spent a great deal of effort learning to differentiate psychopaths from other individuals for the purpose of performing useful research. I will not try to describe all of his relevant findings here (Hare, 1980; Hare & Cox, 1978; Hare and Schalling, 1978), but a simple summary will suffice. In essence, what Hare has found is that the criteria specified by Cleckley in 1941 have both validity and interrater reliability (using a scale described by Hare, 1980). Those criteria are enumerated for the reader in Chapter 1. Those criteria are the ones I suggest clinicians use as their indicators of psychopathy when confronted with new clients.

There are other psychiatric conditions that can mimic psychopathy, however, that must be investigated before a determination of psychopathy is made (Lion, 1981b). These conditions are often overlooked because the client's antisocial behaviors seem to dominate the clinical picture.

One such condition involves what the DSM-III refers to as the Organic Personality Syndrome. Based on the official criteria, clients with this problem can show "emotional lability" and "impairment in impulse control" without any signs of "clouding of consciousness," "delusions," or "hallucinations" (American Psychiatric Association, 1980, p. 120). This combination can resemble psychopathy.

For instance, I once had an incarcerated client who had been diagnosed antisocial personality disorder for many years before I came to know him. He was also known to have occasional seizures, but apparently no one drew a connection between the two. The client was known to have suffered an accidental damaging blow to his head when he was age 12 (i.e., before age 15, presumably affecting his behavior in ways outlined for the antisocial personality disorder). His recorded history did not specify if his antisocial behaviors began before that accident. Even so, I came to suspect that his impulsivity and emotional lability were related to his seizure disorder. Given that his brain damage was already documented (through a CAT scan and EEG), I tentatively altered his diagnosis to Organic Personality Syndrome with the purpose of adding pharmacological forms of treatment to his treatment plan. Sure enough, after he began appropriate pharmacological treatment, his emotional lability and impulsivity decreased notably. His remaining psychological issues were then treated without significant interference from his brain damage. If the diagnosis of antisocial personality disorder (in this case, psychopathy) had been continued, the client would have been unlikely to show any benefit from therapy. The reader is cautioned to investigate any reported history of brain trauma from a client to avoid mislabeling an organic problem as psychopathy.

How did I come to suspect that this client was not psychopathic but suffering an organic problem instead? Largely by the type of interactions he and I had. My interactions with psychopathic clients typically leave me with the perception that they have been attempting to have some kind of battle with me, usually verbal. More specifically, during many interactions with psychopathic clients, I feel a push on my emotions to make me feel defensive, guilty, attacked, beaten up, or convinced of something I am not willing to believe.

Interactions with clients suffering brain damage, however, do not usually feel the same. Instead of the psychopath's attempts to "win" in the interaction by putting me on the defensive, the brain-damaged client is more likely not going to understand all that he is being told, such that his verbal persistence simply feels like he has not grasped what I said to him. Instead of feeling defensive, I am typically left feeling frustrated and a little helpless.

Those latter emotions are what I felt while interacting with the case described. I engage in verbal battles many times each day with psychopathic clients, but the interactions with this client felt different. Over time, I had the strong impression that he just *could not* understand or implement the feedback people gave him, unlike the psychopaths who more clearly *chose not* to give other's feedback inportance. My emotional reactions to the client, over numerous interactions with him, told me I needed to reconsider my conceptualization of the client.

A similar situation can occur with psychological (versus organic) conditions such as Post-traumatic Stress Disorder. The official criteria of the disorder (as enumerated in DSM- III, p. 238) do not seem to resemble psychopathic behaviors except for the possibility of "constricted affect" (p. 238) which can appear like the "general poverty in major affective reactions" listed by Cleckley (1941). The official criteria do not tell the whole story, however. I have seen various cases where someone appropriately diagnosed as suffering post-traumatic stress disorder has exhibited various aggressive acts towards others without apparent compunction, significant unreliability, poor judgment and a failure to learn from experience, and an apparent pathologic egocentricity. All of these descriptors have been listed by Cleckley as partially defining psychopathy. How, then, does one differentiate the two conditions?

The foremost concern in differentiating post-traumatic stress disorder from psychopathy should be the determination of whether or not the individual ever experienced trauma; that is, "a psychologically traumatic event that is generally outside of the range of usual human experience" (American Psychiatric Association, 1980, p. 236). If no such event can be verified, and the client's report does not suggest suffering trauma, then the diagnosis of post-traumatic stress disorder can be ruled out.

More problematic diagnostically is the case where a client has apparently experienced a traumatic event. Then one can be presented with the problem of trying to decide if the client represents a case of post-traumatic stress disorder, antisocial personality disorder, or both.

Sometimes the only way to get a handle on the problem is to find a relatively accurate source of information about the client's life before the traumatic event. The issue to be addressed with that information is whether the client exhibited antisocial/psychopathic behaviors before the traumatic event. If the information gathered does not demonstrate an antisocial/psychopathic past before the traumatic event, then one can likely rule out psychopathy. Of course, finding that the client was psychopathic before the event does not rule out his suffering post-traumatic stress disorder, but at least one can then expect to be encountering the treatment issues and psychopathic behaviors described in Chapters 8 through 10 along with any post-traumatic problems.

A sensitive clinician can also find evidence that will assist his differentiation of post-traumatic stress disorder and psychopathy from his emotional interaction with the client. Posttraumatic clients typically do not attempt to engage their interviewers or therapists in discussions of the stressful event on their initial few contacts (with the exception of clients who have already experienced a substantial degree of relevant psychotherapy). The event is something post-traumatic clients would rather avoid and be rid of rather than discuss and integrate as a part of themselves. The only exceptions I have witnessed to this trend occurred when some Vietnam war veterans were applying for benefits from the Veterans Administration. Even in those cases, the veterans who were considered to be legitimate examples of Vietnam war-based post-traumatic stress disorder usually demonstrated a significant *emotional* reluctance to go into details of what they experienced. When interacting with those people, clinicians often found themselves feeling a strong sense of sympathy for the clients. When veterans did not solicit that kind of emotional response from their interviewers/therapists, the clients were often perceived as simply psychopathic and not suffering a post-traumatic stress disorder.

In both of the examples cited, I described a lesson learned from my experiences: that a clinician's emotional reaction to a client is a valuable tool in diagnosing a client, including, if not especially, a psychopath. I suggest that anytime you find yourself "having battles" with a client, you should consider the possibility that your client is psychopathic.

CHAPTER   8

General Treatment Issues

This chapter is designed to enumerate the general treatment issues a clinician will encounter with psychopathic clients. The first major section describes the typical settings and presenting problems of most psychopathic clients. Following that is a discussion of the usual psychological issues of psychopaths, borrowed from the conceptualization of the integrated theory of psychopathy described in Chapter 6. Finally, there is a section devoted to what might be described as the self-preservation of the therapist; how to recognize and avoid getting emotionally involved with your client's psychopathology. This section will lead into Chapter 9 and 10's discussion of the psychopath's behaviors designed to gain control over the therapist.

WHERE AND WHEN PSYCHOPATHS ARE LIKELY TO BE SEEN FOR PSYCHOLOGICAL TREATMENT

Any experienced mental health clinician is aware that psychopathic clients are likely to be found in certain settings, and unlikely to be found in others (Reid, 1978). Given the psychopath's tendency to view sources outside of himself as the cause of his problems, he rarely refers himself for psychological treatment. His typical perspective concerning problems is to try to change his environment, either by changing the characteristics of the one he is in or by leaving it entirely. Neither of these behaviors seems to correspond with the idea of a psychopath sitting down on a regular basis to discuss his problems with a stranger.

Correctional Institution

So where does a clinician find this kind of client, and under what circumstances? One of the locations is within a locked environment, specifically a prison or forensic hospital. Once a psychopath is incarcerated, he recognizes that his options for affecting his environment are substantially decreased (as does anyone under those conditions). Within such a setting, he may perceive some utility to "playing the game" of therapy. Consider the following case example.

The client had been on parole after committing one of his many armed robberies. His parole revocation occurred because of "a technicality" (his term), meaning he did not follow one or more of the conditions of his parole (as opposed to committing another criminal act). During the prison's intake psychological screening, the client described a need for therapy. Specifically, he reported a need to overcome his tendency to commit illegal acts. (Interestingly, the result of a psychological test, the Minnesota Multiphasic Personality Inventory, indicated a severe tendency toward endorsing a host of psychological problems, an outcome that was interpreted as an attempt by the client to appear in dire psychological stress.)

By the end of the second session, I came to the conclusion that the client was a psychopath. During the third session, his true "motivation for therapy" became evident; he asked me to write a letter to his case manager (the person who could arrange for a parole hearing or the client's move to a less secure institution) indicating how involved the client was in therapy and he therefore could be trusted. Needless to say, I did not write the letter. Rather, I used his desire to convince me to write the letter as "the challenge" that kept him coming back for therapy. This technique is described later in this chapter.

As this case exemplifies, the mental health clinician should be prepared to encounter psychopathic clients within a correctional institution. Trying to get a positive written report from you is only one reason for their "participation" in therapy. There are various other common reasons that are typically considered by therapists as extraneous to treatment concerns.

One of these is boredom. As described in Chapter 6, the psychopath seeks stimulation and enjoys interpersonal challenges. A correctional institution can be a very boring place. Sometimes a psychopath will enter therapy simply because he expects to enjoy the verbal debates. Therapy represents something to do that can help pass the time. If treatment is to occur at all, and if the meetings are to continue for any length of time, then the therapy sessions must remain stimulating to the client. Therapists who discover themselves with a boredom-motivated psychopathic client usually find they are either working too hard or getting bored themselves from the lack of effort by the client.

Another enticement into therapy for the incarcerated psychopath is to earn "good time," a decrease of the amount of time he is to serve behind bars because he is "involved" in therapy. (Some states have laws that allow for the accumulation of good time, or extra good time, based on the prisoner's participation in work, education, and/or therapy activities). This motivation can be somewhat difficult to tease out because the client never has to tell you about it (unlike the desired written report mentioned previously), and typically will not. There are, however, some warning signs that the clinician can note.

Early in therapy, the client will have difficulty deciding on the goal of his treatment, or even the issue his therapy is to address. A flippant response stating a desire to stop his illegal behaviors (most often phrased as a desire to stop getting locked up) is a common reaction to the client's need to describe a reason for his therapy involvement.

As the therapy continues, the clinician is likely to note a storylike quality to the client's comments. He will not seem to have much emotional attachment to what he is saying, even if the content of the story seems shocking or upsetting to the therapist. The client may even smile at times where other emotional responses would be expected.

Later in therapy, this type of client will usually show one or more of three kinds of behavior (if he is still attending sessions): (1) his stories will become repetitive, (2) he will ask a substantial number of questions of the therapist with the purpose of getting the therapist to talk, or (3) he will talk more and more about trivial topics. All of these behaviors signal that the client is not willing to do any therapeutic work. When coupled with his earlier difficulty setting goals for his treatment, one can be rather sure that the client was in therapy for some secondary gain.

Finally, besides the clients who do not desire therapy, there are some psychopathic inmates who recognize that they are at least partly responsible for their repeated incarcerations (or loss of jobs, etc.) and are getting tired of being imprisoned (or being unemployed, etc.). These are the clients who will manage to give their therapists something with which to work. If a clinician believes a client fits this category, it can be tested early in the therapy by giving the client an assignment to do between sessions. Most psychopaths simply "playing the game" of therapy will find any of hundreds of reasons why the assignment could not or did not get completed the way the therapist requested.

The Forensic Hospital

Besides the correctional institutions, another place where psychopaths are imprisoned and willing to involve themselves in therapy is the forensic hospital. The reasons for psychopaths' involvement in treatment within this setting depends in part on the reasons they are there. The possibilities are discussed in chronological order relative to the patient's trial.

One function of many forensic hospitals is to perform assessments of defendants' competency to stand trial. A psychopath may enter the mental health system here by appearing to the judge or defense counsel (1) not to understand the legal charges against him or their potential consequences, (2) not to understand the roles of the people involved in a trial (i.e., the judge, prosecuting attorney, and defense attorney), (3) not to be able to participate in his own defense, and/or (4) not to be able to withstand the stress of the trial or the period of incarceration before and during the trial.

The most difficult issue for the psychologist or psychiatrist doing a competency for trial evaluation with this type of patient is determining that one is evaluating a psychopathic patient. Except for the notably mentally retarded psychopath, there is no inherent reason why a psychopath is not always going to be (or cannot quickly become) competent to stand trial, given the criteria of competence just discussed. There may be complications at times because the patient is found to have destroyed a sufficient number of his brain cells through his chemical abuse to affect his cognitive functions (such as his memory, ability to attend, or ability to think without paranoid ideations). Usually, however (given that the patient was not sent for an evaluation simply to buy time for the defense, a practice that is too common), the main assessment issue will be that of malingering.

The psychopath appearing in a forensic hospital for an evaluation of his competency to stand trial is often playing a game of challenge involving high stakes. The challenge is to convince the professionals that he is really unable to stand trial. The challenge seems to take one of three forms: (1) the patient goes mute, (2) the person reports auditory and/or visual hallucinations, or (3) the patient reports amnesia for the events surrounding his alleged crime. How to cope with each of these behaviors is described below.

If a patient remains mute at all times, there is no way to determine his psychopathy except by his history, and that may be difficult to ascertain in the time allotted by statute for the evaluation. About the only issue relevant to the court, however, is whether or not the patient could participate in his own defense if he wanted. In other words, the judge needs to know if the muteness is by choice or psychological trauma (given no physical reason). Therefore, the evaluator needs to concentrate on the presence or absence of other symptoms of psychological trauma, including sleep disturbance, hyperalertness or exaggerated startle response, constricted affect, and difficulty concentrating. The mute patient who beats everyone else on the ward in chess, seems to laugh at appropriate and frequent times, and shows no sleep disturbance (as was true of a case I saw) is probably mute purely by choice to avoid assessment.

The "competency for trial assessment" patient who reports auditory hallucinations raises a few issues for the evaluator. First, the evaluator must realize that auditory hallucinations in and of themselves do not make someone incompetent to stand trial. They only become an issue when they appear to interfere with the defendant's understanding of the roles of the people in a courtroom (such as through reported paranoid vocalizations that are believed by the defendant) or his ability to assist in his own defense. Second is the issue of whether a true psychosis or organic personality syndrome is present. Psychological, neuropsychological, and neurological testing all can serve to differentiate these possibilities. Third, there is the issue of malingering; the defendant (who, in our discussion, is a psychopath) feigns psychiatric symptoms in an attempt to "beat" the legal system. Given that the defendant can be experiencing auditory hallucinations and still be competent to stand trial, however, means that the evaluator should not need to deliberate much in these kinds of cases.

That leaves the patient who claims amnesia about the events surrounding his alleged illegal act. Before even trying to determine the honesty of the patient's report, the evaluator should discover how his legal jurisdiction deals with this type of claim. Some jurisdictions allow reported amnesia to serve as evidence of incompetency to stand trial. (The issue being the defendant's ability to assist in his own defense.) Many jurisdictions, however, do not. When the evaluator needs to determine the honesty of the report of amnesia, the process is similar to that of muteness. The assessment will largely concentrate on determining if there are any concomitant symptoms of the various reasons for amnesia. Assessing the degree to which the patient is psychopathic will typically give the evaluator useful information as well.

The second time a psychopath may enter the forensic mental health system is after being adjudicated as incompetent to stand trial. He is then committed for the purpose of "treatment to competency to stand trial." If the patient falls into one of the categories mentioned previously then the "treatment" phase of his commitment will largely involve an in-depth assessment along the lines described, largely to demonstrate that the original legal determination was in error.

However, occasionally there is a case where the judge, prosecuting attorney or both do not want the psychopath to be found competent to stand trial. The reasons differ from case to case, though they usually involve a desire to keep the defendant off the street for as long a time as possible. (Time spent committed to a hospital as incompetent to stand trial is sometimes not credited to any sentence later imposed, thereby lengthening the time the person spends incarcerated.)

One such case I saw was a young male adult gang member with a history of various misdemeanors and a felony. He was charged with first degree murder in the death of an opposing gang member. After he had been at the forensic hospital for a month, the professional staff sent a report back to the court stating that the patient was competent to stand trial. (The defendant was found to be psychopathic and borderline mentally retarded.) Not only did the judge eventually continue the defendant's commitment as incompetent to stand trial, but, before the hearing, the prosecuting attorney sent a rather nasty letter to the hospital staff indicating he believed our professional competence was in question. This process repeated itself, sans the nasty letter, six months later after another report was sent to the court. Considering that the murder case against the defendant was virtually open and shut, the prosecuting attorney's reaction was not based in a fear of bringing the case to trial. In cases such as these, there seems to be nothing more one can do without becoming the defendant's advocate.

The third time a psychopath may be seen in a forensic hospital is after an adjudication of not guilty by reason of insanity (NGI) (labeled in various states by other names such as not guilty by reason of mental disease or defect). In these cases, the patient has been committed to the hospital for treatment for his "dangerousness based on his mental illness" (defined with different standards in different states).

The NGI psychopath's motivation for treatment will often seem clear—to get himself released from the commitment. One should obviously become strongly suspicious of any newly committed NGI patient who shows a rapid recovery from his reported mental illness, especially if that patient has a substantial criminal past. Such can be the sign of a psychopath.

Many states have, and many more did have, statutes that committed "sexual psychopaths" (or "mentally disordered sex offenders," "mentally disturbed sex offenders," "criminal sexual psychopaths," sexually dangerous persons," "psychopathic personalities," "defective delinquents," "sex offenders," or "habitual sex offenders," depending on which state one is in) for treatment. These psychopaths were convicted of an offense considered sexual by the committing court, but instead of being incarcerated in prison, they are sentenced to be treated in a psychiatric setting. (Depending on the state, the period of treatment can occur at the beginning of the sentence, near the end of the sentence, or for the whole period of the sentence.) Problems of and techniques for treating psychopaths committed in this way will be discussed in Chapters 9 and 10.

Finally, forensic hospital clinicians typically have some people under their care who have been transferred from a correctional setting such as a county jail, state prison, or federal prison. The reason for the transfer will only sometimes alert you to the possibility that you are working with a psychopath. For instance, a common reason for transfers from correctional institutions is continued suicide attempts by the inmate (i.e., patient). As any clinician knows, suicide attempts can be motivated by reasons ranging from severe depression to conscious social manipulation. The latter category opens the door for a psychopath into a forensic hospital where he may believe that his "time" will be easier than it was in the prison or jail. Unlike the previous statutory methods of becoming a forensic hospital patient, however, psychopaths entering the hospital as a transfer from corrections may find they are soon transferred out of the hospital when their deception is discovered.

Court-Referred Outpatient Therapy

People are required by a court to participate in outpatient therapy in two ways, as a condition of probation and as a condition of parole. In both cases, the "client" may have little desire to be in your office and even less desire to self-disclose to you about anything. When this "client" is psychopathic, these characteristics are often strikingly obvious from the very beginning. Chapters 9 and 10 describes potentially useful techniques the clinician can use to form a therapeutic relationship with psychopathic clients in this setting, though the problem is admittedly very difficult.

Outpatient Marital–Family Therapy

If there is one tried and true finding about psychopathic clients involved in this kind of therapy, it is that they did not come in without a lot of "pushing" from someone else. Typically, the psychopathic client sees the problem as someone else's, or, at best, one he had but does not have any longer. Correspondingly, the someone else who "pushed" will not believe the psychopath's statements of innocence.

The "push" that got the psychopath into marital/family therapy will often be essential to determine if therapy is going to be effective. Common motivators include threats of divorce, threats of legal prosecution (i.e., for assaults), and "blackmail" involving threats of disclosure to certain people of a detail of the psychopath's history he would rather not have divulged (e.g., a wife's threat to inform the husband's employer of the husband's history of theft). The "push" can be used by the clinician to ensure that therapy does not end abruptly after a couple of sessions when the "push" may have otherwise lost its immediacy (e.g., by reminding the husband that his wife may bring up the same threat at a future time if their relationship does not change soon).

Substance Abuse Treatment Program

Psychopaths do not seem to resist acknowledging their substance abuse any more than other clients. Based on my colleagues' and my clinical experience, however, psychopaths' perseverance in continuing their abuse even after treatment seems worse than the average abuser.

That finding might lead one to the conjecture that psychopathic clients typically do not really wish to stop their chemical abuse. This conjecture is supported to the extent that psychopaths get involved in substance abuse treatment only after being "pushed" by someone else (as described under the previous subsection) or, in the case of inpatient care, when winter approaches (to get out of the cold). I know of no study describing this phenomenon with psychopathic clients, but it is supported anecdotally at one Veterans Administration Medical Center.*

* Black, John. Personal communication, January, 1983.

General Psychiatric Hospital

Psychopaths are not typically found in general psychiatric hospitals for treatment distinct from the categories enumerated previously, at least when speaking of adult clients. (Children who "act out" in ways that their parents find unmanageable such as severely hyperactive youngsters may be hospitalized by those parents, but those clients are not being considered psychopaths here, at least not as long as they are children.) When one does find a psychopathic client in a general psychiatric setting, the issue of malingering often arises. The purposes for that malingering vary, but include (1) to escape being found by the police, (2) to escape the winter's cold, and (3) to get "three hots and a cot" (prison slang for three meals a day and a place to sleep). Generally a psychopathic client who seems to have a legitimate reason for being treated in a general psychiatric hospital is probably going to be treated for something other than his psychopathy.

GENERAL TREATMENT ISSUES OF PSYCHOPATHS

"Over a period of many years I have remained discouraged about the effect of treatment on the psychopath." (Cleckley, 1964, p. 476)

"The traditional therapeutic procedures have not been effective in changing the behavior of psychopaths." (Hare, 1970, p.118)

"Even a quick review of the literature suggests that a chapter on *effective* treatment should be the shortest in any book concerned with psychopathy. In fact, it has been suggested that one sentence would suffice: 'No demonstratably effective treatment has been found.'" (Suedfeld & Landon, 1978, p. 347)

These statements bespeak the frustration clinicians experience during attempts to alter psychopathic behavior. Occasionally, however, a writer still suggests that there are therapeutic techniques that facilitate the alteration of psychopathic behavior through treatment:

It is possible that therapy with these individuals could be made effective by convincing them that their behavior is self-defeating, increasing their appreciation of the future consequences of present action, and exerting complete control over the administration of rewards and punishments.

(Hare, 1970, p. 112)

Similarly,

It appears that in verbal therapy of various sorts, the data urge us to establish situations in which the psychopath is given firm but not oppressive rules that are enforced consistently, and a therapist who is warm and understanding but understanding in the full sense of the word, not in the partial sense that uses it as synonymous with uncritical. The effective therapist will make it clear that he sees through the manipulative attempts of the patient and will continue to be realistically rather than gullibly supportive. A limited use of drugs for inducing temporary changes in mood and for opening the patient to increased rapport with his therapist seems reasonably well supported, as is the use of stimulants particularly with juvenile psychopaths. While the data on mileau therapy are quite mixed, there does appear to be evidence that the appropriate kind of therapeutic community, in which the individual is given responsibility and is expected to live up to it, can be useful. An alternative is the institutionalization of the individual until he reaches the age where antisocial behavior diminishes or disappears. Still another, socially preferable, is to move him into an environment where the psychopathic characteristic becomes productive and valued. One fairly reliable finding is that therapy works best with those who need it least.

(Suedfeld & Landon, 1978, p. 369)

And

The principles of successful inpatient treatment . . . [involving psychopathic patients] . . . are relatively simple, although hard to implement successfully.

(Reid, 1985, p. 835)

These statements make it clear that psychological therapy designed to alter the behavior of psychopaths has been difficult and often unsuccessful. Can this situation be improved?

This section describes the control theory's potential contribution to psychotherapy techniques and successful outcomes with psychopathic clients. Relevant concepts to be described include (1) preoccupation with perceived challenge and control, (2) a limited behavioral repertoire, (3) the tendency to persist in acting when frustrated, (4) an attentional deficit, and (5) the perception of other people as objects and obstacles. A discussion of the application of these concepts to therapy follows.

Preoccupation with Perceived Challenge and Control

Before individual or group therapy can proceed, one must have the client or clients in attendance, preferably ones who wish to be there. (Although my experience has taught me that the client does not need to "want" to be in therapy for it to have effect, it seems obvious that a willing client is easier with which to work.) Psychopaths, however, do not often refer themselves for therapy due to their persistent belief that their troubles are caused by others. Psychological treatment of psychopaths is therefore often performed through some external constraint on the client, such as a court order or incarceration (as described earlier in this chapter). Such circumstances do not typically facilitate the intrinsic motivation of the clients to attend therapy sessions or to change their behaviors.

Therefore, the first step in therapy with psychopaths is to increase their "intrinsic desire" to attend and benefit from treatment sessions. This is not done by actually changing their "desire to benefit from treatment," but by taking advantage of their enjoyment of an interpersonal process that can be made part of the clinician's therapeutic technique. Specifically, the control theory suggests that a therapist can take advantage of the psychopath's perception of challenge and control as rewarding. The therapist sets himself up as a source of that challenge. This is accomplished in either or both of two ways: (1) through setting oneself up as someone the psychopath wishes to manipulate, or (2) by early confrontation of the client's verbalizations and behavior, with the idea of being perceived as playing verbal games that the psychopath will want to win. Either way, the psychopath's interest in therapy participation should increase to workable levels.

For instance, I began confronting the verbalizations of one incarcerated, psychopathic client during his second weekly therapy session, far earlier than I use such a procedure with other kinds of clients. (I had diagnosed the client as a psychopath by the end of the first session.) Nine months later, the client was still attending therapy, having been absent no more than other clients. The confrontation served to keep his interest in the therapeutic process while encouraging him to verbalize his perceptions and rationalizations. As new psychological material was elicited through these rationalizations, the client was in turn confronted on those topics.

What did that confrontation look like? Mostly it consisted of statements like "I don't understand how you thought that your action would get you what you wanted" and "That game won't work on me. You'll have to find something else that works." (I use the term "game" with psychopathic clients a lot, in the same way it is used in Transactional Analysis, mostly because the clients often find it a challenging term.) In both cases, I eventually followed the statements with a description of behavior that was likely to have been more effective in getting what he wanted than what he had done. In this way the confrontation necessarily led to his education.

In another case involving an incarcerated client, I used a different kind of confrontation, basically a challenge to his sense of being one of the most "macho" guys around. He was already a leader of half of his fellow prisoners (through intimidation, strong-arming, and simply playing the "tough" guy) when I entered his life. To confront his effectiveness in getting what he wanted would not have been useful because he already did get what he consciously wanted.

Therefore, I challenged him in another way. First, I told him constantly that I believed he could become the leader of the whole unit in which he lived if he would only learn a few things about dealing with people. (In other words, I addressed his apparent strength as the factor that would increase his participation in therapy.) Coupled with that statement was another about how a "true leader" does not lead only half a pack (thereby challenging his "macho" image). Once given the assumptions of those statements, he either had to learn to lead "the whole pack" or acknowledge that he was not as tough as he wanted me to think he was. After two years of therapy, he was still participating in group and individual therapy, even though he threatened to drop out of all treatment about every two months along the way.

Both examples demonstrate that the psychopath's tendency to perceive and respond to interpersonal challenge can be utilized in therapy to keep the client coming back for more.

There is another lesson implied in both examples as well, however: Challenge is simply the vehicle to keep the client coming back and *not* the therapy itself. This is probably an obvious statement to the reader while reading it, but it may not feel so obvious while the clinician is in the process of doing therapy. I have witnessed various therapists using confrontive techniques when they seemed to serve no purpose but the expression of the therapists' negative feelings about their clients (i.e., the expression of the therapist's countertransference, defined broadly as therapists' emotional reactions to their clients). Confrontation can be an excellent mechanism for expressing anger (such as at the client for his attempts to manipulate the therapist), dislike or hate (such as at the "SOB" who keeps doing rotten things), fear (such as about the client who does threatening actions), and frustration (such as at the lack of behavioral change by the client after all of the effort by the therapist). The clinician's challenges to psychopathic clients must primarily serve the purpose of promoting interest in the clients or the comments will be therapeutically destructive.

Another danger in using persistent confrontation is the idea that the therapist should always "win" in those verbal exchanges. This danger is described in detail later in this chapter under the rubric "Traps to Avoid." Let it suffice to say here that the overall idea of verbal challenges to the psychopathic client is to keep him interested in the process you know to be influencing his behavioral change, not to demonstrate your verbal acuity, intellectual prowess, or high school debating skills.

A third caveat needs to be mentioned about the technique of

confrontation. The therapist must feel comfortable enough with the procedure to avoid feeling threatened by the psychopath's occasionally hostile retorts. If the therapist makes a practice of "backing off" when confronted by the client, the therapist will be too easily manipulated and thereby become an insufficient challenge to the client.

Limited Behavioral Repertoire

What does a clinician concentrate on while challenging the psychopathic client? The answer is largely the psychopath's behavioral repertoire, what may be termed his social skills.

Do I really mean to suggest that a client who is known to be manipulative of others, almost by definition, lacks social skills that he needs to be taught? Do I really mean to say that someone who has the skills necessary to fool "most of the people most of the time" needs to learn other interpersonal skills? Absolutely. To understand this, one needs to avoid confusing behaviors that are effective only in the short term with those that are effective in both the short and long run.

For instance, Hare (1981) states that psychopaths have "a larger repertory of actual behaviors than does the normal person" (p. 58). His evidence is the fact that psychopaths engage in criminal actions more often than do nonpsychopaths. *With the assumption that both groups share the same noncriminal behavioral repertoire,* one could then conclude that Hare is correct; psychopaths do have a larger behavioral repertoire than the rest of us. However, that assumption is clearly not correct.

Anyone who has worked with a number of psychopathic clients knows that they (as a group) tend to act aggressively and passive-aggressively when attempting to satisfy their desires. Assertiveness is not typically part of their behavioral repertoire (without therapy), and one rarely sees a "passive" psychopath.

This is one of the points to social skills training for psychopathic clients. Aggression and passive-aggression typically serve to satisfy short-term desires, but many times cost a lot in the long run. Psychopaths, therefore, can benefit from assertiveness training for the same reasons as any client with a social skill deficit.

Similarly, psychopaths typically have a diminished ability to discriminate among superficially similar situations (i.e., to note the relevant details of their environment) compared to the rest of us. For example, one incarcerated client tended to see any action he did not like by the institution staff as an expression of their desire for "power," in particular when it directly affected him. It did not matter how reasonable the action was to others who were incarcerated, how much the action was necessitated by circumstance, or how much the staff stated they would have preferred being able to do something else. His perception was limited. Psychopaths need to learn how to discriminate among situations to make more effective attributions about them.

However, does training psychopaths to be more assertive and discriminating amount to training them simply to be better manipulators? Why would I want to train psychopaths to be able to take even more advantage of people than they do already?

These are typical questions asked of me when I teach psychiatric hospital employees about therapeutic interactions with psychopathic clients. The employees perceive a moral dilemma: their duty to treat clients who are psychopathic will lead to making the clients "better psychopaths." I consider this dilemma valid only to the extent that the employees believe that they do not all manipulate other people through the use of well-timed assertiveness and useful situation discrimination. Once the employees recognize that the skills psychopaths need to learn are simply those that we all use everyday for the same purpose (of satisfying our desires without "violating" others), the moral dilemma seems less intense. (To those employees who still feel a strong objection to teaching psychopathic clients these skills because of the perception of an immorality in making the clients "better psychopaths," I recommend that they avoid working with such clients. Their countertransference issues will otherwise interfere with, and be destructive to the clients' treatment.)

Tendency to Persist in Acting when Frustrated

This characteristic of psychopathy can be one of the most frustrating for clinicians. They see the clients making a great deal of effort with destructive results when a little patience and a few thought-out actions would get the clients what they want.

To exemplify, I had one incarcerated client who wanted to be transferred from his unit of residence to another. He initially received a negative response from his case manager. The client then came to me, his therapist, to intervene, which I refused to do (after keeping the possibility open for a while that I might help, so that he would tell me in therapy what he was doing and why.) The series of events after that was almost amusing. There were repeated requests made to both his case manager and me, as well as contacts with the social worker and unit chief to make the same request. He even wrote letters to the institution's highest administrators to make his request. Basically the client repeatedly contacted any relevant person he could find who might listen. In therapy, he explained that people would eventually get tired of hearing the same old thing from him and would acquiesce simply to "get him off their back." That persistence when frustrated probably often succeeded for him (though it did not in this case), though it also brought him much animosity. When this result became clear to him (after much confrontation), we concentrated on more useful and effective methods to appeal request denials.

A different incarcerated client showed a similar tendency to go from one staff member to another over many days when he felt frustrated. Usually, in this case, the client's frustration occurred when the staff did something he perceived as an injustice against him (which was, initially during therapy, often). The pattern was something like this: (1) the staff would take some action that this patient did not like (not always directly involving him), (2) the patient reacted with anger, frustration, and many abusive verbalizations and inaccurate, derogatory accusations, (3) the patient selected staff members to confront with his anger, always one at a time, going from one to another at times he chose for maximum effect (in front of other patients), (4) the staff members would tell him that he needed to speak to the staff collectively about the issue he had with the collective staff, recommending to the patient to fill out the request form to speak with the collective staff, (5) the patient would not fill out the form, but would continue to attempt to confront individual staff members until days passed and he cooled down or moved on to another issue.

Needless to say, the staff found this reoccurring event to be obnoxious. A host of unsavory characteristics were attributed by the staff to this patient based on their countertransference. Getting the treatment staff to be willing to interact with this patient became a major hurdle in his therapy.

Over time, however, we developed a coping strategy that involved "giving ourselves permission" to walk away from the patient most times he did this *after* we told him "that is not the way to handle this situation—you know what to do." Not unexpectedly, it still took the patient a while to change his behavior based on ours. But he did change. The staff still gets a number of the patient's requests to speak with the staff collectively about his issues, but when he speaks with them, he is able to finish his discussion about the issue then and there without belaboring the points later with individual staff members. The staff and he have gotten along far better last I knew.

Deficiency in Ability to Understand Consequences of Their Behaviors

This characteristic of psychopaths can be treated hand in hand with their tendency to persist in acting when frustrated. Their persistent acting in self-defeating ways demonstrates their deficient ability to understand the consequences of their actions. As the control theory describes, psychopaths do not typically see negative environmental reactions (e.g., punishments) to their behavior as natural consequences of their own actions. Hence this issue often arises in therapy.

As with the issue of persistent action when frustrated, therapists often find this characteristic deficiency frustrating. The therapist typically puts in hours of work and emotional effort to have the psychopathic client become aware of the consequences of his actions only to witness the client repeating the same behavior and blaming others for the consequences. Watching a client do this time and again can easily raise a therapist's doubts about his own competence. After all, with all that effort. . . .

Effective treatment of the psychopath's deficiency in understanding the consequences of his behavior follows a similar course as that with his tendency to persist acting when frustrated. One does not appeal to the client's "common sense." Rather the therapist should consistently focus on pointing out what the client could do that would likely be effective and useful in obtaining what he wants without destructive outcomes, and then "challenge" all of the rationalizations the client has for maintaining his current set of behaviors.

The "challenging" can take many forms. In the previous example it was the staff's walking away from the client before the client could argue his perspective. In individual therapy, it can be a direct confrontation with the client's repetitive failures from ignoring the consequences of his actions.

Statements by the client attributing negative consequences from his actions to other people can often lead to useless debates with a client not willing to accept responsibility for his behavior. As described in Chapters 9 and 10, I suggest you avoid such debates. Rather describe reality to the client in a different way. Each relevant event can be described as including the patient's behavior *and* other people's behavior which he does not like. From that perspective, discuss with the client the possibilities for realistically avoiding those events and, therefore, the negative outcomes he does not want.

A case example can illustrate the point. One psychopathic client followed the pattern of acting in rule-violating and limit-testing ways until he received a negative consequence from the institution staff. At that point, he made claims to anyone who would listen about how the staff was discriminating against him and "picking on" him. Initially, as his therapist, I attempted to have him see how he caused the staff's reactions. This effort was useless. In fact, I risked being seen by him as part of those who "caused" him problems.

After a while, however, I learned to help him conceptualize these events in a different manner. From that point on, each "event" consisted of: (1) his set of actions coupled with the anticipated staff reaction and (2) his feeling victimized. The client showed little resistance to that idea once he felt clear that he was not being singled out as the only source of the problems. Then we focused on what he could alter to avoid feeling victimized. There were two issues here: (1) his actions and (2) the staff's perception of him. He was quickly willing to acknowledge he could not change the staff's perception of him (in keeping with his sense of being victimized by those in authority), so we were able to focus our efforts solely on his behavior without significant resistance by him.

Attentional Deficit

This will be a treatment issue to the extent that therapists need to be aware of it and mold their efforts accordingly. Specifically, psychopaths often simply get bored of the therapeutic process. They need to be stimulated as the process continues, or they will find something else to do with their time.

How should therapists deal with this problem? As stated in the previous sections, the use of confrontation and verbal challenge as an integral part of the therapeutic process will be experienced by the psychopath as generally stimulating. This technique alone often keeps the client coming back for more.

However there is one caveat. No one, including a psychopath, likes always "losing" in their interpersonal battles. The therapist must be willing to "win a few, lose a few" when doing therapy with a psychopathic client. The therapist should be willing to acknowledge when the client has a good point. Set up certain challenges such that even though the client may perceive himself as "winning," he will still be engaged in a therapeutic activity. (For example, in situations when the psychopath is openly challenging your ability to know who he is, state that you believe he will *not* be able to perform a certain therapeutic action, in effect challenging him toward "proving" you wrong). Likewise, the therapist should ensure that he "wins" sometimes. Ultimately, to counter the psychopath's attentional deficit, therapists should strive to be perceived by their clients as potentially beatable challenges.

Some mental health workers may resist the idea that all of this is necessary to work successfully with psychopaths. Therapy with a psychopathic client cannot, however, be successful with a passive therapist (Persons & Pepinsky, 1966). Simply sitting back and reflecting clients' feelings on the rare times they speak of feelings will lead to boredom and the waste of much time by the clients.

Perception of People as Objects and Obstacles

One issue will be guaranteed to stand in the way of changing psychopaths from being psychopathic, given our current state of knowledge about behavior change. Psychopaths will come into therapy viewing other people as objects and obstacles, and they will very likely leave therapy the same way. Treatment can alter how psychopaths interact with others, but it cannot teach them to love, to empathize, and to feel guilt when they never have before. Those emotions are minimally felt before treatment, so there is virtually nothing to build on and shape. Psychopaths can learn to act "as if" they experience those emotions, but they cannot learn to feel them.

What does this mean for treatment success? Does this mean that all therapy with psychopaths is doomed either to failure or simply to making them into better "cons" than they already were? The answer to this question depends on the goals of the therapy.

If the therapy goals are to make the psychopath into an upstanding citizen who will care about others, feel what others feel, and feel guilty when he hurts someone (i.e., to increase his superego functioning, to use psychoanalytic terminology), the therapy *is* doomed to failure. I have never seen it happen. Nor have I ever heard of it happening.

If the therapy goals are to get the person acting "as if" (a phrase from Adlerian therapy) he is empathic and does not wish to hurt others, this can happen. Some mental health professionals, however, view this as making the client even more manipulative than he was before therapy, and that outcome is considered bad. I strongly disagree with this perspective. We all act according to our feelings and thoughts in ways we believe will get us what we want. I view the social adeptness involved in this process of our everyday lives as no different from the kind I teach to psychopathic clients. As long as no one gets hurt in the process (which would be true as long as the client continues to act as if he is empathic), does the "sincerity" really matter? Our alternative as professionals is to let the psychopaths continue victimizing others without training the psychopaths in how to stop that process.

"TRAPS" TO AVOID

This section enumerates five destructive interpersonal processes that happen often during therapy with psychopathic clients. Not only should clinicians who work with psychopaths be cognizant of these processes before beginning therapy, but a periodic review of them during the middle sessions of therapy is highly recommended as a self-protective device/therapeutic reminder.

Battling to Win, Especially if You Are Winning

The terms "winning" and "losing" were used in the previous discussion of the therapeutic challenging of psychopaths. What exactly do these terms mean?

In any challenge, the challenger can get a desired outcome or fail to do so. When a therapist challenges a client's self-perception of being an innocent victim of other people's injustice, the client may either remain steadfast in his self-perception or begin to alter that self-perception. In the former case, the therapist will probably experience losing while the latter case will probably be experienced as success or winning.

Similarly, when a clinician confronts a psychopath with the therapist's interpretation of the client's behavior, the client may or may not accept the interpretation as having some validity. In the former case, the clinician is likely to experience a sense of progress or winning while the latter case would represent a failed attempt or losing. In both this and the preceding example, the client would probably experience the opposite result from the therapist's; that is, winning when the therapist lost and losing when the therapist won.

There seems to be a natural tendency for clinicians, like anyone, to want to win (to want to be right, to want to see progress from their efforts, etc.) This tendency is easily exacerbated when performing therapy with a psychopathic client. The psychopath already views the world in extreme terms (win-lose, right-wrong, good-bad), as do most character disordered clients. He will therefore react to his therapist in those extreme ways. Many clinicians all-too-easily fall into the trap of responding to the client in those same extreme ways, with the exception that the clinician can typically make sure he or she wins the battle.

Although winning against a psychopath can be emotionally gratifying at the time (especially after a series of frustrations involving that client), continual battling by the therapist to win is counterproductive to effective treatment. This is especially true if the therapist is constantly winning. The clinician's "ego" may be satisfied through that process, but the client will effectively discontinue therapy from that point on. (Even though clinicians then typically ascribe blame to the kind of client with whom they were working, the outcome of termination was not usually necessary.)

To avoid this process, clinicians should do their best to anticipate before a therapy session what verbal "battles" or challenges will occur in that session, and make plans to win only the major ones. In other words, the effective therapist with a psychopathic client plans on losing some verbal interchanges (from the client's perspective), though there is an attempt to choose beforehand which issues will be lost and which will not. If you find yourself battling to win, stop what you are doing, especially if you find you are winning.

For example, one psychopathic client with whom I worked was moody, often expressing anger when in the mood over any issue available at the moment. He would go from one topic to another as needed with the effect of "beating up" the listener with words. (The listener was typically someone the client considered the cause of all of these problems, or at least someone who could remedy all of his problems.) The listeners (colleagues and myself) found themselves continually getting defensive, upset, and/or angry. The client's tendency to find issues to justify his anger was pointed out to him various times, but his resistance to "insight" made such interpretations have little effect.

When I became aware of what he was doing, I took a different tactic. Labeling his process to myself as "trying to win," I began my sessions with him with a self-statement that gave myself permission to acknowledge he could be "right," whether or not I agreed with him (except in extreme cases). During one such session, he began the conversation telling me about how he had been wronged by my colleagues. His affect and statements told me this was a familiar tune, even if the topic was new. I therefore acknowledged that he had a point and I would have to discuss it with my colleagues. He immediately paused, then "argued" one more statement at me. The subject was then changed by him to another such issue. When I quickly remarked that he had some good points, his mood changed. (He told me later that he had run out of issues even though he still felt like arguing.) I was then able to bring up a topic that was therapeutically more meaningful. If I had been absorbed in winning (being right), we would not have gotten beyond the superficial topics that masked the real issues.

Becoming the Advocate, Especially if You Mean It

Another trap when working with psychopathic clients is represented by your becoming their advocate with others. This can take various forms.

Probably the most common is when the therapist believes the client is making real progress and the therapist does not want other people to mistreat or be countertherapeutic to the client "just because of his reputation." In cases such as this, the clinician typically goes out of his or her way to protect or get something for the client. When questioned about this practice, the clinician may have some rationale involving positive reinforcement for his or her client's progress.

If this were true, clinicians would do this for all of their clients showing progress. I have never read about a therapy technique (with the exception of treatment for victims of sexual assaults) that involves protecting the client from the world of consequences of his behavior. Most therapists, in fact, have as a central tenet the concept of getting the client to be more aware of the real world.

Therapists who believe their protection of, or advocation for, a psychopathic client should be part of the treatment should reexamine their motives. While I am not prepared to state emphatically that any therapist who advocates for a psychopathic client who is progressing is making an error, I do recommend that any such therapist be constantly suspicious of his own motives.

A second common form of therapist as advocate is when the therapy has just begun. Most good mental health professionals wish to give their clients the best chance of benefiting from treatment possible, and rightly so. As therapy with a psychopathic client begins, the therapist is probably most ripe for giving the client "the benefit of the doubt." While I do not disagree with this perspective, I also believe that a significant portion of therapy is getting clients to solve their own problems. One can give a new client "the benefit of the doubt" near the beginning of therapy without becoming that person's advocate or mediator in interpersonal problems.

A rarer form of therapist as advocate is when the mental health worker becomes enamored by the client. This situation is typically not therapeutic for the client no matter what kind of client it is. The situation is not different with a psychopath. In fact, it can serve to reinforce that individual's tendency to use other people (including the therapist) to get what he wants. Whenever a therapist's feelings become that extreme about a client, the therapist should seek guidance from another mental health professional and/or refer the client to someone else.

Why does it matter if a therapist is an advocate for the client? Because it is typically a countertherapeutic process, especially if the therapist takes on the advocacy position with the intention of winning for the client. The client has simply gotten the clinician to take up the client's usual fight, without the client even having to enter the battle zone. Even if the therapist gets the desired outcome, the client has learned that he does not have to risk fighting all of his own life battles. This is especially true if the clinician communicates to the client how much effort was put into the fight by the therapist. Hence my recommendation to avoid becoming the client's advocate, especially if you mean to do so.

For example, in a forensic hospital unit, one psychopathic client was able to get his therapist to argue the client's perspective in staff discussions concerning the client. The therapist's rationale was that the patient was in need of trust from others, so that he could see that other people were not "out to get him." The other staff members disagreed with that argument, but periodically allowed the therapist to win.

What did the therapist get for his trouble? Initially, a lot of spoken gratitude from the patient and some self-gratification as a "good guy." Over time, however, the therapist found himself getting burdened with increasing complaints from the client that he expected the therapist to "fix." It was then that the therapist recognized he had started down the wrong road with this client.

Believing What You Hear, Expecially if the Story Seems too Complicated to Have Been Fabricated

Most people recognize that they cannot always tell a falsehood from a truth. Some things have the sound of truth to them; others are clearly lies. Most of what we hear, however, we just assume to be true without any clear knowledge that they are.

But when we are not sure, what do we do? I remember that my experience with multiple choice tests in school taught me to choose the longest response because typically that represented more than the professor was willing to invent. In conversations with other people, I think that I still generally accept as truth those statements that involve a large variety of potentially verifiable facts.

My experience as a clinician, however, has taught me that that practice is not at all reliable when dealing with a psychopathic client. Lies from psychopaths, as far as I can tell, come in all shapes and sizes. Some of the most complicated and fascinating lies I have ever heard (of which I am aware) came from the mouths of my psychopathic clients.

For instance, one such client was found out by the staff at the institution he was incarcerated in to have lied repeatedly about his age, claiming he was five years older than he was. This was unimportant. However, a day after he was confronted with that lie, he had an incredible explanation for why he lied. The story started with statements about how there was another person in the military the same time he was with a very similar full name. The client stated the other person's name. When that other person died, shortly after retiring from the military, that person's widow recognized that she was not going to get as much money from the government as she would have (with her husband) if her husband had continued to live. My client was made aware of this situation by this woman. Through the goodness of his heart, he fraudulently let her use him to sign documents and make it appear that her husband was still alive. He, of course, asked for nothing in return. What this meant was that when he was subsequently arrested for a crime, he needed to report his age in keeping with his other identity. This was why the staff found a discrepancy in the files with two different birth dates recorded.

What a complicated explanation for why he chose to lie about his age! From the best the staff could later ascertain, the entire story was another lie. We never did learn why he lied about his age.

How should clinicians determine what is the truth? Probably in the same way clinicians should win in their sessions with psychopathic clients, that is, selectively. Usually, during the process of therapy, it will not matter. The content of the client's presentation is rarely of greatest importance during the session. Only when there seems to be a therapeutic need for the clinician to know the truth should there be any real effort to discover it.

This is not to say that clinicians should believe what is told them. To the contrary, as with any other client, therapists should always assume that "the truth" as reported by psychopathic clients is distorted by their psychopathology. Sometimes they will be lying and sometimes they will not, but they will always be giving you a sample of themselves for your therapeutic interpretation. This section was to inform you that complicated samples of themselves may still involve content that was never accurate.

Fearing Manipulation, Especially if You Do Not Believe You Are Being Manipulated

One of the major topics discussed among mental health professionals working with psychopaths is manipulation. The therapists wonder if they "have been manipulated," wonder if the clients' actions were attempts at manipulation, make statements about how they hate "being manipulated," and express doubts about their professional competency if they find they "have been manipulated." Often these comments sound as if the staff are afraid of being beaten in some kind of psychological battle measured according to a yardstick they can only partially comprehend.

This is the problem with the common lore about psychopathic clients. Most therapists see themselves as ill-equipped to fight the forces of the "great manipulators" who disguise themselves as patients and clients. When these clinicians sit down to do therapy with such clients, they are already in a battle with themselves, to treat this client like any other or to stay constantly alert for "signs of manipulation." Even then, most therapists still have that sense of impending doom that they, too, will fall victim to these great manipulators.

To avoid this problem, we need to start from scratch. What is meant by the term manipulation? Typically we use the term to imply something sinister, calculated, and with resultant behavior that we otherwise would not have predicted. As the term is often used in conjunction with psychopaths, manipulation is something to be avoided at almost any cost if one is to keep one's professional integrity.

This perspective is not only utter nonsense, but counterproductive to any therapeutic endeavor. Manipulation does *not* necessarily imply something sinister (though such motives may be present). The definition I prefer to use instead is "a calculated attempt to affect someone else's behavior for one's own benefit." The way through which we conduct business in this country is manipulative. The process of seduction is manipulation. The steps I took to get this book published were manipulative. (I hope my editor did not perceive me as sinister!) Using my definition, I can say that we all manipulate other people each day.

So what is it that we fear as therapists with psychopathic clients? We fear being manipulated by an untruth. We fear "being conned" when somehow or another we expect ourselves to have "known better." Typically, our perceived inexperience with people who often lie is felt as a dilemma that goes something like this: "If I don't accept what my client tells me as an accurate representation of how he perceives his world, then I will have no basis on which to begin therapy, no basis on which I can make interpretations of what this client needs and the psychological issues with which he is dealing. On the other hand, if I accept what the client says as an accurate representation of how he sees the world, then I stand the high risk of being made to look foolish both professionally and personally."

This brings us to the second point. Where in people's training as clinicians do they get the idea that being in a win-lose combat with a client's psychopathology is part of therapy? We are typically trained to promote "transference" (loosely defined as a client's process of interacting with his therapist as the client typically does with other people significant to him or her). For instance, we usually know we are making progress when a borderline personality disordered client describes perceptions of the therapist that are representative of "splitting" (i.e., seeing people in extreme ways such as all good or all bad) even though that perception is part of the person's psychopathology. Similarly, when a passive-aggressive client continually arrives late for appointments, we feel we have something with which to work.

When it comes to the psychopath, however, we react to the client's lying and shrewdness as something to be avoided. To "fall victim" to it is considered awful even though the analogous therapist who is waiting for the overdue passive-agressive patient to arrive for the appointment does not typically think twice about his or her own professional competence.

Being manipulated by a psychopathic client means that you have a potentially successful therapy in process. The client is involved enough with you to have invested energy into your relationship. In so doing, he has exhibited his psychopathology. In other words, when you discover you have been manipulated, congratulate yourself! You have made progress!

Of course, a therapist cannot continue to be manipulated by a client and expect therapy to progress. In the same way that the therapist for the borderline client must help the client to see the therapist more realistically (instead of splitting), clinicians working with psychopathic clients must help them interact with other people in ways that are more effective in the long run. Manipulation by psychopathic clients is not something to be feared and avoided, but something to be used for therapeutic gain. A therapist's fear of manipulation is countertherapeutic, especially if the clinician is doing his best to avoid being manipulated.

Becoming Fascinated, Especially if You Are Being Entertained

The final "trap" to be described in this chapter concerns the apparent opposite of the fear of being manipulated. In this trap, the clinician becomes fascinated by his or her psychopathic client. This fascination can take many forms.

Probably the most common is the therapist who finds the client's outrageous (and sometimes criminal) actions intriguing; in particular, intriguing enough to daydream or wonder about what it felt like to do those behaviors. Many psychopaths' actions are of a kind that most therapists dare not do for fear of the social consequences (if not for other reasons involving one's self-image and sense of guilt). Some of us, however, like hearing about these clients' exploits. A kind of vicarious entertainment is derived.

The problem with this kind of fascination is that it typically interferes with therapy. Psychopathic clients usually find it easy to relate stories about their experiences (both true and false). A therapist who is fascinated by those stories is likely to promote their being told without dealing with the therapeutic processes that need to occur.

A second kind of therapist fascination involves "falling in love" with the client. In essence, the clinician stops viewing this person as a client, seeing instead a person who "really knows about people and how to live life to its fullest." The fascination is felt as a longing to be a part of that client's life, to share the excitement.

The therapeutic problems with this reaction by the mental health worker are obvious. A "therapy" relationship no longer exists. The therapist has stopped focusing on the client's needs and has become focused on his or her own.

A relatively rare form of fascination can occur with therapists who also plan to report the case in a professional forum (as a case study in a professional journal or a case presentation at a professional conference). In these cases, the therapist sees the client's progress as a measure of his or her own professional abilities. Because the case outcome will be made known publicly, the therapist becomes invested in each event in the client's life, with the not-so-subtle attempt by the therapist to shape the client's world so that progress (as measured by the professional forum's standards) is almost assured.

The therapeutic problem with this kind of clinician is that he or she often acts as an advocate for the client (with the concomitant problems previously described), and coddles the client during their sessions together. The client quickly learns that he has a protector in his therapist instead of someone who will push him to better himself.

In all three cases, the mental health worker who becomes fascinated by a psychopathic client stops performing effective therapy. Although I believe that it is important for clinicians to enjoy their work, they need to be alert to the possibility that they are being fascinated by their psychopathic clients. The kind of entertainment that is spawned by that fascination usually makes therapeutic endeavors nonviable.

CHAPTER 9

Specific "Direct" Behaviors of Psychopaths Designed to Obtain Environmental Control

An integral part of any therapeutic encounter is the set of feelings the therapist has about the client, what is called the therapist's countertransference. The issue of countertransference is particularly important when discussing psychopathic clients because of the continual challenges inherent in having therapeutic relationships with them. Unfortunately, very little has been written about countertransference involving psychopathic clients to coach mental health workers through their emotional bouts (Lion, 1981a, being an exception).

This chapter concentrates on enumerating behaviors typical to psychopathic clients that are designed to gain interpersonal control. These actions typically lead to significant countertransference by clinicians. Both the client's behaviors and the likely therapist's reactions are described for each type of interaction. Finally, recommendations for effectively handling these client behaviors are described.

The chapter is divided into two sections according to the type of behavior exhibited by the client: (1) direct and verbal, and (2) direct and nonverbal. Chapter 10 describes psychopathic behaviors which are (3) indirect and verbal, and (4) indirect and nonverbal. This list of behaviors is not considered exhaustive of the actions psychopathic clients use to gain control, but it probably includes sufficient examples for any mental health worker to learn how to identify such "counter-transference hooks" (my term for such behaviors).

DIRECT AND VERBAL

Verbal Aggression

Probably the psychopathic client's most easily identifiable attempt at interpersonal control second only to outright physical aggression is verbal aggression. In my definition, direct verbal aggression includes direct threats of physical violence, implied threats of physical violence, statements that are vague in meaning but nevertheless threatening, cursing at someone in front of that person, describing a person to his or her face with a derogatory label, and strong sarcasm. Examples I have heard include:

"If I weren't behind these bars, you'd be in big trouble."

"When I get out of this (seclusion) room, there are going to be a few busted heads."

"If you try that again, you'll wish you were dead."

"I'll see you in June" (from an incarcerated client who was scheduled to be released in June which was a few months away).

"I'll get even. You just wait."

"If you walk away now, you'd better just keep walking."

"You're tough now, but just wait till I get my chance."

"Don't you dare call me a liar."

"You _____" (fill in your favorite, or least favorite, curse phrases).

"Fuck you."

"Don't play your head games with me, or you'll be sorry."

"You're a fool."

"You're a goddamn liar."

"And you call yourself a psychologist . . . " (with heavy sarcasm in his voice).

"Ooh, you're so tough. . . ."

"You think you know so much. . . ."

"If you think I'm going to listen to you, you're more stupid than I thought."

In each case, the effect of these kinds of words on a therapist can include shock, fear, indignation, and helplessness. Most of us do not experience these kinds of statements during our daily lives, so when they come in therapy we usually feel professionally and personally unprepared for them. Even clinicians who have had years of professional experience with other kinds of clients often recognize a sense of uncertainty and helplessness when confronted by a client's hostility in this way.

There is not much one is going to do to prevent countertransference on those occasions unless one begins each interaction with each psychopathic client with an expectation of hearing such comments. This expectation can minimize one's sense of helplessness and anger.

Even so, one may react viscerally when such a comment is made based on one's perception of a real threat to one's physical safety. To deal effectively with your countertransference in these cases, it is strongly recommended that you speak to other mental health professionals involved with the client about your reaction. You need to reality test your perception of danger. In most cases, such clients voice a great many threats that are never acted out. Eventually you may come to recognize that you are in more danger driving your car to work than you are from your client, irrelevant of his statements.

So how should you handle these comments during therapy? This partially depends on your assessment of the dangerousness of the situation, but not significantly. There should be three major points in your response: (1) you acknowledge the client's ability to cause harm to others, (2) the client will not get what he seeks with such comments, and (3) you suggest he try (specific behavioral suggestions) next time to get what he wants. The first idea is to challenge the client to find a way to "hook" you without expressing doubt about his destructive physical abilities. (Such expressed doubt would only challenge the client to prove you wrong by acting out his stated intention.) The second idea is to instruct the client in ways to act more appropriately, to expand his behavioral repertoire. An exemplary response is "While I don't doubt you could do what you say, that kind of statement is not going to get what you want from me. I suggest that next time you (fill in the blank with a specific behavioral suggestion)."

Intimidation

Sometimes the aggression is not so overt. The client's comments may not even be said with notable hostility in his voice. The effect on the clinician, on the other hand, may not significantly differ from that of the most overtly aggressive statement. Examples of such statements are:

"I've killed before."

"I've taken hostages before."

"I've started a riot before."

"I could call one of my (motorcycle gang) buddies and have your family messed up if I wanted."

"You can do what you want to me. I'll never surrender to the system."

"You'd better not [do that] anymore."

"I could mess up your treatment program if I wanted."

"Don't mess with me anymore."

"You'd better quit messing with me, or you'll be sorry."

"Come here and say that!"

"Who's going to make me? You?"

In all of these examples, the clients were challenging the listeners with statements that seemed to say far more than they did. When such statements are made, the implications are typically not difficult to specify. Even so, the client may deny the implication if directly questioned about it. This seems especially true if the mood of the interaction is not overtly conflictual and hostile.

What are effective ways of reacting to these kinds of comments? As with direct threats, there are two important ideas you need to convey in your responses to statements designed to intimidate. The first is that you will not be controlled (hooked) by that kind of statement. The second is that the client must find a different kind of behavior to get what he desires from you. Tied into the second message should be various examples of appropriate behaviors from which the psychopath can choose and implement.

The most difficult aspect of the outlined response is usually the first message—you will not be hooked by such comments. Sometimes your emotions and nonverbal cues will communicate your response before you formulate anything to say. You *will* feel intimidated from time to time, and your reaction will show. In those cases, you should not deny your reactions. Chances are you will not be able to pull off such a deception (meaning you will just increase the message that you were hooked), nor should you try. Lying to your client will not protect you or facilitate his therapeutic growth.

To cope with feeling intimidated by a psychopathic client, you must be prepared in two ways. The first is to recognize that this possibility exists each time you interact with such a client, in the same way it was described earlier that you need to prepare for the possibility of threats of physical aggression. This preparation alone can make a comment less intimidating than it otherwise might be. This process makes the unpredictable feel more predictable and, therefore, controllable.

The second form of preparation is to have another mental health professional available for you to share your reaction. Often the "reality testing" that occurs through that process can lessen the intimidation one feels from these statements.

Exemplary verbal responses to intimidating comments from psychopathic clients may be helpful. If one does not feel intimidated, an appropriate statement might be "Your comment seemed designed to intimidate me, make me fear you. From my perspective, you should not expect me to give you what you want (or whatever statement is relevant to the situation) by making such comments. You need to try something else to do that such as making direct statements to me about your feelings without making threats." If one does feel intimidated by the comment, then something like the following will often suffice: "Your comment seemed designed to intimidate me. I can tell you that your making such statements will not result in [something positive] for you from me, as it does not now. For that, you will need to. . . ."

Present the Proof, or "Catch Me if You Can"

One of the more frustrating aspects of working therapeutically with psychopaths is their ability to keep some of their worst misbehaviors secret from those who would do something about them. At times, a staff member or family member may believe he or she has finally caught the client misbehaving only to have the client react with indignation and adamant denial. The psychopath's statement at those times can be paraphrased as "You're accusing me falsely. If you really think you have something, prove it!"

There are two common reactions by therapists in those situations. The first is to "play detective" and try to prove your claim. What mental health workers often discover, however, is that they cannot "prove it" to the client's satisfaction. If you present a witness or two, the client claims that the witnesses are lying, trying to get on the therapist's "good side" by lying about the client. If you present a relevant substance (e.g., drugs, contraband, or something that had been stolen), the client's claim is that the item was "planted" to make him look guilty by those people who do not like him. (He might even name specific people, though not typically.) If you present your own notes from a previous interaction with the client, he will claim that those are simply notes that you could have made up at any time; they mean nothing to him. Most often, there is no way to win.

Without proving it to the client's satisfaction, it may seem that any further therapy discussion about the alleged misbehavior typically leads nowhere. At those times, you will find you are in a battle with the client where the rules are that one side will win and one will lose. Each side needs to get in the final word about the "truth," meaning that therapy begins to resemble a debate where each side presents its arguments with no view toward the original goals of therapy. For a clinician, it's a worthless battle.

The second common therapist reaction to these situations is to feel helpless, as if there is nothing that can be done to take the client's denial and use it therapeutically. As described in the previous discussion, the therapist buys into the concept that the specific behavior at the center of the current situation must be the topic upon which their discussion is focused. Since the client adamantly denies the behavior, there seems nothing relevant to the situation left to discuss in therapy. The client's prove it to me stance becomes successful in its goal of avoiding recognition of the repercussions of his behavior.

The trick for the clinician is to avoid the win-lose battle by not concerning oneself about proving the accuracy of your claim. You can expect that the client will still attempt to persuade you that you are wrong, but you need not respond in kind. The following is an example of an interaction that can take place.

THERAPIST: Yesterday I became aware of your having lied to the nurse so you could get a second dose of your medication.

CLIENT: I didn't lie to her. What are you talking about?

THERAPIST: About your statement to the nurse yesterday that you had not gotten your medication when in reality you had.

CLIENT: That's crazy. Who's feeding you that stuff? Who told you that, anyway?

THERAPIST: The nurse.

CLIENT: Well, then, she lied to you.

THERAPIST: No, I think not. You lied, and you are continuing to lie to me now.

CLIENT: Oh man, if you are so sure, prove it. It's her word against mine.

THERAPIST: I could attempt to do that, but I won't.

CLIENT: So I'm guilty until proven innocent?

THERAPIST: Neither guilt nor innocence is the issue here. Your attempt to get something you wanted through lying is the issue. What other ways could you have tried to get what you wanted?

CLIENT: But I didn't do anything of the kind.

THERAPIST: You may or may not have this time, but are you denying that you ever lie to get what you want?

CLIENT: Well, no, but I didn't lie yesterday to the nurse.

THERAPIST: Well, then, what other ways besides lying can you get what you want?

CLIENT: You mean from the nurse?

THERAPIST: That example will do, or any other time you lied that you're willing to describe.

The reader will note that the therapist concentrated on the behavioral issue (of lying) rather than the prove it debate the client tried to initiate. Typically, the therapeutic bottom line is that it does not matter if the client did the behavior on that occurrence or not. The general topic your claim involves is the key issue with which to remain. Although you may be positive that the client did the action in question, you will frequently find it is not useful to "battle" with the client in demonstrating your position.

The following case example might illustrate the usefulness of this approach. One client was known to lie on multiple occasions, though the staff of the institution were typically not able to prove that he was lying. He, of course, always denied it (and, thereby, lied about his lying). The staff's approach to this situation was to enumerate those topics about which we believed the client had lied on at least (though usually more than) one occasion. We then met with the client to let him know that we knew we could be wrong about any one of these topics, but overall there was an obvious pattern of his lying at least on some occasions. During that meeting, the client continued to deny the accusations. My response to his denials was that he was just continuing to lie and that that behavior was no longer going to work. In response to his demands that we prove our claims, I repeated our original statement that we could be wrong in any specific area, but that the pattern still remained clear. Through this conversation, the client eventually acknowledged that he sometimes lied (though he still argued against specific accusations we had made). The outcome from that meeting was that it opened up therapeutic discussion for months concerning his lying to get what he wanted and the natural consequences from that behavior (of not being trusted by those who know he lies). This connection between his actions and their consequences proved invaluable in positively influencing other therapeutic changes.

Negative Comparisons

This "countertransference hook" can occur whenever the client lets you know that you probably do not "measure up" in some way. The psychopath's statements relevant to this area typically occur during

the first few sessions of therapy, though the comments can be made at
any time.

The comparisons made by the client can be of three forms: (1) to
one or more therapists from his past, (2) to one or more therapists that
are your colleagues, and (3) to some standard the client reportedly
believes is in the profession. Each of these areas are described in the
following.

The most common negative comparison of which I have been aware
is between the current therapist and one or more therapists from the
client's past. The comparative statements typically sound like one of
the following (with the same beginning for each): "Well, my therapist
at (such and such hospital, clinic, or institution) used to . . .

1. make me feel more comfortable during our sessions than you do,

2. be able to get me to feel better between sessions than you do,

3. understand me better than you do,

4. give me better feedback than you do,

5. be more active in helping me than you are,

6. be more willing to let me do what *I* think is best than you are,

7. help me more than you do,

8. trust me more than you do.

Clinicians' reactions to these statements vary, but most often
involve a defensive stance such as "Well, I'm not your previous
therapist" or "I do what I think is best for you." With responses like
these, therapists buy into their clients' challenge for control of the
conversation and, in essence, the therapy session. These answers are
not useful for the psychopath's treatment. (They do not typically help
the therapist feel better either.)

Rather the perspective must be maintained that the client's
comments are representative of his pathology and not in need of direct
answers. Direct answers only suggest to the client that his behavior is
useful and should be maintained.

So what is a better way to handle those kinds of comparative
statements? By recognizing them for what they are: the client's
method of testing his environment for its parameters and limitations,

and not a reflection on the therapist's real or imagined professional capabilities. With this interpretation in mind, clinicians can avoid a defensive response and reflect something more useful to the client. For instance, if your desire is to help the client pay attention to details of his environment, a question such as "What makes it appear that way?" may facilitate that goal. If your response is to be geared towards his limited behavioral repertoire (i.e., towards teaching the client greater social skills, the assertive expression of his needs), then statements such as "Maybe you could explain to me what it is you want from me. Then I might be able to fulfill your needs better" would be useful. In either case, the clinician's response helps the client focus on *his* perceptions and feelings rather than his therapist's.

A second type of psychopath's comparison is between the current therapist and the therapist's colleagues. While most of the aforementioned applies to this kind of situation as well, there are a few extra dimensions for these comparisons that should be mentioned.

The main features in this situation that differ from that previously described are that it is all in the present and all relevant parties are available for direct comparison. The client, therefore, has the capability of delineating the behavior of the specific colleague that is better than yours. This can have more personal meaning for any clinician than comparisons by the client to unknown people from his past, largely because his comments are more likely to reflect a comparison we or our supervisors are also making. In this case, we are being told that we are on the losing side, and our psychological defenses spring to life.

An additional feature of these situations which can occur in certain settings is a kind of possessiveness by the therapist over the client. An example of the internal dialogue after hearing such a comparison would be: "How would this client know what it is like to interact with (my colleague)? This client is supposed to be mine. Is (my colleague) sticking his or her nose where it does not belong? Second-guessing me perchance? Does he or she think I'm incompetent?"

The presumption in that internal dialogue is that the client's statement reflects something that is real, rather than (at best) his perception of an event. The comments may even represent a lie by the client. Rather than keeping in mind that the client's perceptions are just that and no more, the therapist buys into them as reality and the hook succeeds. The therapist is focusing more on his or her own affect than that of the client's.

The recommended method for handling these kinds of statements from psychopathic clients is the same as previously described for other negative comparisons. Focus on the client's perceptions and behavior and not on some internal reaction that assumes your client's statement has reality for you. Your specific response should reflect your client's current therapy goal.

The third kind of negative comparison that can be made is between you and some kind of professional standard in your client's head. I have seen this process most often when a student therapist or intern is in the process of beginning therapy with a psychopathic client. The client begins to ask various questions about the therapist's credentials or experience. If unprepared, this mental health worker can find himself or herself on the defensive rather quickly. This stance can be very difficult to overcome during the session.

Again the therapist's recourse is based on the concept that the hook represents the client's attempt to test his environment rather than any specific reality that the clinician may feel a need to defend. Helping the client focus on more useful and effective methods for expressing his needs is the way to deal with these types of statements.

Throwing Guilt

"You're the one who went to school. My family didn't have the money yours obviously did. What did your schooling tell you I should do?"

"You're the one who has all those degrees. Why are you asking me how I should handle this problem? I'm here to get your advice."

"You're the one who uses all those fancy words. I don't even understand half of them and yet you're telling me you don't know what I should do. What kind of therapist are you, anyway?"

"Here I'm paying you for your advice. Then you have the nerve to tell me I'm supposed to come up with my own answers. Why am I coming to you anyway?"

"Look, my family sent me here so you could fix me. They keep telling me they don't see any improvement. Don't you know how to do therapy?"

Do any of these sound familiar? If you have worked with psychopathic clients, you probably have heard something of the kind. Each comment reflects the perspective found in most clients that their therapist should have solutions to all of their problems. For instance, in general clients often ask for advice during the early sessions of their therapy. A psychopathic client's comments, however, often contain an extra element—an implicit demand for a defense from the therapist. This is the "challenge" for which therapists must be prepared.

The difficulty in handling these comments effectively is that at first glance, there often appears to be no good way to do it. If the therapist concentrates on the client's expressed need for advice, then a debate often ensues over what the point of therapy is (e.g., "If I'm supposed to have all my own answers, then I don't need to be in therapy with you, do I?"). On the other hand, if the therapist simply gives advice, the client will frequently make sure that the advice fails to work, thereby continuing his "demonstration" that the therapist (i.e., a factor of the environment) cannot control the client.

As with the various types of hooks already described in this chapter, the method for dealing with the comments at the beginning of this section is to refuse to "play the game," to refuse to buy into the client's way of perceiving the world. In this case, simple answers typically suffice to communicate with the client without defending one's therapeutic technique or giving unneeded advice.

The following, based on the previous examples, will illustrate:

You're the one who went to school. My family obviously did not have the money yours did. What did your schooling tell you I should do?

THERAPIST: It didn't.

CLIENT: So you have no idea what I should do?

THERAPIST: Oh, I can think of various possibilities, but only you know what you should do.

CLIENT: Like what possibilities?

THERAPIST: Let's work on this together. What have you seen other people in the same situation do that seemed to be successful for them? (This can lead to increasing the client's behavioral repertoire.)

You're the one who has all the degrees. Why are you asking me how I should handle this problem? I'm here to get your advice.

THERAPIST: Oh? I thought you were here to learn how to handle your problems.

CLIENT: I am, and I'm asking you to teach me. So tell me now how to do it.

THERAPIST: I have a different idea about how people learn to handle their problems. How about if we discuss various possibilities from which you can choose? What are some possibilities you can think of?

You're the one who uses all those fancy words. I don't even understand half of them and yet you're telling me you don't know what I should do. What kind of therapist are you, anyway?

THERAPIST: Someone who is trying to help you.

CLIENT: But you're not helping me if you don't tell me what I should do.

THERAPIST: But you've told me how all your life someone has been telling you what to do, and it has not helped, so I'm helping you stand on your own two feet. Now, what actions do *you* think would be good for you?

Here I'm paying you for your advice. Then you have the nerve to tell me I'm supposed to come up with my own answers. Why am I coming to you anyway?

THERAPIST: You've told me it's because you wanted to change yourself.

CLIENT: Yeah, and you're not helping me do that.

THERAPIST: One of your goals was to learn to make "better" decisions on your own, wasn't it? If I told you what you should do, I would be interfering with your goal. I think it is my role to ensure that you make your own decisions, and that those decisions get "better" over time.

CLIENT: But what am I supposed to do now?

THERAPIST: Let's talk about the possibilities.

Look, my family sent me here so that you could fix me. They keep telling me they don't see any improvement. Don't you know how to do therapy?

THERAPIST: Yes.

CLIENT: Apparently you don't with me.

THERAPIST: Meaning that you don't see any progress. Why do you suppose that is?

CLIENT: Because you're not doing good therapy.

THERAPIST: If you mean the therapy has not been effective, you may be correct. If, however, you mean that I was supposed to control your behavior, then you are mistaken about therapy. I will never take away your control of your behavior. So, do you wish to change your behavior, or not? (Using a challenging comment to facilitate the client's interest in continuing therapy.)

In each of these examples, the therapist does not respond to the comments that set the stage for the guilt throwing. To do so would have been pointless and potentially reinforcing to the client's usual means of expressing himself. Rather the therapist sidesteps those comments and leads the discussion back to something more useful for the client.

Demand for Trust

Comments from a psychopathic client that in essence demand trust from the mental health worker can occur at any time during therapy.

They can be made at the beginning of therapy when the participants are still learning the basics about their relationship. Such comments are relatively common when the therapist confronts the client about misbehaviors such as lying. Finally, clients sometimes "demand" trust after meeting with the same therapist for a large number of therapy sessions, with the presumption that duration of contacts should imply an emotional tie and hence, trust. Recommended responses for clinicians, however, are similar in each of these contexts.

The client's comments typically sound something like the following (in time order from early to late in the therapy):

1. "Don't you trust what I say? I don't see how I can work with someone who doesn't trust me."
2. "Just because I say something that you think doesn't sound right, you automatically think that I am lying. It makes me feel like I shouldn't say anything or if you don't happen to like it, you're going to accuse me of lying."
3. "I don't understand how you can say you don't trust my word, after all the time we've spent together and all the therapy I've gone through."

What makes these comments from a psychopathic client different from those of other clients is that, by definition, psychopaths are known to lie and be untrustworthy. Their demands for trust, therefore, take on a "catch-22" nature. If you do trust the client (i.e., to be honest and reliable), you are likely to find yourself disappointed or betrayed, making it more difficult for you to remain productive with this client. If you openly keep the perspective that you do not trust the client, he will feel hurt, feel that the therapy is a sham, and quit. In either case, the situation can seem like no matter what you do, the therapy is in jeopardy.

This outcome is true only if you buy into the client's perspective about "trust." The psychopathic client tends to view such concepts as "either–or, yes–no" concepts; either people trust you or they do not. (This lack of knowledge about the nuances of concepts such as trust reflects the psychopaths' partial helplessness learning where "extremes" were the only salient features of their environments worth giving attention.) Rather than responding to the client's demands for trust with a defensive statement concerning one's level of trust for the client, the therapist needs to concentrate on assisting the client develop greater knowledge of the "details of his environment," the nuances of his world.

This kind of assistance usually involves a set of discussions regarding different forms of trust; (1) about the client's not committing a physical attack, (2) about the client's not committing a property crime, (3) about the client's following authority's directives, (4) about the client's telling the truth, (5) about the client's not trying to hurt someone emotionally, (6) about the client's showing up for each therapy session, (7) about the client's continuing in therapy, or (8) about the client's willingness to make personal changes through therapy. Chances are that you as therapist do trust the client in some of these ways and not in others. *This* kind of feedback may be useful for the client *after* he has come to understand the nuances of "trust."

The following case examples illustrate the point. One incarcerated client persistently made general statements that the staff was always going to blame him for everything because they did not trust him. He included me in those comments. Over time, he made various inquiries to me about my trust for him. Each time, I responded with "it depends what you mean by trust" as a lead-in for such discussion. Eventually the client got the concept more clearly and those inquiries changed to more specific ones (almost always within a context of his wanting something) such as "You know I'm not going to hit anyone, don't you?" (I answered "absolutely" because I believed that the feedback was useful for him, as well as because that is what I believed.) Because he knew that I was well aware of his tendency to lie, he knew not to ask general questions about my trust in that area.

A second client, referred to treatment by his wife (with whom marital therapy was eventually done), stated early in therapy that he believed that no matter what he did, I (as his therapist) would not believe him. This comment followed shortly after I expressed doubt about the accuracy of what he had just said. Following his comment, I reflected on his tendency to feel helpless when it came to being trusted, but also explored with him the various kinds of trust. He was soon able to recognize that many people trusted him in many situations, with only a specific few being problematic for him. (This particular client was an exceedingly charming fellow on first impression, such that I pointed out to him that people usually trust him fully initially.) We explored ways in which he could positively affect those specific situations so that he no longer felt helpless in dealing with them. I never did need to answer his demand for my trust afterward.

"Yes, But . . ."

Any experienced therapist has heard a client respond "yes, but . . ." followed with a rather complete denial to what had just been agreed. The psychopathic client has no patent on this kind of statement.

What is more unique to the psychopath, however, is the frequency with which the "yes, but . . ." is followed by a statement of someone else's fault, what is often termed (from the psychoanalytic literature) as projection of blame. Typical examples are:

THERAPIST: So, you did not follow through on your week's therapy assignment.

CLIENT: True, but I couldn't because my wife needed me to fix a bunch of things around the house, so I didn't have the time.

THERAPIST: I thought we agreed that you would not go out to drink any alcohol this week.

CLIENT: Yes, but I only went out to play cards and the guys kept pushing me to drink until I did.

THERAPIST: I thought we agreed that you would follow staff directives this week.

CLIENT: Yes, but they were being so unreasonable, I felt it only made sense to do what I did.

In each case, the client in effect denies the responsibility for his failure and attaches it to some outside cause. In psychopathic clients, this can occur both because they are consciously attempting to "get away with something" and because they truly see outcomes as caused by forces outside of themselves (based in their earlier partial helplessness conditioning). Consider this example:

THERAPIST: I thought we agreed that you would follow staff directives this week.

CLIENT: Yes, but when I did they kept on my case anyway, so I figured what's the use. It didn't seem to make any difference.

Here the client is not denying his agreement, but his willingness to stay with it after its initial failure (or *perceived* failure). As alluded to previously, the therapist needs to concentrate on the client's difficulty seeing connections between his own behavior (i.e., his behavior of not following staff directives) and their consequences (i.e., staff not accepting his initial willingness to comply with directives as real), as could be understood from the effects of partial helplessness learning.

The hook for mental health workers when the psychopathic client states "yes, but . . ." is to give feedback to the client about his responsibility for his behavior. This often leads to a debate, a verbal battle, that is fruitless. The client will have a variety of reasons why he could not accomplish what he was supposed to while the therapist will have a sense of morality and professional wisdom from which to argue the other perspective. Debates such as that do not "challenge" the client so much as make him feel diminished.

In keeping with this perspective, a useful response to the last example would be: "Well, let's explore why it failed so that we can make it work next time." Using such a comment, the therapist avoids a debate about responsibility with a concentration on setting the expectation that the client will try the behavior again.

Purposeful Misinterpretation/Misquoting

This form of psychopathic hook can occur any time during therapy, though it is more common during the initial and middle sessions rather than the later ones. Typically the comments are said to a third party such that you as the therapist only hear about them second hand.

Periodically, however, you can expect to hear purposeful misinterpretation or misquoting of your words directly from the client. In any case, the client's behavior can be viewed as directly related to his desire to challenge his environment for control over what he wants.

The following description is an example of how this process works. During a therapy session (or, within an institutional setting, it can occur during offhand conversations), you say something to the client suggesting your perspective on the appropriateness of his or other people's behavior, an institutional rule, a law, or the like. The client later decides to use that comment to his advantage, perhaps by telling other institutional staff that you said it was okay for him to do something in exception to the rule. You learn of this misquoting later through the staff's anger expressed in your direction. Most therapists find it difficult not to translate that anger into anger towards the client. That, in turn, often turns into a debate over what you said and what you did not say. All in all, the therapist's countertransference is what ends up needing treatment before the client is going to gain anything from the interchange.

Sometimes that purposeful misinterpretation/misquoting can occur solely within the therapy sessions:

1. After some discussion about the client's recent misbehavior: "Doc, I thought you said last time that I should do what I feel is best rather than listen to someone else's rule" (when the original comment was probably couched in a rational-emotive approach concerning irrational self-statements involving "shoulds").

2. (After physically striking another individual): "Hey, I did as you told me. I expressed my feelings honestly and directly to the person who was bothering me."

While the cases involving third parties often lead to anger, the within therapy occurrences many times lead to exasperation. *You* know what you said, and you know that the *client* knows what you said, but what do you do with a client who purposefully misinterprets what you say for his own gain?

The first impulse of some clinicians is to make a comment

correcting the stated interpretation by the client. This usually leads to both parties acknowledging that the client had an excuse for his actions because of his misinterpretation. After all, if the therapist needs to explain his or her statement again, then there is an implicit acknowledgment that the client could have made an error in interpreting it. In other words, the clinician has only served to reinforce the psychopath's deliberate tendency to misinterpret what others say to get what he wants.

Recommended instead is that clinicians make a statement contending that the client knew what was being said all the time and that the misinterpretation/misquoting was deliberate. The client will likely disagree with you, stating that you are falsely accusing him. This situation can then be treated as any case of "present the proof, or catch me if you can" described earlier in this chapter.

Following the previous example where there was a discussion regarding the client's recent behavior:

CLIENT: Doc, I thought you said last time that I should do what I feel is best rather than listening to someone else's rule.

THERAPIST: You know perfectly well that I was referring to the rules you told yourself in your head and not those written down for all to see.

CLIENT: How was I supposed to know what you meant? You didn't make yourself clear.

THERAPIST: You knew what I meant. You're just using this as an excuse for your misbehavior.

CLIENT: That's not true. You're wrong.

THERAPIST: Are you denying that you ever even slightly change people's words, on purpose, in order to get or do what you want?

CLIENT: Well, maybe a little sometimes, but not this time.

THERAPIST: Then let's talk about those other times.

In this example, as with those for any catch me if you can denial, the therapist focuses on the general behavior rather than the specific instance. Many times that successfully avoids the debate over who is right and who is wrong.

Of importance, some clients will continue to deny *any* occurrence of the behavior being discussed. In those cases, the therapist should simply state that that is an issue they will need to come back to in therapy, and go on to something else. The client will get the message that a debate is not going to occur, but that the therapist did not "surrender" in the challenge either. If the issue is an important one, it will resurface.

Exaggeration

Some psychopaths' approach to controlling their environment is to try to impress others with how wonderful the clients are. This section will concentrate on what that looks like and how to handle it effectively when the psychopath's attempts do not involve out-and-out lies, but rather exaggerations of the truth. Lies as a psychopath's technique for controlling his environment is described in the following section.

Impressing others through exaggeration has two forms of expression: (1) through comparisons to others and (2) through statements of some absolute (versus relative) level of ability. Only the first form is discussed here, as the second almost always could just as easily be labeled as a lie and will, therefore, be described in the next section.

Probably the most annoying form of exaggerated comparison made by a psychopathic client is between himself and you, his therapist. Illustrative examples include:

"You're not so smart. I'm smarter than you are, even with all your years of school."

"I'm better at understanding people than you are, and I only went to the school of hard knocks."

"I'm probably better at getting people to do things than you are, and that's supposed to be your job."

"I'm probably better than you in almost anything I do."

The reader may note the not-so-hidden hostility that underlies these comparisons. This, in my experience, is common. The exaggeration coupled with the hostility usually appear like a purposeful put-down to the therapist rather than a bona fide attempt by the client to build his own self-esteem. Since most therapists are sensitive enough to detect the degrading nature of the statement, a defensive reaction by the clinician is also common; that is, the clinician gets hooked.

This hook works whenever the mental health worker gives the client's words meaning beyond being representations of the client's pathology. Few of us like to hear ourselves denigrated in some way, but we need to keep the perspective about a psychopathic client (as well as any other) that his words about us do not say anything about us but only say something about him. When the therapist gives those words meaning beyond that, then the client's method of challenging his environment for control gains some reinforcement.

When the clinician is able to keep the appropriate perspective on the client's words, however, a useful and therapeutic process can ensue. For instance, after the client makes one of these kinds of comments, the therapist can respond with any of the following depending on which therapy goal (in parentheses) is valued most at the time:

1. "Your attempt to get me upset with you did not work. You will have to find another way if that was your goal." (Goal: To challenge the client in his interaction with you.)

2. "Your expression of anger was noted, but I believe you could have expressed it more directly without putting me down in the process." (Goal: To increase the client's behavioral repertoire and social skills.)

3. "I do not believe that that kind of comment will lead to the outcomes you most desire." (Goal: To teach the connection between the client's actions and their consequences in the therapeutic attempt to overcome the effects of partial helplessness conditioning.)

A second type of comparison involving exaggeration is toward people besides the clinician. These exaggerations are usually easier for therapists to handle because the comments do not feel as personal. Sometimes the statements are as simple as "I play chess a heck of a lot better than John" (when that situation is not true). Other times, the comments represent put-downs to beloved colleagues.

No matter what the exaggeration, the current primary goal of therapy should be kept in mind in determining your response. As stated previously, those goals are likely to include variations on challenging the client to get him invested in your interaction, increasing social skills, or teaching the connection between one's actions and their natural consequences.

Lying, or "Have I Got a Story to Tell You"

Psychopaths are probably best known for their lying. They seem to lie to avoid punishment, to gain rewards, to manipulate people, and, sometimes, "just because." For some psychopaths, lying can appear to be their way of being, their normal method of verbal interchange.

Not only do psychopaths often lie, but their lies frequently appear absolutely incredible (when exposed). Psychopaths who are impostors live their lives with one fantastic lie after another. Consider the following example written by the Associated Press and quoted from the *Wisconsin State Journal* of January 27, 1985:

> Lakeland College accounting students apparently liked the teacher who called himself Stephen Marshall Barton and apparently he did a good job of instructing them.

> But, officials of the small northeastern Wisconsin liberal arts college said, Stephen Marshall Barton was not the person he claimed to be.

> Dr. Richard Hill, president of the college, said the balding, heavyset man in his mid-40s was dismissed this month after the college learned of the deception.

> "Student evaluations given at the end of the terms were very positive," he said of the man who was hired last February to teach upper level accounting courses. "I guess you don't become a con man unless you can make friends and influence people."

> Keith Striggow, the college's academic dean, described the man, who also taught a course on computers and accounting, as a "sort of computer whiz."

> "The quality of his work is verified by the students taking the certified

public accountant exams, who did better than students had before he came," Striggow said.

The teacher was hired after answering an advertisement in the *Chronicle of Higher Education*.

"His credentials were great, better than we expected we would be able to attract," Hill said.

The man produced transcripts and letters of recommendation from the University of Connecticut, where he claimed to have earned a bachelor of science degree, and from the University of Nebraska, where he said he had earned a master's degree in business administration.

He also said he had earned a doctorate in accounting and information services at the University Systems of England in Manchester.

Lakeland said there is a Stephen Marshall Barton with bachelor's and master's degrees, but he lives in Meriden, Conn., where he works for Hartford Insurance Co.

"But our Stephen Marshall Barton. We don't know who he is," Hill said.

Hill said the school began to question things after a student at Lakeland mentioned he had Barton as a teacher at UW–Eau Claire several years ago. Hill said that was puzzling since Eau Claire had not been mentioned on the man's resume.

James Wenner, dean of UW-Eau Claire School of Business, said the man identifying himself as Barton was there from January of 1980 until August of 1981.

"To my knowledge there were no problems that we were aware of, no things that would bring questions to mind," Wenner said.

The UW-Eau Claire dean said the man resigned suddenly.

"It was my understanding that he had an opportunity to join a firm in Asia doing some kind of information systems work," he said.

Hill said the man was confronted with the Eau Claire matter, and said he had been involved in a messy divorce at the time and had not wanted that to mar his credentials.

The man who posed as Barton could not be reached for comment Saturday. Hill disclosed the dismissal Friday. It took place Jan. 16.

"I said to him, 'With all your ability, it is a shame you can't just be yourself,'" Hill said he told the man. "He replied something like, 'I know it sounds like a hollow answer, but something happened 20 years ago. I wish I could undo it.' There was a very quiet acceptance of all this, it seemed to me."

The real Stephen Marshall Barton, who is 6-foot-1, weighs 195 pounds and a full head of hair, said he never taught and had lived in Connecticut since leaving Omaha, Neb., in 1969.

"He's got a lot of moxie," Barton said of the impostor.

Barton said he had been contacted in July by Larry Holtzman, an investigator for a bank in Omaha who had been looking for him for three years.

"It seems someone using my name had run up a MasterCard or Visa bill for several thousand dollars and skipped out on it," he said.

Barton said he had recently been contacted by an Eau Claire police detective, James Olson, who was investigating the deception there and put the two men in contact with one another.

"I think it is kind of hard to believe that today, being such an information society, with all that's known about all of us, that someone could pull this off," (the real) Barton said.

Difficult to believe indeed, but pull it off he did. As it can be with many lies from psychopathic clients. Consider the following example concerning an incarcerated client with whom I worked. The client anwered a local newspaper advertisement from a woman who indicated that she was willing to correspond with someone who wished such a relationship. Very early in their correspondence, she apparently informed my client that she had recently lost her husband to cancer. In his next letter, George (not his real name) wrote that he had also lost his wife to cancer just a year before. Elizabeth (not her real name) began to visit George in the forensic hospital where he was incarcerated on a maximum security unit, thinking that she and he had something important in common.

During those visits as well as through telephone calls, George told Elizabeth that he was at the hospital because he had had a nervous breakdown after the death of his wife. He stated that he had been there for nine months, but could not leave because the hospital staff were lying to the authorities about him. He emphasized his desire to help himself by pointing out that he was seeing a private therapist in a nearby city at his own expense once per week.

George described some details about his current business ventures, asking her assistance for some minor errands, given that he was living in the hospital for the time being. She complied with his early requests. According to information later learned by the hospital staff, George had apparently strongly suggested to Elizabeth that he would form a long-term relationship with her, including the possibility of marriage, when he left the hospital. Within those discussions, he indicated it would help his business greatly if she would obtain some credit cards in her name which he, with her permission, could then use for his business. He would, of course, pay her back for everything he bought. This arrangement was just to simplify his business transactions. Elizabeth was contemplating applying for the credit cards when the hospital staff learned of what was transpiring and spoke to Elizabeth about all of it.

In fact, George's wife did not die of cancer a year earlier. In fact, she was alive and well and still married to George when he was "forming a relationship" with Elizabeth. Likewise George did not enter the hospital nine months earlier after a nervous breakdown but many years earlier after he was convicted of rape and sent to the hospital under a statute calling for psychological treatment for certain sex offenders. He was not at all likely to leave the hospital in the near future, with many years to his scheduled release date and little chance at being paroled early due to his having "done his time" poorly. His lack of intention to pay Elizabeth for anything he charged in her name was quickly uncovered when she received a bill for over $100 of food she did not order, with no statement from George that he had placed such an order. Similarly, the food was something he consumed rather than something that was part of his business.

What Elizabeth came to recognize, over time, was that George had lied to her about almost everything. If the hospital staff had not intervened when they did, Elizabeth probably would have found herself with some large bills on her newly acquired credit cards as her one keepsake from a relationship that never really was.

Seeing one of your clients use someone like that can cause a variety of countertransference reactions, most of which interfere with therapy. The process of remaining therapeutic can be even more difficult when you encounter a psychopathic client who tells fantastic tales directly to you.

One such client was already known to lie, so I thought myself prepared for his attempts at deception. But not so. One morning as I entered the institution where I worked, I learned from the staff that Hank (not his real name) reported receiving a telephone call the evening before from his sister informing him that his mother died after a lengthy illness. Hank had apparently not slept much during the night, asking for aspirin on occasion. I spoke to Hank later that day during which he repeated the details I had been told by the staff. He had tears in his eyes. We spoke of the process of grieving. I was sure that all was as it appeared to be.

To follow through on some administrative detail gathering a day after Hank's report of her death, however, a staff member from the institution had reason to call the household where Hank's mother lived. To the staff member's shock, Hank's mother answered the telephone. She obviously had not died. She had not even been ill. The staff member learned from Hank's mother that he had not had contact from his sister in over seven years, so any kind of reported telephone call from her was doubtful.

How should you as a therapist react when you learn that one of your clients feigned grieving with you about the death of his parent, especially when you cannot even guess as to why he would do such a thing? The countertransference hook potential is great: (1) feeling like a fool for being "duped" in this way, (2) feeling confused in attempting to understand your client's unusual behavior, (3) feeling anger for being lied to about such a significant topic, (4) feeling satisfaction in finally "catching" your client in his behavior, and/or (5) feeling like a failure as a therapist.

Each of the first three types of countertransference represents a human response to interpersonal deceit. Those feelings suggest that the therapist saw the relationship between the client and himself as involving mutual trust which has been broken. To elaborate, the perception of a client-therapist relationship usually works with most clients as long as the clients can say to themselves "I can trust my therapist." The issue of whether or not the therapist can say to himself "I can trust my client" is often not overtly considered by therapists as they conduct treatment. With most types of clients, it does not matter. With psychopathic clients, however, clinicians' tendency to want to trust their clients is confronted by the untrustworthiness of their clients. Lies are one of the most overt demonstrations of this untrustworthiness. The mental health worker who expects to form mutually trusting relationships while performing therapy is likely to find himself experiencing a sense of betrayal from his psychopathic clients. To avoid this pitfall, therapists need to remember not to trust what their psychopathic clients say, no matter how simple or elaborate the story.

The fourth countertransference response, of the detective, usually occurs when the therapist strongly wants to be able to have "proof" of a client's misbehavior with which to confront him. Many times this reaction is based in a kind of frustration of wanting, just once, to be able to say to the client "Ah ha! Got you! And I can prove it this time." Sometimes the motivation to be a detective is based in feeling that trying to solve the mystery is fun, especially when you find the proof you need to solve the mystery. In either case, therapists feel satisfied with themselves, with finally "getting their man."

Getting proof about a lie can be used therapeutically, but the internal gloating associated with being a "satisfied detective" often interferes with the process. The proof can be used to instruct the client that he needs to find a better way to get what he wants because lying will not work for him in the long run, as "this" one did not. The therapist can then describe alternative behaviors that would be more appropriate.

The danger in being a satisfied detective is that your internal "gloating" will often be interpreted by the client as "ah ha! I won this round!" which is exactly what it is. That communication serves to perpetuate the perception of the therapist as a challenge to the client, but in a way that says that "scoring points" is the whole concept behind your treatment approach. The "challenge" becomes the therapy instead of being a vehicle for the therapy.

Finally, the countertransference reaction of feeling like a failure as a therapist assumes that your client should not show any of his old misbehaviors once you invested your time in him. Phrased this way, most clinicians recognize the absurdity of their response. The usual corrective action is to have the therapist simply tell himself: "My client will lie to me. His lying represents part of his psychopathology. Like any symptoms of his psychopathology, his lies will simply be grist for the therapeutic mill."

In summary, therapists need to expect (1) their psychopathic clients to lie, (2) that the lies will usually be simple but may be incredibly intricate, (3) that you as therapists will not be able most of the time to demonstrate that your clients are lying, (4) that you do not need to trust your clients for them to trust you or for you to perform successful therapy, and (5) that your clients' lying simply represents a symptom of his psychopathology and not a sign of your incompetence.

Playing for Sympathy

Of all the countertransference hooks described up to now, this is the first in which the therapist's emotional reaction has a likelihood of being inappropriately positive toward the client. This section elaborates on the common tendency of psychopathic clients to see themselves as the victims of others' prejudices, especially those of people in authority. This tendency, an outgrowth of the psychopaths' life experiences of partial helplessness and therefore involving what they find to be unpredictable negative reactions from others, can have a strong effect on therapists over time.

The process has a typical pattern. Initially, during one of the therapy sessions, the client expresses his frustration about being subjected to the discriminatory/prejudicial practices of someone who has authority over him. From his perception, he keeps being blamed, punished, or picked on unfairly. He does not see, or at least is unwilling to acknowledge responsibility in causing the other person's actions. (A client who has been involved in therapy for a significant period of time will usually acknowledge some responsibility in causing the other's actions, but not to the extent he feels persecuted.)

Initially therapists usually interpret these statements appropriately, as reflections of their clients' psychopathology more than some reality of systematic persecution or consistent misattribution of blame by "the authorities." Over a period of many therapy sessions, however, the clients' statements begin to sound like there must be some reality to them. Clinicians notice that these clients *are* subjected to a disproportionate loss of privileges compared to nonpsychopathic clients. Simultaneously, therapists are typically privy to conversations by the authorities that suggest strong negative feelings towards the psychopathic clients. Drawing the conclusion that there is some prejudice against psychopathic clients that serves to discriminate against them is then not difficult.

Unfortunately, the "accuracy" of that conclusion probably has not changed over time. The authorities' reaction has probably not altered from where it was when therapy started. The negative feelings are just as much a part of the natural consequences to the clients' misbehaviors as anything else; and just as predictable (from our perspective, not the clients').

What changes is the therapists' interpretation of the clients' statements. Over time, it is as if therapists say to themselves, "Given all of these examples given me by my client, there must be some truth here." One should examine and reexamine that sentiment when it is felt.

On most occasions, this conclusion simply represents being worn down by the psychopath's tendency to persist in acting when frustrated. The client can keep up the same behavior with little overt reinforcement for quite a long time. Partial helplessness conditioning has guaranteed this. The consistency of therapeutic interpretations is not as great.

This hook can be a difficult one to spot until one is confronted by other mental health workers' judgments. The process of being "worn down" is an insidious one. A tell-tale sign of being hooked, however, and one to be remembered, is when you as therapist become the client's advocate with the authorities. Are you asking for considerations that make sense to you, but to few other people, considerations that you would not and have not asked for when it comes to other clients? If the answer even approaches being affirmative, reexamine your interpretation of your client's situation.

Miraculous Insight, or "You Were Wonderful, Doc"

We all want to be successful in what we do. Most of us like hearing about how well we have helped someone. With most clients, being thanked for our efforts makes all the work worthwhile.

There can come a time, however, when we need to disbelieve the good things we are being told, even when the present comes in the fine wrapper of "insight." I refer to this situation as "miraculous insight," when the client seems to have learned too quickly many of the things you hoped he would eventually learn.

There are some obvious examples that are not difficult to spot. One such type occurs shortly after a client has been admitted to a forensic hospital after being adjudicated not guilty by mental disease or defect for a crime. He now needs to convince you that his "dangerousness" has passed, he is "cured," and he can be released safely to the community. Through his miraculous insight he hopes to convince you to recommend his discharge.

A similar situation occurs in correctional institutions shortly before an inmate is to face the parole board. He may want a letter from you or similar notice added to his file so that the board will release him. This circumstance is also easy to spot.

More difficult cases occur where no obvious motive is apparent. We, as people who have dedicated a significant part of our lives to improving people's mental health, may pat ourselves on the back for the good work we have done. Unfortunately, the client expressing the insight has only learned the words to say without making any significant change in his behavior. Nothing important has been accomplished.

The client's comments can sound absolutely wonderful, as in this example:

> With your help, Doc, I think I finally understand why I sexually molested that 9 year old girl. I was feeling lonely, very lonely, with no one to turn to who would understand me. My wife and I had just had another of our arguments and we weren't communicating very well. I always felt that my mother never listened to me. She just lectured me on how I should straighten up my act. I had no real close friends,

certainly none that I could tell I felt lonely. That wouldn't be macho. You know how you pointed out to me how important that was to me, though I have seen how stupid it is since then. Well, anyway, I decided to wash my car and my neighbor's daughter came over to watch. She and I had talked many times before, but I hadn't thought much about it before that day. I thought that day that she seemed able to understand me, in a way that nobody else did. I know now that it was simply my desire to have someone close to me that got me to perceive her in that way, but it seemed so real then. After a short while, based on my feeling a little better talking to her, I viewed her as an adult, able to understand adult kinds of things. Because I felt close to her, and saw her as an adult, sexual contact was something sort of natural. I know now how stupid I was. To make sure that I don't do that kind of thing again, I need to make sure that I seek out an adult any time I feel lonely, including therapy with a professional if I feel I have no one else to turn to. I know a child just cannot understand adult relationships and shouldn't be made to. You've been a great help to me in learning all of this. I feel confident that I can make it out there without hurting anyone.

But does this insight alter his behavior? Is he really even going to remain aware of his feelings, especially his loneliness, enough to know when he should seek help? Is he going to care enough to seek help when the time comes that he needs it? Those are the questions that typically matter, not if the client has insight into his problem or if you have done a good job as a therapist. The temptation to congratulate oneself for an accomplishment with a client known to be difficult with which to work needs to be kept in check until the real work of therapy is done. The insight, especially relatively early in therapy, is probably not insight at all, but just some intellectual understanding of his circumstances.

A variant of these types of cases involves the clients who have been in therapy for years (usually because they have been incarcerated that long) such that they can tell you "why" they have done what they have done, all in language that sounds like true insight, but their behavior has not appreciably changed from before they started therapy. Here, the amount of time invested in therapy may have been extensive, so the insightful comments do not seem so miraculous. On the other hand, the lack of significant behavioral change lets you know that the "insight" is really just intellectual understand.

In all of these kinds of cases, the question for thera₊ one of where does one go from here. Assuming that you client's understanding is accurate, you may ask yourself ` ₋₋₋ent already knows why he does something, knows that it can get him in trouble, but still chooses to do it, what can I do?"

This is a time when you can use your knowledge of the discrepancy between what the client says he has learned and his behavior as a challenge to him. By confronting him with your knowledge of this discrepancy, by setting yourself up as a challenge for him, he will feel a need to pursue answering the question of why he would willingly be so self-destructive, or demonstrate to you that he is not. In either case, the therapy has progressed from the apparent standoff.

A caveat for my readers. There are likely to be occasions when you will find clients who will not accept the challenge described in the last paragraph. They will simply tell you that they like their life and do not wish to change, though it may have been important to them to understand why they had done what they did. At those times, you are likely to find that there truly is little you can do to affect change in the relevant behaviors.

Everything You Always Wanted to Hear, and More

This is the general case compared to the special case of miraculous insight. The previous section described how psychopathic clients can sometimes tell therapists just the insights that the therapists wish to hear (though a bit earlier than expected). This section explains the more general case of clients stating just what they believe their therapists wish to hear.

There are various kinds of examples which could be enumerated. Probably the most common type involves a comment beginning with "you are the only one . . . " such as the following:

1. You are the only one I can trust.
2. You are the only one I can talk to.
3. You are the only one who understands me.

4. You are the only one who cares about me.
5. You are the only one who has been able to help me.

A second type of "everything you wanted to hear" statement involves the client's reported perception of the mental health worker's personal attributes:

1. You seem like someone who really cares about people.
2. You seem like a really fun kind of person.
3. If you weren't my therapist, I would probably want you as my friend.
4. You're really intelligent, aren't you!
5. I hope you make a lot of money at what you do, because you are really good at it.

A third type of comment uses comparisons where the therapist is elevated to a "better than" position:

1. I've been in therapy before, but you're a hell of a lot better than the other therapists I've had.
2. I find you amazing. You have a better understanding of people and life than anyone I've ever known.
3. I have the impression that you could make a mint if you just wrote a book about what you know about people. A lot of people are looking for the answers you seem to have.

In all of these examples, the process is the same. The client tells the clinician something that it is hard not to feel proud about. Under other circumstances, the compliment would serve as a boost to one's self-esteem. These, however, are not other circumstances. The hook works when clinicians forget that fact.

Usually the effect of these statements, when they cause a countertransference reaction, is rather insidious. Because there is no immediate demand or expectation implied in these kinds of comments, it is easy for therapists to accept these statements as nothing more than the clients' perceptions of reality. After all, we all know that we are good at what we do. It feels good when a client recognizes that fact and expresses his perception directly.

The insidious effect can typically be found when, some time after the comments were made, the therapist needs to make a judgment about the client. For instance, a mental health worker (with an incarcerated psychopathic client) may find himself writing a routine report for the parole board that somehow seems a little more positive than other institutional staff would have expected. In the midst of writing that report, the therapist may find it difficult to say all the nasty things that otherwise would be said if it were not for the fact that the client seems "to be doing so well in therapy." If you feel that sentiment when evaluating your client's progress, be sure you can clearly state how it is that you have come to that conclusion. One can find it difficult to think poorly of a client who apparently sees one in such a positive light.

If the clinician views these kinds of comments as examples of how the client challenges his environment for control, however, then an appropriate response is rather easy to formulate. For instance, a statement such as "Although I appreciate your comment, we need to concentrate on you rather than me during our sessions" would suffice to deflect the attempt to control in this way. More confrontive statements, such as "Those kinds of comments will not get us off the topic of you" and "Those attempts to sway my sentiment about you will not work" can be used if the client persists in telling you what he thinks you want to hear.

Charm, or the Fascinating Client Syndrome

This section is dedicated to all of my readers who find that they enjoy working with psychopathic clients. More specifically, this section represents my warning to those of you who find that some psychopathic clients are charming and fascinating.

Let's take "charming" first. Many psychopaths strike us as being charming. This is true by definition, according to Cleckley's original set of descriptors for these kinds of clients. However, some of us more than others find them so.

The greatest danger here for mental health workers is "falling in love" with your client. I have seen this occur particularly when the mental health worker is in a rather needy state in his or her own personal life and the time alone with the client is all too convenient. Many rationalizations are employed by the therapists to excuse their stepping over the limits of proper professional conduct. The client's charm wears off over time, however, as all but one of those relationships of which I have been aware ended in a relatively short period of time (i.e., a few months). In each case, however, the mental health worker's career was at least notably tarnished.

Being fascinated by one's client is a form of positive counter-transference that similarly clouds one's interpretation of events. For instance, in one case with which I am familiar, the clinician viewed the client as a particularly fascinating case about which many professional papers could be written. Indeed, all of the staff working with this client agreed he was a "one-of-a-kind" type of case. Over time, however, that clinician's judgments concerning the client grew to be more and more apart from those of the other staff, reaching the point where the other staff believed that the clinician was "overinvolved" with the client. The clinician's retort was that the staff held a strong prejudice against the client and that he was one of the few (if not the only one) who could do effective therapy with the client. In this case, the therapist's fascination with the client strongly influenced how he viewed his fellow workers and their judgments.

A similar case occurred when a clinician saw that his efforts to change a psychopathic client were starting to have some effect. That clinician saw this case as a potential demonstration to his professional colleagues that he could be effective in changing even a "hard-core classic" psychopath. Once some behavioral change was noted, the therapist found it difficult to view the client with the same critical eye used for other clients in making the needed institutional judgments about the client. Likewise, the clinician was more willing to give a great deal more time to this client than other clients, thereby giving this client "power" among others incarcerated within the institution. (The client used that power rather frequently both with the other staff and his peers.) In this case, the therapist's desire for personal glory interfered with his judgment concerning the case.

In cases where being charmed or fascinated is potentially a primary issue, corrective action should not wait until the problem already exists. Many times, it is too late by then to do much that is fully constructive. Rather, such clients need to be labeled by mental health workers as early as possible, before anyone has been hooked by the client's charm. Periodic reminders are also useful, such as statements on the client's treatment plan that get reviewed on a regular basis. Open staff discussions concerning their feelings about these clients can also be useful. Without such prophylactic action in an institutional setting, one can feel certain that it is only a matter of time before one or more of the staff become overinvolved emotionally with these clients.

If, after those efforts, it is found that a staff member has become fascinated by a psychopathic client anyway, one should consider the situation imperative that that staff member be confronted about the problem. Ideally this should happen not only by that person's superiors, but by co-workers as well. The confrontation should include an offer of facilitating support in alleviating the problem as well as the strong message that the overinvolvement must be terminated.

Physical Complaints, or "I Know Some Things You Can't Ignore"

This hook occurs almost solely in an institutional setting. The process occurs after a client has attempted various methods to get control over the people in his environment, but has been largely unsuccessful (at least in *his* evaluation). He then resorts to making a complaint of a somatic problem, almost always involving relatively nonassessable pain such as a headache or gastrointestinal discomfort. Because most institutions are sensitive to claims of physical mistreatment, and because most medical professionals feel an obligation to treat ailments that come to their attention if at all possible (or risk a lawsuit), these physical complaints do not get ignored. Rather, the psychopath learns that he *can* get some control over the people in his environment by habitually reporting minor ailments.

Staff reaction to these complaints, over time, typically becomes annoyance, disbelief, and frustration. The annoyance is based in the client's continual complaining that necessitates repetitive efforts by the staff. Disbelief that the complaints represent reality often ensues when staff become diligent in their observations and find that the client is not acting as if he is in pain at times other than when he makes his complaints to them. Finally, frustration is common when the staff find themselves spending a great deal of time trying to manage this fellow with only some success and much concern regarding lawsuits that could affect their licenses.

Unlike most of the previous examples of countertransference hooks, this type does not directly involve individual therapists. Large numbers of people, mostly consisting of medical staff, are usually involved in complicated cases. In some cases, where there is difficulty ascertaining if the complaints represent part of a delusional system (implying that the determination that the client is a psychopath has not been made), psychiatrists addressing questions about psychotropic medication may also be part of the picture. As one might expect, the countertransference reactions typically increase as more and more people get hooked into the situation.

Because the problem is regularly a collective one, the solution also needs to be collective in nature. Specifically, meetings of all involved staff are recommended during which all available information is discussed and an agreed on course of action for everyone is determined. Individual countertransference reactions of the involved parties are usually curtailed when each person feels part of the concerted effort to deal with the problem.

NONVERBAL BEHAVIORS

Various forms of nonverbal challenges for environmental control are described in this section. In almost all cases, the suggested therapeutic approach to dealing with these behaviors involves orally acknowledging the behavior with an accompanying statement about how that behavior will not accomplish what the client is seeking. Because of the similarity of some of the following categories with those described previously coupled with the similarity in recommended therapeutic responses among the following, the discussions of direct and nonverbal psychopathic behaviors in the following sections are relatively brief.

Intimidation

Many forms of intimidation do not involve verbal threats. We are all familiar with certain hand signals that indicate someone's hostile dissatisfaction with someone else. Likewise virtually anyone can recognize the facial expression that communicates hostility (e.g., staring from partially closed eyes, tight jaw muscles). What many therapists are not accustomed to, however, is being the recipient of those nonverbal behaviors from a client.

As with verbal intimidation, being the recipient of nonverbal actions designed to intimidate can be disconcerting, especially if unprepared for them. Typical countertransference reactions from mental health workers range from fear to anger, with the concomitant behaviors ranging from avoidance to hostility. Clearly none of these reactions are useful to the client's therapy.

The recommended approach for dealing with nonverbal actions from your client that are designed to intimidate is similar to the response suggested for verbal intimidation. First, a statement needs to be made acknowledging the client's actions and your interpretation of them. Second, the therapist should indicate that the client's behavior will not be effective in getting him what he wants. A follow-up statement then needs to be made enumerating to the client appropriate ways he could have chosen to act that were more likely to get what he wanted as a result.

As with verbal intimidation, mental health workers need to be prepared, and come to expect that their psychopathic clients are going to try to intimidate them. Without that expectation, therapists will find it very difficult to react according to the previously discussed therapeutic guidelines. With that expectation, however, therapists regularly find that they are less intimidated when challenged by their clients. Therapeutic interventions are then an easier task.

Deliberate Defiance

One of the most challenging of all of the psychopaths' behavior repertoire short of violence and threats of violence is their deliberate defiance of those they perceive as "authority." In an institutional setting, this description would include virtually all staff not easily controlled through other means. Within a therapy session, it includes the therapist.

The most common form of defiance occurs when the psychopath deliberately acts against a law, rule, or policy. When confronted by someone "in authority," the psychopath's response is essentially one of "Oh yeah, make me!" This can be verbalized or, as described here, it can take the form of passive resistance. For example, if a client is told he should not be in a certain area and that he is now to leave that area, he may just continue to sit where he is.

Most of the time a client is deliberately defiant, he will mark himself as a management problem for those in authority. As such, getting him to follow rules, or at least not be severely disruptive to the institution will become higher priority than his psychological treatment. You as his therapist will often find yourself discussing what occurred with your client much after the event rather than at the time it was happening. It is recommended that you concentrate on what the client could have done that would have been more effective for him in the long run.

More problematic for clinicians, however, is when their clients are deliberately defiant in interacting with them. This most typically occurs when clients view their therapists as extensions of "the establishment," as in a forensic hospital or prison setting. Although what the client is in effect saying at these times is "I cannot trust you because you represent to me the kind of person who periodically punishes me for no reason," clinicians often see the client's actions simply as a passive expression of hostility to be met with confrontation. This approach can be useful on a short-term management basis, but it only serves to reinforce the psychopath's perception.

When the situation allows it, and I recognize that management concerns can often take precedence, a more therapeutic approach would be to answer the implied message directly. For instance, in response to the client who is refusing to move from a restricted area, statements by his therapist similar to the following can be helpful: "I recognize that you do not trust me at this moment, but I have no desire of seeing you harmed in any way. If you move from this area now, no harm will come to you. (Do not say that if it isn't true.) If you do not move now, however, I can guarantee that you will get sanctioned in some way. The choice is yours." Through such statements, the therapist addresses the real issue, shares his perception of reality, and places the selection of consequences to the psychopath's behavior on him. No matter what choice the client makes, he will get to see that your word was accurate, making you more trustworthy in his eyes (though not necessarily in his words, for a while). Similarly, one can later use whatever happens as a therapeutic example to the client concerning the predictability of the consequences of his actions.

Malicious Obedience

I was once playing volleyball with a number of clients and some fellow staff members as part of a recreational therapy program. One of the clients, with a psychopathic character structure, was asked by the recreational therapist to move a shirt away from the boundary line, presumably because someone might slip on it and hurt himself. The client went over to the shirt, picked it up, and moved it about two inches from where it had been, away from the boundary line. He then walked back to the game court as if he was again ready to play. His action may have been considered humorous if it were not for the obvious hostility with which it was done.

In essence, malicious obedience can occur whenever you use a phrase that implies more than it says or can be taken literally when you did not mean it so. Some examples are:

"Take this form to the admissions office" when you also mean, but do not say that the form should be left at the admissions office as well; leading to the client's taking the form to the appropriate office, but not leaving it there.

"Keep a diary of when and why you get angry. Make an entry in the diary every day, even if you have to write that nothing happened that day"; leading to a week's worth of entries stating "that nothing happened that day."

In both cases, what was implied and how it was (purposely mis-) interpreted were not at all the same. In these examples, and whenever malicious obedience occurs, one can get a strong impression that the misinterpretation was deliberate and hostile. As with other nonverbal challenges for control, clinicians should handle this type of behavior from a client by acknowledging its implied message and stating that it will not work in getting what he wants. The long-term utility of more appropriate interpretations and behaviors by the client should be enumerated to him.

Limit Testing

Any parent is familiar with the process of limit testing. Virtually all children do it. The common tales of the "terrible twos" exemplify this point.

Psychopathic clients can bring this characteristic into adulthood. The conflict between those in authority and themselves can look very much the same as the struggles between parents and children, though the stakes are often much higher.

The basic event involves the client doing something he knows those in authority, including his therapist, do not want him to do. In effect, he asserts his independence from others' rule. (Sometimes the clients will even state so when asked.) I am not referring here to open defiance, as described previously, but the taking of actions that are known to be just outside the boundaries of approved behavior.

As in the case of deliberate defiance, management issues often take priority in dealing with these misbehaviors. When mental health workers do get involved, however, there is typically room for some therapeutic growth.

Initially, the therapist needs to ensure that the topic of the misbehavior is discussed. From my experience, you can expect that the client will disavow prior knowledge that the behavior was not allowed or inappropriate. This is likely to be a lie. However, there is no reason to get into a debate about the truth or falsity of the statement. Given that the perspective of therapy is to change future behavior, arguing over the past is not useful. (This topic is discussed in detail under the subheading "Present the proof, or catch me if you can.")

A clear statement can be made by the therapist at the times the client's misbehavior is discussed that he now knows what is expected of him in the area concerning his inappropriate behavior. If he has any questions, he should feel free to ask them. Similarly, if he has any objections to acting in accordance with others' expectations in the area of relevance, he should voice them. If there are no voiced objections, then a final comment should be made by the therapist stating an expectation that there will not be any future transgressions in the relevant area. If there are voiced objections, then the clinician should teach the client how he might pursue voicing his objections in useful ways to the correct people. In this way, the client can learn useful ways of working toward the changing of rules in his environment without simply violating them.

The hook for mental health workers concerning limit testing by the client is in three areas. The first concerns the potential debate with the client concerning the issue of the client's prior awareness that his behavior was beyond the limits of what was acceptable. (See the discussion in the subsection entitled "Present the proof or catch me if you can" for details on how to handle this form of countertherapeutic interaction.) The second hook concerns the feeling of tedium and lack of fulfillment when a mental health worker sees the client limit testing over and over, only in slightly different areas. Finally, there can be anger toward the client when he seems to be acting in an "unreasonable" manner during therapy.

The second hook, the feeling of failure and tedium after viewing the client continue to misbehave, can in its extreme form totally interrupt a useful therapeutic process. If the therapist takes the attitude of "what's the use," then little that is therapeutic for the client is likely to happen afterwards. The first approach in dealing with this hook is preventive, doing what one can to prevent this countertransference. An expectation that the client will *not* learn from his experience and what you have told him during therapy can be useful in this regard. A second approach to coping with this hook concerns what to do once you find yourself feeling this way. I have found that a written letter to my client (that also was placed in his records and, therefore written accordingly) describing my perceptions of his actions has been useful. In that letter, I describe his behaviors that I have witnessed or heard about that were inappropriate, my interpretations of those behaviors from a psychological perspective, and my frustration at making efforts to help my client when he seems determined to repeat his mistakes.

This kind of letter has served many purposes. First, it has opened direct discussion with the client concerning his lack of desire to change himself. Usually a client will not state directly that he does not want to change at all. If that occurs, however, then you have every reason to terminate therapy (and get you off the hook). When the client states he wants to change, then you can challenge him to demonstrate how, as you have not seen him act on that desire. This challenge results either in his demonstrating some change or your being able to continue the challenge with his lack of demonstration.

Second, the purpose of the letter is to give you an opportunity to formulate what it is that is bothering you, your countertransference issues, and use them in a way that may be therapeutic for the client. If used constructively, the letter can be more than just a place for you to vent your feelings, though it can serve that purpose as well.

Finally, by placing the letter in the client's file, you have in effect entered a progress note that is likely to say far more to future readers than most progress notes. Future therapists can learn not only what the client was like and his typical problem, but also what it was like to work with this client.

The reaction of anger to one's client because of his continual misbehaviors suggests that the therapist sees himself in the role of someone who is suffering an injustice; that the client is not being fair to the therapist given all the effort that the therapist has made on behalf of the client. When phrased this way, most mental health workers see that the reaction borders on the absurd, based on the expectation that your clients owe you behavioral change for your efforts. If that were true, then your clients would be in therapy to satisfy you rather than to satisfy themselves. Mental health workers typically know better than to believe their clients are in therapy to please their therapists, but periodically some get angry anyway when their clients do not act according to the therapists' desires.

Facial Expressions, or "You're Not Good Enough"

The use of facial expressions to convey displeasure seems to be a favorite behavior of some psychopathic clients and hardly ever noted from others. As described here, the facial expression involves the communication that you, as his therapist, have not obtained the client's approval. Various facial expressions actually can convey this message such as: (1) a tilting of the head to a side and downwards with an upward movement of the eyebrows and a movement of the eyes toward the top of the head, (2) a tilting of the head straight downward with an accompanying wrinkling of the forehead, a squeezing of the lips, and a movement of the eyes toward the top of the head, or (3) a simple, but extreme movement of the eyes toward the top of the head, though slightly off-center, for a short period of time.

Some clinicians might consider these behaviors too quick and too inconsequential with which to bother. On the other hand, from my perspective, countertransference reactions can result from these behaviors quite readily.

The recommended approach to handling these facial expressions is to bring the apparent message out into the open with the client. Even if the client denies trying to communicate the message you received (which, from my experience, occurs often), you will have then made the challenge to the client to find a more effective way of communicating his feelings.

Laughs and Grunts

Without belaboring a point, this section covers a similar topic to that of facial expressions previously discussed. A well-timed laugh or grunt of displeasure can often effect an uncomfortable emotional reaction from its recipient. As with facial expressions, the recommended action for the therapist is to mention the behavior and the communication it conveyed. The effect should be the same as just described.

Silence

How do you react when a client just stares at you, saying nothing, after you have made a statement to him concerning your perception of him or his behavior? Our training as clinicians often gets us accustomed to periods of silence during therapy, but this situation involves more than the usual silence. In the cases described here, there is a notable hostility in the silence, an implicit statement from the client telling the therapist to get lost.

Therapists' frequent first attempts to deal therapeutically with the silence involve saying something like "You seem to have a reaction to what I said." The continued silence by the client can then become particularly disconcerting. What do you do when the client refuses to respond even to simple statements such that you know he is being passively aggressive toward you?

As with many of the previous examples of psychopathic methods to gain control, this is an example where mental health workers become confronted by their own expectations of how therapy sessions should run. Therapists tend to find themselves getting annoyed at the client's silence, or at what is many times referred to as the waste of time. In fact, the client is communicating with you through every passing moment. Therapists often ignore this point because the communication is not the kind that they enjoy. It also seems unfair, being one-sided from the client toward the therapist. After all, therapists are not supposed to be passive-aggressive toward their clients. Our expectations of therapy do not usually include the client's sitting there being silently aggressive toward us.

What should you do under these circumstances? As always, openly reflect the communication you are getting. Most likely, the client will continue to remain silent (though a negative facial expression might be noticed). Pointing out how it would be more effective for him to express his dissatisfaction openly is recommended. Some examples of how he could do that could be useful. At some point, however, with a particularly persistent client, you may find that the situation has not changed from before you started reflecting the communication you received from his silence.

That is when you need to make sure that his "silent communication" is not effective, to ensure that your previous statements have accuracy. This can be done by turning your body from facing your client so that he is not in your field of vision. Just sit and ponder about whatever you happen to enjoy thinking. Be sure that if the client is going to communicate with you, he will have to make it verbal.

This kind of challenge to a psychopathic client can be experienced by some clinicians as rude and inappropriate. My counterargument to that reaction is that your client is already acting rude and inappropriate from the perspective of general interpersonal interactions. Something needs to be done to gain his attention in order that this type of behavior will not be successful in getting him what he wants from others. As long as he captures his therapist's full attention, he has no reason to change. The therapist is likely to sit there and feel uncomfortable as long as he or she faces a client who is relishing the therapist's discomfort. Therefore, forcing a change in the form of communication is necessary to facilitate a change in the client's behavior.

On rare occasions, the client will simply remain quiet throughout the remainder of the session. The session will end without any processing of what just occurred. That is as it should be, because it is the *responsibility of the client* to begin the communication after you have stated how he might do so effectively. The choice must be his, or he would still be effective in controlling his environment with his silence. Hence, at the end of such a session, a simple "see you next week" should be all the therapist says to the client, conveying the expectation that this ending is only temporary. Of course, if the client does voice virtually anything during the session (including open hostility toward the therapist), the therapist's verbal and nonverbal cues should again be geared toward establishing and maintaining communication with the client.

Charm, or the Apparently Good Listener

This example is a specific case of the charm described under "Direct and Verbal" efforts at control by psychopathic clients. Sometimes, mental health workers can find a client charming because he seems to be such a good and understanding listener. Most often this occurs with paraprofessionals, because it is difficult to make this assessment during formal professional therapy sessions. As in the discussion in the previous subsection, the mental health workers who make attributions about psychopathic clients being such good listeners are often in a needy state in their own personal lives. That attribution represents the mental health worker's own desire to have someone from whom he or she can feel emotional support.

Most often this attribution does not come to other staff workers' awareness until either the hooked individual discovers the error of his or her ways or that individual's behavior shows too great an emotional involvement in the case, both cases being beyond where simple corrective actions are meaningful. This is why it is important that preventive action be used to ensure that these kinds of attributions are not made by one's fellow staff members. Staff education concerning the "charm" of psychopathic clients can be helpful. Similarly, ongoing periodic staff discussions about their feelings concerning these clients are recommended.

Physical Problems, or "How I Can Use My Body to Control Yours"

We usually think of people as hypochondriacal when they report a lot of physical pains and ailments that either do not appear to exist or are not as severe as they would have us believe. The term manipulative is frequently employed at the same time, indicating our perception of the reason those people complain as they do is to get something they want from us through this form of devious behavior. Many who have worked with psychopathic clients, especially in an institutional setting, know that hypochondriacal behaviors can also be found among psychopaths.

The client's issue is the same here as in all of the previous examples and in those examples that are to follow—to control the environment and the people in it. The well-timed grunt of pain from the client can do much to interfere with what otherwise would have been a productive therapy interaction. Similarly, a pained look on the client's face can bring sympathy his way when he was about to be confronted about a misbehavior. The feigning of any of various pains can also serve as an excuse for inappropriate interpersonal behavior such as verbal aggression and accusations that no one cares.

The countertransference problems in dealing with this situation are very similar to those described under "Physical Complaints, or I Know Something You Can't Ignore." Typically the problems are collective and need to be handled in a collective manner with everyone potentially affected involved in determining the solution. Likewise, the client needs to be made aware that his hypochondriacal behavior is not the most effective way he can act to get what he wants.

When the client continually uses physical complaints to interfere with individual therapy sessions, either by altering important ongoing discussions or by missing the sessions entirely, then a direct interpretation of the client's actions needs to be made. Of course, the therapist should expect the client to deny the accuracy of the interpretation. When the accuracy is denied, the clinician can challenge the client to demonstrate that he is correct by not repeating the behavior under those circumstances. In that way, either the client changes the behavior or he acknowledges the accuracy of your interpretation. Most often, the client will choose to prove you wrong by changing his behavior rather than let you be right. You will then have succeeded in using a challenge to effect behavioral change in your client.

CHAPTER 10

Specific "Nondirect" Behaviors of Psychopaths Designed to Obtain Environmental Control

This chapter expands the list of psychopathic behaviors started in Chapter 9. The following examples were considered "indirect" (versus "direct") behaviors for one of two reasons: (1) either the action taken is only partially done by the client himself and another person or persons are also involved in the action or (2) the action is not done directly to you, but in a way that incriminates you to some degree. As the reader will see, the enumerated behaviors are different in character from those described in Chapter 9. Similarly, recommended therapeutic responses also differ in type.

VERBAL BEHAVIORS

Legal Outlets

Many of us feel comfortable with our professional skills until we are threatened to have to defend them in court. The phrase "I'll see you in court" can send a shiver of fear through the backs of many fine clinicians. At least, that is what psychopathic clients think.

If you have never been threatened with a lawsuit, then you have missed an experience during which you can learn a great deal about yourself. Being threatened by a lawsuit can lead one to second-guess one's judgment, double-check one's records, and/or generally avoid the threatening client. On the other hand, the same experience may lead you to do nothing differently from your general practice, as if you do not take the threat seriously or you are confident the judge will see things your way.

Receiving notification of a lawsuit can be an event that shakes you. All of a sudden, the topic is more than hypothetical. You may really find yourself defending your actions in front of a judge and jury. The thought of cross-examination may make you shudder. On the other hand, you may laugh at the subpoena in your hand, believing that it is just an example of a "nuisance" lawsuit and will be thrown out of court during its preliminary review.

Whatever your reactions are to being threatened by and actually being sued, you need to come to know them before they occur. I have seen an unprepared therapist thrown for an emotional loop the first time a client threatened him with a lawsuit. He was afraid his new career was in jeopardy, until his supervisor told him how such threats were relatively common from such clients. It took a full week when he next saw that client and the client did not even mention the lawsuit before he finally recognized the emptiness of the threat and began to feel calm again.

There are two forms of preparation that are useful toward avoiding strong emotional reactions to threats of lawsuits from psychopathic clients. The first involves keeping a legal perspective on all of your actions and writings concerning litigious clients. Specifically, one constantly needs to ask oneself how well what you do would stand up in court. If you feel shaky in your answer, then alter what you are doing, or at least consult a fellow professional for suggestions as to how you can improve what you are doing. Then record the fact that you made a professional consultation. There is almost no better defense in court than to have had a concurring judgment from another professional at the time an action was taken. Similarly, you will find that you are unlikely to try atypical forms of therapy with litigious clients once you take a legal perspective on those cases. Such forms of therapy would be more difficult to support if you needed to do so on the stand. On the other hand, if you have a second professional opinion, either stemming from a documented conversation or written professional literature, then you can feel more confident about what you are doing.

That confidence is most of the issue when dealing with threats of a lawsuit. The second area for preparation, the emotional realm, pertains largely to whether or not you feel threatened by comments concerning lawsuits. If you find that you have reacted negatively to a client's threat of a lawsuit, I suggest that you reality test your fears with another professional. Keeping a legal perspective on all of your work with psychopathic clients, however, can go a long way toward preventing strong fears when such comments get made.

There is one other countertransference reaction that should be mentioned here—betrayal. After a clinician has spent a lot of therapy time with a client, the therapist's receiving notice of a lawsuit against him or her filed by that client can lead one to feel betrayed by the client. Although this reaction makes sense in the world of mutually sharing relationships, one needs to remember that therapy (with a psychopathic client) does not involve such a relationship. You can only be betrayed if there was mutual trust in the relationship. I expect that no therapy with a psychopathic client involves a mutually trusting relationship in the full sense of the word trust. Hence, if you find that your emotional reaction to a lawsuit is betrayal, I recommend that you reevaluate your perception of the relationship you have with the client. A consultation with an unbiased colleague can be helpful in this regard.

The Messenger

Every now and then you may notice that there seems to be a third party giving you messages that seem to stem originally from your psychopathic client. This can happen in an institutional setting where an inmate or patient different from your psychopathic client makes various statements to you that seem to represent your client's views. Similarly, therapists can see this process in community settings such as a probation and parole office or private practice when someone from the client's family or ring of friends contacts the therapist to relay a message.

This process would not be important to discuss if the messages were typically positive or neutral in nature. Frequently, however, the messages are complaints or accusations. When the psychopathic clients are questioned later about this process, they deny ever having sent the third party your way. Mental health workers, therefore, find themselves in the situation of being on the receiving end of an unpleasant communication without having the opportunity to react directly to the original sender. Therein lies the potential for frustration that just grows as the process repeats itself over time.

The client's messenger may or may not recognize his role. If the client was relatively skillful in his manipulation of that person, the messenger will see the complaint or accusation as his or her own, as well as the client's. Hence confrontation of that person may not be useful.

As with virtually all of the other psychopathic behaviors designed to gain control of his environment, it is important for the clinician to let the client know that this form of communication will not work to get him what he wants, and to offer suggestions as to what behaviors would be useful. In the case of third party messengers, I suggest (1) that you let the messenger know that, whether or not the issue being raised is valid or not, it needs to be discussed by you and the client, and not someone else speaking on behalf of the client, (2) that you inform your client that the third party contacted you, (3) that you wondered if your client was aware of the third party's actions, (4) that you believe your client should always be responsible for communicating with you directly on whatever issues arise, even if someone else is willing to do his communicating for him, (5) that you will be willing to listen to direct communications from the client but not third parties, (6) that you believe your client should tell the third party not to repeat what occurred, and (7) that if the client has any objections to this, he should voice them or you will conclude that the two of them have an agreement.

Note that throughout this message, the therapist does not give the client much room to deny responsibility effectively. Even if the client states he had no awareness of what the third party was doing, your message will still have been communicated. Likewise, you have set up the conditions such that if the process should occur again, you can confront your client about how he has not acted according to your agreement.

Purposeful Misquoting to Third Parties

This and the next two subsections describe three forms of what has often been termed "staff splitting" in institutional settings. The concept largely implies that an otherwise unified set of staff members find themselves becoming polarized on, or arguing over issues pertaining to the one client. In essence, the client sets up conditions such that he gets to sit back and watch other people in conflict.

One of the ways that this can happen occurs when the client purposefully misquotes to one staff member what was said by another. In the cases described in this subsection, the misquotes typically paint some staff member or members in a negative light.

For instance, I have heard "quotes" that one staff member said specific, nasty things about another staff member. (The client, of course, reports the quote either to the other staff member or to their mutual supervisor.) Other "quotes" concern statements acknowledging active discrimination by the staff, or certain staff members, toward certain clients (almost always including the reporting client). Still others indicate a specific staff member is the source of a vicious rumor concerning another staff member.

Some of these examples can represent outright lies by the client. What is being referred to here, however, is where there was a conversation between the client and the staff member, but what is being quoted was not what was said. The originally stated qualifiers such as "not" and "may or may not be" are conveniently forgotten in the "quoted" statements. Needless to say, such misquoting by a client can be very annoying to the staff.

This form of staff splitting, as with the other two described in the following two subsections, can be very difficult to prevent in total. However, making it a practice to guarantee staff communication before conclusions are drawn any time a psychopathic client reports potentially upsetting quotes can minimize the effects of this behavior. In essence, this suggests that the staff should always keep a suspicious perspective on reports stemming from these clients. This perspective will help protect the staff from strong negative interactions among themselves that are set up by the client.

This does not do anything to alter the client's behavior, however, at least not directly. Over time, the client may come to recognize that he did not get the desired effect and therefore go onto something else, but that can take a while. Psychopathic clients are not known for their ability to learn from the consequences of their actions quickly. What is needed is some direct feedback to the client that tells him: (1) that his misquoting will not work to get him what he wants and (2) that the misquoting will only serve to keep the staff suspicious of him, thereby making it more difficult for him to communicate effectively with them in the future.

Most psychopathic clients will, of course, deny that they misquoted anybody. They will adamantly state that what they quoted is what was said. As with other such denials, there is no reason to debate with the client about the truth or falsity of his statements. Rather, you can tell him that you are simply informing him of your perspective on misquoting someone, whether he did it this time or not.

Claiming Nonexistent Authority

A second form of staff splitting occurs when the client claims he has the approval of a specific person in authority to do something that he otherwise probably could not do. This, of course, occurs only when that person in authority is not available for verification. What should a staff member do under these circumstances?

I ran into this situation while working in a management position of a treatment unit on which resided some psychopathic clients. On weekends, or at times I was not available, a client would tell another staff member that he had permission from me to do or have something, something that he would otherwise not be allowed to do or have. Because I frequently spent a lot of time talking with the various clients on the unit, the staff did not know whether to believe the patient's report or not. They became very frustrated with the situation, and me, as these situations continued.

Luckily for me, this was an easy management problem to solve. I informed my staff that I would take full responsibility for informing them ahead of time if I gave special permission to anyone to do anything. If the staff did not have a written report from me on such permission before the client made his report, the client's report should be considered inaccurate. If I failed to inform the staff when I should have, thereby meaning that the client would not be believed, then I would apologize to the client as soon as I could later. The only problem remaining, then, was for me to be sure I was responsible in reporting to my staff.

This a priori communication with the staff solved the problem. Some clients continued to try that ploy for a while, even showing a great deal of emotion when they were (appropriately) not believed by the staff, but the clients' process of claiming my permission when they did not have it soon dropped out (except initially when there was a new staff member on the unit). Similarly, I had a much better relationship with my staff, as they did not feel set up by my actions. My suggestion is that all similar situations be handled in a similar fashion.

Altering Written Materials

A third form of staff splitting involves the altering of documents. Most institutional settings use written notices for a variety of items, from policy changes to scheduled activities. The idea of posting such notices is to ensure accurate communications to their readers. Unfortunately, some of the institution's residents may have other ideas.

I first learned of the effect of an altered posted notice when a fellow staff member was telling me that a policy was the opposite of what I knew it to be, and that he could show me where it was written. I was escorted to a notice I had posted. The document had been changed "ever so slightly" from what I had originally posted. The word "not" had been inserted, with the appropriate "^" symbol, in a place that significantly altered the intended meaning. The insert was done very neatly. I was both annoyed and amused. I learned to respect my clients' power to disrupt the efficient running of my unit more that day.

On numerous occasions, I also found that posted notices had simply disappeared, with some clients reportedly (and conveniently) never having seen them (and thereby not having an awareness of a new policy). The staff found it difficult to enforce a policy when it could not be ascertained if a violating resident had had prior notice of the rule or not. This form of indirectly taking control of the environment by psychopathic clients became annoying until the staff formulated a solution.

The most simple and straightforward solution, we found, from a management perspective, was always to post notices in places where they were protected from alterations or being stolen. This included on the inside of office windows facing into another room or hallway, and underneath Plexiglas where the first option was not possible. Duplicates of all posted notices were kept in a secure location.

That largely solved the issue from a management perspective. Although that solution did not serve to change our psychopathic clients' behavior (in that we would expect them to engage in the same behaviors again if given the opportunity), it did wipe out the problem. Considering that we could never ascertain which of our clients was responsible for our problem, we never knew who to confront. I expect that the situation would be the same whenever the problem is found. Hence this countertransference hook must be considered so indirect that it can only be handled effectively from a management perspective. You cannot win them all.

Lying, or the Psychopath as a Witness

A primary factor to remember about psychopathic clients is that, virtually by definition, they will lie without guilt or even a second thought. The potential gain they believe they will get from their lies will be nearly immediate, but it may not be directly obvious. For instance, having someone indebted to them (for a lie supporting the debtor's story) can represent a reward to be cashed in at some later date (for monetary, sexual, or other favors). The debtor may not even be aware of what the psychopath's charge will be later, or even that there will be some abstraction of "payment" for the verbal support. Of course, once the psychopath lies to help cover another's story, the latter can be blackmailed by the former.

Obtaining some direct knowledge that this process is occurring can be very difficult. I have frequently heard an institutional staff voice suspicions about such a process by one or more of their residents, but rarely is someone caught at it.

For that reason, I strongly suggest that you avoid using psychopathic clients as witnesses concerning another persons action. If that situation cannot be avoided, then the psychopath's report should be taken with a large grain of salt pending verification from other sources.

NONVERBAL BEHAVIORS

The last set of behaviors used to gain environmental control to be discussed in this book are those that do not involve any direct verbal interchange between you and your client. One of the following necessarily involves using a third party, but most of the actions enumerated represent attempts at control from a distance. As such, they can become difficult to "pin" on a specific psychopathic client. This issue is often the source of great frustration for the affected personnel.

The "Bug" or Long Distance Surveillance

This attempt at control comes in two forms, human and mechanical. The first utilizes a third party to eavesdrop on conversations or events of staff or other clients (in an institutional setting) and then report the happenings to the psychopath. In this way, the psychopathic client keeps an alibi (i.e., "I wasn't there") without missing out on any information he can use in his battle to gain environmental control. The third party is virtually always another client, though he may not be aware of how he is being used by the psychopath. Such third parties typically report they were just doing the psychopathic client a favor or simply making conversation with him about current events. In these cases, the staff can sometimes get a handle on what is happening by affecting change in, or at least getting information from the third party. This situation can be handled in ways similar to those described under the previous subsection entitled "The Messenger."

Not so when the surveillance is mechanical. I have seen this form of attempt to gain control on numerous occasions, including having been personally subjected to it twice, that I am aware. The process is simple. A client brings in, or smuggles in (depending on the setting) a wireless microphone that broadcasts on an FM frequency. (They easily fit inside a loose fist.) These can be obtained readily from local electronics stores for about $20. The microphone is taped to the underside of a table, chair, desk, and so forth, when no one is looking. From that point on, all the client needs to do is keep his radio set to the appropriate FM frequency whenever he wishes to listen to conversations in that room. (For their own protection, these clients usually move their radio dials to some other frequency when they are not listening in, so as never to be caught as having knowledge of the microphone.)

One should not believe that because you happen to work in a rather secure institution, you are immune to this process. In fact, I would venture to guess that the greater challenge to the psychopath in such a setting increases the likelihood of such an attempt. I can say that my two occurrences were in a maximum security institutional setting. I have also learned of microphones being found in a medium security facility, though I have yet to hear of any being found in a minimum security unit. (Of course, it is debatable whether the crucial issue here is the greater challenge to the psychopath or the fact that more secure institutions do better security checks and are therefore more likely to discover such a device.)

The countertransference issues in reaction to finding a microphone can be intense. People feel angry that their privacy has been invaded, especially when they learn that they not only broadcast over the radio, but could have been recorded on a tape recorder at the same time. The most outspoken of staff (during broadcast meetings) can believe that someone is going to try to blackmail them based on such tape recordings. Other clients may feel that their safety is jeopardized because certain knowledge may have become public that should not have.

Catching the person responsible for "planting" a microphone, or even getting a reasonable list of suspects, can be an impossible task. Most of the time, there is little chance of confronting someone effectively.

Instead, a meeting of all available clients can be useful during which the problem is brought out, with the expectation that other clients should be outraged as well. The purpose of the meeting is to attempt to solicit the assistance of the other clients to prevent this from reoccurring, or at least being reported quickly if it reoccurs. (From a management perspective, the problem can be alleviated if no FM radios are allowed in the vicinity of the workplace, as on a treatment unit. From a treatment perspective, however, this may only serve to point out to the psychopathic client the extent of his power and the degree to which he can get a strong reaction from those in authority.)

Dealing with staff countertransference, or one's own for that matter, can be more difficult once it has developed. As in the cases of verbal threats and intimidation, mental health personnel need to expect that their psychopathic clientele will attempt to control them through some form of long distance surveillance. That expectation can prevent some of the stronger countertransference reactions from occurring. Likewise, it can make a staff vigilant in their awareness of possible microphone locations.

The Third Party Intimidator

An offshoot of the previous form of controlling behavior involves the use of a third party, usually another client (sometimes psychopathic himself), to deliver a nonverbal message of intimidation. I have only witnessed this behavior in an institutional setting, thus I will concentrate on its process there.

The way it works is through a third party's attendance at formal client meetings and informal conversations where that third party is not there just for his own reasons. He, by his association with the psychopathic client, serves as a reminder to the rest of the clients and/or staff that the psychopathic client will hear about everything that gets said. Implied in such a nonverbal message is that any comments that could hurt or hassle the psychopathic client will be punished by him, even though he is not within earshot at the moment. If the psychopathic client has a reputation for vindictiveness and aggression, this form of nonverbal controlling behavior can be very effective.

It can also be very difficult to combat. Neither the psychopathic client nor his messenger are likely to acknowledge to the staff what the clients are doing. Similarly, those people who are the target of the intimidation are not likely to risk physical injury by reporting what they know. Attempting to obtain relevant facts can be a hopeless cause.

Even so, the situation does not preclude using this information as part of therapy with the psychopathic client. As with the previous examples, the therapist does not need to debate the truth or falsity of the allegation that the client is participating in this kind of intimidation. Even after the client denies his participation in such activities (usually with a great display of anger at having been accused wrongly), the clinician can say:

> Well, I'm glad you have such a strong reaction against such behaviors and the idea that people think you are involved in these behaviors. Given your strong reaction, can we then agree that you will not do such things in the future, and that you will take appropriate actions against others who try such things? I think that your doing so would serve to protect yourself, as well as stop these obnoxious actions.

From this perspective, therapists can clearly state their message without getting into a verbal battle about the accuracy of the allegation.

Countertransference reactions from long distance intimidation are frequently not very strong, probably because the target of this form of controlling behavior is usually other clients. When a staff member is the target, allowing that staff member to confront both the psychopathic client and the messenger directly can be useful. In those cases, the message from that staff member should contain at least three points: (1) that he has noticed the actions of the messenger and the psychopathic client, (2) that he does not believe their approach to him should be reinforced by allowing it to continue, and (3) that he or she, therefore, will take the necessary actions to avoid interacting with the two of them in the way that has been occurring. I suggest that a description of more appropriate behavior also be offered to the two clients, as the kind of behavior that will be effective in interacting with this staff member. The staff person's confrontation should not be tainted with that person's countertransference reactions.

The Set-Up

Probably the most devastating behavior associated with psychopathic clients beyond physical aggression is the "set-up," the methodical procedure by which an innocent party becomes accused, and sometimes judged guilty of a major infraction of a law, policy, or rule. The results can range from a temporary blemish on one's reputation to potential loss of one's career and possible legal involvement.

Most often, the set-up involves a major issue of the setting in which it takes place. For instance, within a secure penal institution, the set-up can involve secretly placing one or more contraband items in a therapist's office, to be found by someone else. Within a forensic hospital, where confidentiality of patient records is usually dictated by law, spreading rumors (with a small degree of substantiating evidence learned from an innocent source) about a therapist giving patient information to the public is not uncommon. In a community setting, making reports to official bodies concerning sexual contact between a clinician and his or her clients can serve the same purpose.

These situations are similar to that described earlier concerning a mechanical "bug" because there is virtually no way to trace the set-up back to its source, the psychopathic client. Unlike that previous example, however, the set-up can involve two causes for frustration and anger: (1) not being able to demonstrate who was responsible and (2) the process of having to defend oneself based on the set-up itself. At times, if the set-up is well planned and executed, this can be a rather drawn out procedure.

I expect that the only effective way to handle the possibility of a psychopathic client setting you up is through good preparation. This should include discussions with co-workers about which clients are likely to have the desire to act in this way, and how might they do it. Limiting access to avenues of potential set-ups is suggested, such as ensuring that therapists' offices are not accessible when the therapists are not around. Scheduled supervision time for any mental health workers who are meeting with psychopathic clients is recommended both to remain constantly aware of any countertransference issues and to keep a third party appraised of what is occurring in therapy. This information from an outside source can be useful if one ever needs to defend oneself. Finally, if a psychopathic client ever suggests to you that he could "make things difficult for you if he wanted," I strongly encourage you to inform other staff members of what you were told, as well as document the conversation. This "ounce of protection" can go a long way.

Limit Testing, or Discovering the Real Perimeter

Deliberate rule breaking is probably the most common and well-known behavior psychopaths use to gain control of their environment. Although I will not reiterate the points already explicated previously in the subsection entitled "Limit Testing, or finding out what you will do," there is one issue I believe is important to address under the heading "Indirect and Nonverbal." This issue pertains to the inmate and forensic hospital patient who is soon to be released or discharged because his mandated sentence is about to expire.

At about that time, many psychopathic clients (i.e., those you have been unable to affect significantly through therapy) feel a great sense of freedom based on their realization that virtually all of the negative consequences that could follow their misbehaviors no longer apply. For instance, a fixed time period of being restricted from a favorite activity loses its meaning when the person is going to be released before that time period expires. Most restrictions that imply some sort of compliance by the client are simply no longer of concern to him. He, therefore, tends to break rules at will, typically in a way that flaunts his new freedom.

At these times, the client's behavior can be infuriating to an institution's staff. They feel a loss of control, a threat to their authority, and, sometimes, a sense of fear and danger about what this person may do next. Typically everyone begins counting the days until the client's release.

Some sense of control can be reinstilled to the staff through a collective meeting with them and jointly deciding your course of action. Even though at times you may need to allow a rule infraction without a meaningfully sanctioning reaction, having everyone collectively determine which areas are such and which are not can give the staff a sense of not being alone in their frustration. Similarly, being able to predict the psychopath's behaviors can also elicit a positive reaction from the staff. At least, by the end of such a meeting, the staff members should feel as if they know what to expect to see from the client, what is expected of them as staff, and that they are going to do the best that can be done under the circumstances.

Given that your recalcitrant client is soon to be released, there is little reason to attempt further therapy with him. If he has only a month or so left in his time in the institution and he is still deliberately breaking various rules, you might as well use your month of time with someone more likely to benefit from it.

Playing for Sympathy

The nonverbal "poor me" is the final psychopathic behavior designed to gain environmental control to be discussed here. In this form of action, you might say that the client pouts, or puts on an air of trying to hold back tears after he has just been hurt. The immediate purpose of this behavior is to gain others' sympathy.

The classic circumstance occurs after the client has largely been rejected by other clients and/or staff members. He acts in a manner that suggests he feels hurt, but he says little to anyone. A compassionate soul (i.e., a staff member) comes over to console him. At the end of their conversation, the psychopathic client states that he feels better knowing someone cares. This whole series of events repeats itself numerous times with the same compassionate soul. After a short while, the staff member has strong positive feelings about that client, sometimes to the point of feeling in love with the client. Bringing that staff member's countertransference back to some neutral point can be a nearly impossible endeavor.

Another type of countertransference reaction to the same situation is disgust at the client's "obnoxious" attempts to gain sympathy. People reacting strongly in this way have usually forgotten that what they are witnessing is a form of the client's psychopathology, not a message to be taken personally.

As with all of the indirect, nonverbal behaviors described, the best way to cope with this form of controlling behavior and the related countertransference is before they begin using preventive work with one's fellow staff members. (If you are working alone with such a client, obtaining some supervisory guidance on a regular basis is recommended as a similar preventive measure.) Labeling clients likely to employ such actions is necessary. Periodic reviews of staff feelings about those clients can also be useful to assist those with extreme (positive or negative) reactions to reality test their perspectives.

Therapeutic responses to the client's poor me behaviors include the same three segments enumerated throughout this chapter: (1) voicing the otherwise unspoken communication from the client, (2) informing him that that behavior will not get him in the long run what he seeks, and (3) offering him suggestions of better ways to seek what he wants.

CHAPTER 11

A Final Word

This book has been designed to offer an understanding and method of treating a client population most often considered untreatable. In writing the book, I have tried to convey that the situation is not hopeless, just difficult. Most of the efforts needed to treat psychopaths effectively revolve around the therapists' counterproductive reactions to the clients' psychopathy. With these in check, many psychopathic clients can receive the help they need, even as they deny they need any therapy.

This is not to suggest that the process is considered a routine, short-term matter. To the contrary, a great deal of work by the therapist should be expected before even minor behavioral changes are noted in the client. (I usually tell therapists to give themselves at least one year, and sometimes two, before they look for any substantive behavioral changes in their psychopathic clients.)

There are a few key points to remember from the perspective explicated in this book. First, the therapist should employ the process of challenging the client to gain his interest, attention, and intrigue, but the therapist must also remember to allow the clients their small "victories" to keep them interested in coming back for more. (In more behavioral terms, the therapist must employ partial reinforcement.) Once you have been working with a client for a substantial period of time, and progress has been noted by both you and the client, the client may even come to recognize and acknowledge his tendency to "challenge his environment" whenever he feels emotional pain or perceives a threat to his self-esteem. This recognition of his main psychological defense can be used to facilitate further behavioral changes through teaching the client alternate ways to satisfy his desire for "challenging" situations.

Second, an important factor of therapy with a psychopathic client is his limited behavioral repertoire. The reader should note that throughout the discussions of behaviors designed to gain environmental control (Chapters 9 and 10), the recommendation was made to instruct the client about how he could act more appropriately and effectively. Such actions by clinicians can effectively treat the client's deficit in this area. Clinicians need to keep in mind that they are very much in the role of teacher and socializer when working with psychopathic clients.

Even with training by their therapists, however, psychopathic clients will still tend to persist in acting when frustrated and their actions will often be the old, destructive ones. I have heard it said that someone who treats psychopathic clients needs a great deal of patience and persistence. This may be so. In any case, mental health professionals who find themselves working with such clients need to keep their expectations about the clients realistic, almost always suggesting a long-term process with little change initially noted.

The psychopathic trait of failing to understand the consequences of their actions (based in their partial helplessness conditioning) can be very problematic to some therapists. The clients can seem to be *unreasonable*. What therapists forget when they make such attributions, however, is that we do not expect our other clients to be reasonable (i.e., borderline clients to stop being so suicidal, phobic clients to stop being afraid), thus we should not expect that of psychopathic clients either. They will be unreasonable—that, in part, is the nature of their disorder.

Possibly the biggest issue concerning the treatment of psychopathic clients is the untreatability of their perception of people as objects and obstacles. As much as we may want to affect change in this area, I consider it virtually a hopeless cause from its inception. As I explained in Chapter 8, there is practically no emotional foundation on which to build in this area.

Some mental health workers have a major moral issue with this fact, stating that all therapy can do given this fact is make psychopathic clients into "better psychopaths," meaning that they simply learn how to manipulate more effectively than they already knew. Although I do not argue that this statement is wrong (given that the psychopath's perspective of others as objects or obstacles does not change through therapy), I believe that therapy is extremely useful in making these people less destructive citizens than they would be without therapy. Is that not what therapy with psychopaths is ultimately about?

Third, a statement needs to be made here about the potential success of applying the control theory to clinical work with psychopathic clients. Although other previously attempted techniques have been notably unsuccessful, I have seen substantial changes in psychopathic clients using the above techniques.

This does not suggest, however, that all cases can be treated effectively. Some clients are simply too invested in trying to get their environment to change rather than themselves. An assessment of the degree to which a client's hostility towards others is overtly and persistently expressed can serve as an a priori indicator of his potential benefit from psychological treatment.

The comments of one man exemplify the difficulty one can expect with the more extreme psychopathic clients. When this man was known to me, he was incarcerated on a drug smuggling conviction after having served time on several previous occasions. He was about to be tried on the charge of first degree murder and kidnapping. He spoke about his crimes matter-of-factly. He jested at the idea that he could receive the death penalty if convicted of the new charge. Finally, with a look of certainty on his face, the sound of defiance in his voice, and the expression of challenge in his words, he stated: "They can do what they want with me, but they'll never break me. I'll never surrender to the system."

I expect he never will.

References

Abudabbeh, N.N. (1974). An investigation of the relationship between psychopathy and intelligence, risk-taking and stimulation seeking. *Dissertation Abstracts International, 35*(6-A), 3501.

Adler, A. (1976). Individual psychology and crime. *Journal of Individual Psychology, 32,* 131–144.

American Psychiatric Association. (1952). *Diagnostic and statistical manual of mental disorders.* Washington, DC: Author.

American Psychiatric Association. (1968). *Diagnostic and statistical manual of mental disorders* (2nd ed.). Washington, DC: Author.

American Psychiatric Association. (1980). *Diagnostic and statistical manual of mental disorders* (3rd ed.). Washington, DC: Author.

Ax, A.F. (1962). Psychophysiological methodology for the study of schizophrenia. In R. Ressler & W. Greenfield (Eds.), *Physiological correlates of psychological disorder.* Madison: University of Wisconsin Press.

Bachand, N.L. (1978). Avoidance learning and reaction time as a function of psychopathy and anxiety arousal. *Dissertation Abstracts International, 38*(11-B), 5554–5555.

Bacon, W.E., & Stanley, W.C. (1963). Effects of deprivation level in puppies on performance maintained by a passive person reinforcer. *Journal of Comparative and Physiological Psychology, 56,* 783–785.

Baum, A., Aiello, J.R., & Calesnick, L.E. (1978). Crowding and personal control: Social density and the development of learned helplessness. *Journal of Personality and Social Psychology, 36,* 1000–1011.

Beger, E. (1952). The relationship between expressed acceptance of self and expressed acceptance of others. *Journal of Abnormal and Social Psychology, 47,* 778–782.

Bell, R. (1968). A reinterpretation of the direction of effects in studies of socialization. *Psychological Review, 75,* 81–95.

Bernard, J.L., & Eisenman, R. (1967). Verbal conditioning in sociopaths with social and monetary reinforcement. *Journal of Personality and Social Psychology, 6,* 203–206.

Blackburn, R. (1978). Psychopathy, arousal, and the need for stimulation. In R.D. Hare & D. Schalling (Eds.), *Psychopathic behavior: Approaches to research.* Chichester, England: Wiley.

Block, J. (1978). Review of the Eysenck Personality Questionnaire. In O.K. Buros (Ed.), *The eighth mental measurements yearbook.* Highland Park, NJ: Gryphon.

Borkovec, T.D. (1970). Autonomic reactivity to sensory stimulation in psychopaths and normal juvenile delinquents. *Journal of Consulting and Clinical Psychology, 35,* 217–222.

Cantwell, D. (1972). Psychiatric illnesses in the families of hyperactive children. *Archives of General Psychiatry, 27,* 414–417.

Capute, A., Niedermeyer, E., & Richardson, F. (1968). The electroencephalogram in children with minimal cerebral dysfunction. *Pediatrics, 41,* 1104.

Christiansen, K.O. (1974). Seriousness of criminality and concordance among Danish twins. In R. Hood (Ed.), *Crime, criminology and public policy.* London: Heinemann.

Cleckley, H. (1941). *The mask of sanity.* St. Louis: Mosby.

Cleckley, H. (1964). *The mask of sanity* (4th ed.). St. Louis: Mosby.

Cloninger, C.R., Reich, T., & Guze, S.B. (1978). Genetic–environmental interactions and antisocial behavior. In R.D. Hare & D. Schalling (Eds.), *Psychopathic behavior: Approaches to research.* Chichester, England: Wiley.

Cochrane, R. (1974). Crime and personality: Theory and evidence. *Bulletin of the British Psychological Society, 27,* 19–22.

Cohen, L.M. (1959). The relationship between certain personality variables and prior occupational stability of prison inmates. Unpublished doctoral dissertation, Temple University.

Confer, W.N. (1978). Learned helplessness, locus of control, and presumed source of control. *Dissertation Abstracts International, 39*(2-B), 974.

Conners, C.K., & Eisenberg, L. (1963). The effects of methylphenidate on symptomatology and learning in disturbed children. *American Journal of Psychiatry, 120,* 1458.

Cook, J.O., & Barnes, L.W. (1964). Choice of delay and inevitable shock. *Journal of Abnormal and Social Psychology, 68,* 669–672.

Corah, N.L., & Buffa, J. (1970). Perceived control, self–observation, and response to aversive stimulation. *Journal of Personality and Social Psychology, 16,* 1–14.

Cox, D.N. (1978). Psychophysiological correlates of sensation seeking and socialization during reduced stimulation. *Dissertation Abstracts International, 39* (1-B), 372.

Craddick, R. (1962). Selection of psychopathic from non–psychopathic prisoners within a Canadian prison. *Psychological Reports, 10,* 495–499.

Craft, M.J. (1965). *Ten studies into psychopathic personality*. Briston: John Wright.

Craft, M.J. (1966). *Psychopathic disorders and their assessment.* Oxford: Pergamon.

Crowe, R. (1974). An adoption study of antisocial personality. *Archives of General Psychiatry, 31,* 785–791.

deCharms, R. (1968). *Personal causation: The internal affective determinants of behavior.* New York: Academic.

DeMyer–Gapin, S., & Scott, T.J. (1977). Effect of stimulus novelty on stimulation seeking in antisocial and neurotic children. *Journal of Abnormal Psychology, 86,* 96–98.

Deuel Vocational Institution, Pilot Intensive Counseling Organization. (1956–1958). *Technical report series.* Tracy, CA: California Youth Authority and State Department of Corrections.

DeVellis, R.F., DeVellis, B.M., & McCauley, C. (1978). Vicarious acquisition of learned helplessness. *Journal of Personality and Social Psychology, 36,* 894–899.

Ehrlich, S.K., & Keogh, R.P. (1956). The psychopath in a mental institution. *Archives of Neurology and Psychiatry, 76,* 286–295.

Ellingson, R.J. (1954). Incidence of EEG abnormality among patients with mental disorders of apparently nonorganic origin: A criminal review. *American Journal of Psychiatry, 111,* 263–275.

Emmons, T.D., & Webb, W.W. (1974). Subjective correlates of emotional responsivity and stimulation seeking in psychopaths, normals, and acting-out neurotics. *Journal of Consulting and Clinical Psychology, 42,* 620.

Eysenck, H.J. (1959). *The Maudsley Personality Inventory.* London: University of London Press.

Eysenck, H.J. (1964). *Crime and personality.* London: Methuen.

Eysenck, H.J. (1974). Crime and personality reconsidered. *Bulletin of the British Psychological Society, 27,* 23–24.

Eysenck, H.J. (1975). Genetic factors in personality development. In A.R. Kaplan (Ed.), *Human behavior genetics.* Springfield, IL: Thomas.

Eysenck, H.J. (1977). *Crime and personality* (3rd ed.). London: Routledge & Kegan Paul.

Eysenck, H.J., & Eysenck, S.B.G. (1973). The personality of female prisoners. *British Journal of Psychiatry, 122,* 693–698.

Eysenck, H.J. & Eysenck, S.B.G. (1978). Psychopathy, personality, and genetics. In R.D. Hare & D. Schalling (Eds.), *Psychopathic behavior: Approaches to research.* Chichester, England: Wiley.

Eysenck, S.B.G., & Eysenck, H.J. (1970). Crime and personality: An empirical study of the three–factor theory. *British Journal of Criminology. 10,* 225–239.

Eysenck, S.B.G., & Eysenck, H.J. (1971a). A comparative study of criminals and matched controls on three dimensions of personality. *British Journal of Social and Clinical Psychology, 10,* 362–366.

Eysenck, S.B.G., & Eysenck, H.J. (1971b). Crime and personality: Item analysis of questionnaire responses. *British Journal of Criminology, 11,* 49–62.

Eysenck, S.B.G., & Eysenck, H.J. (1975). *Manual of the Eysenck Personality Questionnaire: Adult version and children's version.* London: University of London Press.

Fairweather, G.W. (1953). Serial rate learning by psychopathic, neurotic, and normal criminals under three incentive conditions. Unpublished doctoral dissertation, University of Illinois.

Farley, F.H., & Cox, Sr. O. (1971). Stimulus-seeking motivation in adolescents as a function of age and sex. *Adolescence, 6,* 207–218.

Farley, F.H., & Sewell, T. (1976). Test of an arousal theory of delinquency: Stimulation-seeking in delinquent and nondelinquent black adolescents. *Criminal Justice and Behavior, 3,* 315–320.

Fenz, W.D. (1971). Heart rate responses to a stressor: A comparison between primary and secondary psychopaths and normal controls. *Journal of Experimental Research in Personality, 5,* 7–13.

Fisher, C.D., & Pritchard, R.D. (1978). Effects on personal control, extrinsic rewards, and competence on intrinsic motivation. *United States AFHRL Technical Report* (report No. 20).

Flavell, J., Botkin, P., Fry, C., Wright, J., & Jarvis, P. (1968). *The development of role-taking and communication skills in children.* New York: Wiley.

Fox, R., & Lippert, W. (1963). Spontaneous GSR and anxiety level in sociopathic delinquents. *Journal of Consulting Psychology, 27,* 368.

Fox, S.S., Kimble, D.P., & Lickey, M.E. (1964). Comparison of caudate nucleus and septal-area lesions on two types of avoidance behavior. *Journal of Comparative and Physiological Psychology, 58,* 380–386.

Gale, A. (1973). The physiology of individual differences: Studies of extraversion and the EEG. In P. Kline (Ed.), *New approaches to physiological measurement.* Chichester, England: Wiley.

Garber, J., & Hollon, S.D. (1980). Universal versus personal helplessness in depression: Belief in uncontrollability or incompetence? *Journal of Abnormal Psychology, 89,* 56–66.

Garlington, W.K., & Shimota, H.E. (1964). The Change Seeker Index: A measure of the need for variable stimulus input. *Psychological Reports, 14,* 919–924.

Geer, J.H., Davison, G.C., & Gatchel, R.J. (1970). Reduction of stress in humans through nonveridical perceived control of aversive stimulation. *Journal of Personality and Social Psychology, 16,* 731–738.

Gilbert, L.A., & Mangelsdorff, D. (1979). Influence of perceptions of personal control on reactions to stressful events. *Journal of Counseling Psychology, 26,* 473–480.

Glass, D.C., Reim, B., & Singer, J.E. (1971). Behavioral consequences of adaptation to controllable and uncontrollable noise. *Journal of Experimental Social Psychology, 7,* 244-257.

Glass, D.C., Singer, J.E., Leonard, H.S., Krantz, D., Cohen, S., & Cummings, H. (1973). Perceived control of aversive stimulation and the reduction of stress responses. *Journal of Personality, 41,* 577–595.

Glueck, S., & Glueck, E. (1950). *Unraveling juvenile delinquency.* New York: Commonwealth Fund.

Glueck, S., & Glueck, E. (1956). *Physique and delinquency.* New York: Harpers.

Gottlieb, J.S., Ashley, M.C., & Knott, J.R. (1946). Primary behavior disorders and the psychopathic personality. *Archives of Neurology and Psychiatry, 56,* 381–400.

Gough, H.G. (1948). A sociological theory of psychopathy. *American Journal of Sociology, 53,* 359–366.

Gough, H.G. (1951). Manual for the California Psychological Inventory. Palo Alto, CA: Consulting Psychologists Press.

Gough, H.G. (1965a). Conceptual analyses of psychological test scores and other diagnostic variables. *Journal of Abnormal Psychology, 70,* 294–302.

Gough, H.G. (1965b). Cross-cultural validation of a measure of asocial behavior. *Psychological Reports, 17,* 379–387.

Gough, H.G., & Sandhu, H.S. (1964). Validation of the CPI Socialization scale in India. *Journal of Abnormal and Social Psychology, 68,* 544–547.

Gray, K.C. & Hutchison, H.C. (1964). The psychopathic personality: A survey of Canadian psychiatrists' opinions. *Canadian Psychiatric Association Journal, 9,* 452–461.

Greenacre, P. (1945). Conscience in the psychopath. *American Journal of Orthopsychiatry, 15,* 495–509.

Gregory, R.J. (1974). The causes of psychopathy: Implications of recent research. *Catalog of Selected Documents in Psychology, 4,* 86.

Guilford, J.P. (1975). Factors and factors of personality. *Psychological Bulletin, 82,* 802–814.

Guilford, J.P. (1977). Will the real factor of extraversion-introversion please stand up? A reply to Eysenck. *Psychological Bulletin, 84,* 412–416.

Hall, C.S., & Lindzey, G. (1970). *Theories of personality.* New York: Wiley.

Hare, R.D. (1965a). A conflict and learning theory analysis of psychopathic behavior. *Journal of Research in Crime and Delinquency, 2,* 12–19.

Hare, R.D. (1965b). Acquisition and generalization of a conditioned-fear response in psychopathic and non-psychopathic criminals. *Journal of Psychology, 59,* 367–370.

Hare, R.D. (1965c). Temporal gradient of fear arousal in psychopaths. *Journal of Abnormal Psychology, 70,* 442–445.

Hare, R.D. (1966a). Preference for delay of shock as a function of its intensity and probability. *Psychonomic Science, 5,* 393–394.

Hare, R.D. (1966b). Psychopathy and choice of immediate versus delayed punishment. *Journal of Abnormal Psychology, 71,* 25–29.

Hare, R.D. (1968). Psychopathy, autonomic functioning, and the orienting response. *Journal of Abnormal Psychology* (Monograph Supplement), *73,* (3(2)), 1–24.

Hare, R.D. (1970). *Psychopathy: Theory and research.* New York: Wiley.

Hare, R.D. (1980). A research scale for the assessment of psychopathy in criminal populations. *Personality and Individual Differences. 1,* 1–9.

Hare, R.D. (1981). Psychopathy and violence. In J.R. Hays, T.K. Roberts, & K.S. Solway (Eds.), *Violence and the violent individual.* New York: Spectrum.

Hare, R.D., & Cox, D.N. (1978). Clinical and empirical conceptions of psychopathy, and the selection of subjects for research. In R.D. Hare & D. Schalling (Eds.), *Psychopathic behavior: Approaches to research.* New York: Wiley.

Hare, R.D., & Craigen, D. (1974). Psychopathy and physiological activity in a mixed-motive game situation. *Psychophysiology, 11,* 197–206.

Hare, R.D., & Quinn, M. (1971). Psychopathy and autonomic conditioning. *Journal of Abnormal Psychology, 77,* 223–235.

Hare, R.D., & Schalling, D. (Eds.). (1978). *Psychopathic Behavior: Approaches to research.* New York: Wiley.

Henderson, J.M. (1972). The doing character. *Adolescence, 7,* 309–326.

Hetherington, E.M., Stowie, R.J., & Ridberg, E.H. (1971). Patterns of family interaction and child-rearing attitudes related to three dimensions of juvenile delinquency. *Journal of Abnormal Psychology, 78,* 160–176.

Hezel, J.D. (1968). Some personality correlates of dimensions of delinquency. Unpublished doctoral dissertation, St. Louis University.

Hill D. (1947). Amphetamine in psychopathic states. *British Journal of Addictions, 44,* 50.

Hill, D. (1952). EEG in episodic psychotic and psychopathic behavior: A classification of data. *EEG and Clinical Neurophysiology, 4,* 419–442.

Hiroto, D.S., & Seligman, M.E.P. (1975). Generality of learned helplessness in man. *Journal of Personality and Social Psychology, 31,* 311–327.

Hughes, J. (1971). Electroencephalography and learning disabilities. In H. Myklebust (Ed.), *Progress in learning disabilities, II.* New York: Grune & Stratton.

Hutchings, B., & Mednick, S.A. (1975). Registered criminality in the adoptive and biological parents of registered male criminal adoptees. In R.R. Fieve, D. Rosenthal, & H. Brill (Eds.), *Genetic research in psychiatry*. Baltimore: John Hopkins Press.

Hutchinson, L.B. (1977). Effects of variation in reward contingency on participation motivation on a perceptual task in psychopathic persons. *Dissertation Abstracts International, 38,*(2-B), 902.

Jackson, D.N., & Paunonen, S.V. (1980). Personality structure and assessment. *Annual Review of Psychology, 31,* 503–582.

Jaffee, L.D., & Polansky, N.A. (1962). Verbal inaccessibility in young adolescents showing delinquent trends. *Journal of Health and Human Behavior, 3,* 105–111.

Jinks, J., & Fulker, D.W. (1970). Comparison of the biometric, genetical, MAVA and classical approaches to the analysis of human behavior. *Psychological Bulletin, 73,* 311–350.

Johns, J.H., & Quay, H.C. (1962). The effect of social reward on verbal conditioning in psychopathic and neurotic military offenders. *Journal of Consulting Psychology, 26,* 217–220.

Jurkovec, G.J., & Prentice, N.M. (1977). Relation of moral and cognitive development to dimensions of juvenile delinquency. *Journal of Abnormal Psychology, 86,* 414–420.

Kaada, B.R. (1951). Somato-motor, autonomic and electrocortigraphic responses to electrical stimulation of 'rhinencephalic' and other structures in primates, cat and dog. *Acta Physiologica Scandinavia, 24* (Suppl. 83), 1–258.

Kabat, H. (1936). Electrical stimulation of points in the forebrain and midbrain: The resultant alterations in respiration. *Journal of Comparative Neurology, 64,* 187–208.

Kahn, E. (1931). *Psychopathic personalities*. New Haven: Yale University Press.

Kelley, H.H. (1971). *Attribution in social interaction*. New York: General Learning Press.

Kelly, G.A. (1955). *The Psychology of Personal Control*. New York: Norton.

Kenyon, J., & Krieckhaus, E.E. (1965). Enhanced avoidance behavior following septal lesions in the rat as a function of lesion size and spontaneous activity. *Journal of Comparative and Physiological Psychology, 59,* 466–469.

Kihoh, L., & Osselton, J.W. (1966). *Clinical electroencephalography*. Washington: Butterworth.

Kimmel, H.D. (1966). Inhibition of the unconditional response in classical conditioning. *Psychological Review, 73,* 232–240.

Knott, J.R., Platt, E.B., Ashby, M.C., & Gottlieb, J.S. (1953). A familial evaluation of the electroencephalogram of patients with primary behavior disorder and psychopathic personality. *EEG and Clinical Neurophysiology, 5,* 363–370.

Krieckhaus, E.E., Simmons, H.J., Thomas, G.J., & Kenyon, J. (1964). Septal lesions enhance shock avoidance behavior in the rat. *Experimental Neurology, 9,* 107–113.

Kurland, H.D., Yeager, C.T., & Arthur, R.J. (1963). Psychophysiological aspects of severe behavior disorders. *Archives of General Psychiatry, 8,* 599–604.

Lacey, J.I. & Lacey, B.C. (1974). On heart rate responses and behavior: A reply to Elliot. *Journal of Personality and Social Psychology, 30,* 1–18.

Larsen, R.W. (1980). *Bundy: The deliberate stranger.* Englewood Cliffs, NJ: Prentice-Hall.

Lindner, R. (1942). Experimental studies in constitutional psychopathic inferiority— Part 1. Systemic patterns. *Journal of Criminal Psychopathology, 3,* 252–276.

Lion, J.R. (1981a). Countertransference and other psychotherapy issues. In W.H. Reid (Ed.), *The treatment of antisocial syndromes.* New York: Van Nostrand Reinhold.

Lion J.R. (Ed.). (1981b). *Personality disorders: Diagnosis and management* (revised for DSM-III). Baltimore: Williams & Wilkins.

Lippert, W.W., & Senter, R.J. (1966). Electrodermal responses in the sociopath. *Psychonomic Science, 4,* 25–26.

Loo, R. (1979). A psychometric investigation of the Eysenck Personality Question-naire. *Journal of Personality Assessment, 43,* 54–58.

Lubar, J.F. (1964). Effect of medial cortical lesions on the avoidance behavior of the cat. *Journal of Comparative and Physiological Psychology, 58,* 38–46.

Luria, A.R. (1973). *The working brain: An introduction to neuropsychology.* New York: Basic Books.

Lykken, D.T. (1957). A study of anxiety in the sociopathic personality. *Journal of Abnormal and Social Psychology, 55,* 6–10.

Lykken, D.T., & Katzenmeyer, C.G. (1968). *Manual for the Activity Preference Questionnaire (APQ).* Minneapolis: University of Minnesota Research Laboratories.

Maier, S.F., & Seligman, M.E.P. (1976). Learned helplessness: Theory and evidence. *Journal of Experimental Psychology: General, 105,* 3–46.

Marotta, C. (1978). Prior exposure to control vs. no control and immunization to learned helplessness in man. *Dissertation Abstracts International, 38*(9-B), 4468–4469.

Martin, I. (1963). Eyelid conditioning and concomitant GSR activity. *Behavior Research and Therapy, 1,* 255–265.

Martinez, J.A. (1976). An investigation into psychopathic aggression through behavioral conditioning. *Dissertation Abstracts International, 36*(11-B), 5806–5807.

Matthey, W. (1974). The effect of observational learning and perceived gain on the imitative behavior of sociopaths. *Dissertation Abstracts International, 34* (9-B), 4669.

McCarroll, J.E., Mitchell, K.H., Carpenter, R.J., & Anderson, J.P. (1967). Analysis of three stimulus-seeking scales. *Psychological Reports, 21,* 853–856.

McCleary, R.A. (1966). Response-modulating functions of the limbic system: Initiation and suppression. In E. Steller & J. Sprague (Eds.), *Progress in physiological psychology*, (Vol. 1). New York: Academic.

McCord, W., & McCord, J. (1964). *The psychopath: An essay on the criminal mind.* New York: Van Nostrand Reinhold.

McDonald, D.C., Johnson, L.C., & Hord, D.C. (1964). Habituation of the orienting response in alert and drowsy subjects. *Psychophysiology, 1,* 163–173.

Mednick, S.A., & Hutchings, B. (1978). Genetic and psychophysiological factors in asocial behavior. In R.D. Hare & D. Schalling (Eds.), *Psychopathic behavior: Approaches to research.* Chichester, England: Wiley.

Megargee, E.I. (1972). *The California Psychological Inventory Handbook.* San Francisco: Jossey–Bass.

Megargee, E.I., & Golden, R.E. (1973). Parental attitudes of psychopathic and subcultural delinquents. *Criminology, 10,* 427–439.

Mehrabian, A. & Russell, J.A. (1973). A measure of arousal seeking tendency. *Environment and Behavior, 5,* 315–333.

Melzick, R., & Wall, P.D. (1965). Pain mechanism: A new theory. *Science, 150,* 971–979.

Mettler, F.A. (1942). Relation between pyramidal and extra pyramidal function. *Research on Nervous and Mental Disorders, 21,* 150–227.

Miller, J.G. (1966). Eyeblink conditioning of primary and neurotic psychopaths. (University Microfilms No. 67–923).

Morrison, J., & Stewart, M. (1973). The psychiatric status of the legal families of adopted hyperactive children. *Archives of General Psychiatry, 28,* 858–891.

Moss, D.J. (1975). Accuracy of interpersonal perception of cognitive complexity of the psychopath. *Dissertation Abstracts International, 35*(9-B), 4658.

Mundy-Castle, A.C., & McKiever, B.L. (1953). The psychophysiological significance of the galvanic skin response. *Journal of Experimental Psychology, 46,* 15–24.

Nygard, N.K. (1975). A test of Hare's temporal conflict model of psychopathy. *Dissertation Abstracts International, 35*(7-B), 3590–3591.

Omenn, G. (1973). Genetic issues in the syndrome of minimal brain dysfunction. *Seminars in Psychiatry, 5,* 5–9.

Omwake, K.T. (1954). The relationship between acceptance of self and acceptance of others shown by three personality inventories. *Journal of Consulting Psychology, 18,* 443–446.

Orris, J. (1969). Visual monitoring performance in three subgroups of male delinquents. *Journal of Abnormal Psychology, 74,* 227–229.

Painting, D.H. (1961). The performance of psychopathic individuals under conditions of positive and negative partial reinforcement. *Journal of Abnormal and Social Psychology, 62,* 352–355.

Palumbo, S.J. (1976). An investigation of social skills in psychopaths in terms of role playing. *Dissertation Abstracts International, 37*(2-B), 981.

Paré, W.P., & Dumas, J.P. (1965). The effects of insular neocortical lesions on passive and active avoidance behavior in the rat. *Psychonomic Science, 2,* 87–88.

Partridge, G.E. (1928). A study of 50 cases of psychopathic personality. *American Journal of Psychiatry, 7,* 953–973.

Patterson, G.R. (1975). The aggressive child: Victim and architect of a coercive system. In L.A. Hamerlynck, E.J. Mash, & L.C. Handy (Eds.), *Behavior modification and families I. Theory and research, II. Applications and developments.* New York: Brunner/Mazel.

Penney, R.K. & Reinehr, R.C. (1966). Development of a stimulus-variation seeking scale for adults. *Psychological Reports, 18,* 631–638.

Persons, R.W., & Pepinsky, H.B. (1966). Convergence in psychotherapy with delinquent boys. *Journal of Counseling Psychology, 13,* 329–334.

Pervin, L.A. (1963). The need to predict and control under conditions of threat. *Journal of Personality, 31,* 570–587.

Peterson, D.R., & Quay, H.C. (1959). Extending the construct validity of a socialization scale. *Journal of Consulting Psychology, 23,* 182.

Peterson, D.R., Quay, H.C., & Cameron, G.R. (1959). Personality and background factors in juvenile delinquency as inferred from questionnaire responses. *Journal of Consulting Psychology, 23,* 395–399.

Peterson, D.R., Quay, H.C. & Tiffany, T.C. (1961). Personality factors related to juvenile delinquency. *Child Development, 32,* 355–372.

Petrie, A. (1967). *Individuality in pain and suffering.* Chicago: University of Chicago Press.

Phillips, E.L. (1951). Attitudes toward self and others: A brief questionnaire report. *Journal of Consulting Psychology, 15,* 79–81.

Powdermaker, F., Levis, H.T., & Touraine, G. (1937). Psychopathy and treatment of delinquent girls. *American Journal of Orthopsychiatry, 7,* 61.

Price, K.P., Tryon, W.W., & Raps, C.S. (1978). Learned helplessness and depression in a clinical population: A test of two behavioral hypotheses. *Journal of Abnormal Psychology, 87,* 113–121.

Pritchard, J.D. (1835). A treatise on insanity. Philadelphia: Haswell, Barrington, & Haswell. As quoted by D. Henderson (1939). *Psychopathic States.* New York: Norton.

Prokasy, W.F. (1956). The acquisition of observing responses in the absence of differential external reinforcement. *Journal of Comparative and Physiological Psychology, 49,* 131–134.

Quay, H.C. (1964). Personality dimension in delinquent males as inferred from the factor analysis of behavior ratings. *Journal of Research in Crime and Delinquency, 1,* 33–37.

Quay, H.C. (1965). Psychopathic personality as pathological stimulation seeking. *American Journal of Psychiatry, 122,* 180–183.

Quay, H.C. (1977). Psychopathic behavior: Reflections on its nature, origins, and treatment. In I. Užgiris & F. Weizmann (Eds.), *The structuring of experience.* New York: Plenum.

Quay, H.C., & Parsons, L.B. (1971). The differential behavioral classification of the juvenile offender (2nd ed.). Washington, DC: Bureau of Prisons, U.S. Department of Justice.

Quay, H.C. & Peterson, D.R. (1964). The questionnaire measurement of personality dimensions associated with juvenile delinquency. University of Illinois (mimeo).

Reckless, W.C., Dinitz, S., & Kay, B. (1957). The self-component in potential delinquency and potential non-delinquency. *American Sociological Review, 22,* 566–670.

Reed, C.F., & Caudra, C.A. (1957). The role-taking hypothesis in delinquency. *Journal of Consulting Psychology, 21,* 386–390.

Reid, W.H. (Ed.). (1978). *The psychopath: A comprehensive study of antisocial disorders and behaviors.* New York: Brunner/Mazel.

Reid, W.H. (1985). The antisocial personality: A review. *Hospital and Community Psychiatry, 36,* 831–837.

Robins, L. (1966). *Deviant children grown up: A sociological and psychiatric study of sociopathic personality.* Baltimore: Williams & Wilkins.

Ross, R.R. (1969). Application of operant conditioning procedures to the behavioral modification of institutionalized adolescent offenders. *Progress Report.* Ontario Mental Health Foundation.

Ross, R.R., & Doody, K.F. (1973). Persistence in the psychopathic personality. *Canadian Journal of Criminology and Corrections, 15,* 292–305.

Rotenberg, M. (1974). Conceptual and methodological notes on affective and cognitive role taking (sympathy and empathy): An illustrative experiment with delinquent and nondelinquent boys. *Journal of Genetic Psychology, 125,* 177–185.

Roth, S., & Kubal, L. (1975). Effects of noncontingent reinforcement on tasks of differing importance: Facilitating and learning helplessness. *Journal of Personality and Social Psychology, 32,* 680–691.

Satterfield, J.H. (1978). The hyperactive child syndrome: A precursor of adult psychopathy? In R.D. Hare & D. Schalling (Eds.), *Psychopathic behavior: Approaches to research*. Chichester, England: Wiley.

Satterfield, J.H., & Dawson, M. (1971). Electrodermal correlates of hyperactivity in children. *Psychophysiology, 8,* 191–197.

Schachter, S. & Latané, B. (1964). Crime, cognition and the autonomic nervous system. In M.R. Jones (Ed.), *Nebraska symposium on motivation*. Lincoln: University of Nebraska Press.

Schalling, D., & Levander, S. (1967). *Spontaneous fluctuations in EDA during anticipation of pain in two delinquent groups differing in anxiety proneness*. (Rep. No. 238). University of Stockholm, Psychological Laboratory.

Schiff, M. (1977). Hazard adjustment, locus of control, and sensation seeking: Some null findings. *Environment and Behavior, 9,* 233–254.

Schmideberg, M. (1978). The treatment of a juvenile "psychopath." *International Journal of Offender Therapy and Comparative Criminology, 22,* 21–28.

Schulsinger, F. (1972). Psychopathy: Heredity and environment. *International Journal of Mental Health, 1,* 190–206.

Schuster, R. (1976). Trust: Its implication in the etiology and treatment of psychopathic youths. *International Journal of Offender Therapy and Comparative Criminology, 20,* 198–233.

Schwartzbaum, J.S., Kellicutt, M.H., Spieth, T.M., & Thompson, J.B. (1964). Effect of septal lesions in rats on response inhibition associated with food-reinforced behavior. *Journal of Comparative and Physiological Psychology, 58,* 217–224.

Seligman, M.E.P. (1975). *Helplessness: On depression, development, and death*. San Francisco: Freeman.

Shagass, C., & Schwartz, M. (1962). Observations on somatosensory cortical reactivity in personality disorders. *Journal of Nervous and Mental Disease, 135,* 44–51.

Shallenberger, H.D. (1976). Orientation response habituation to high intensity emotional stimuli. *Dissertation Abstracts International, 36*(7-B), 3657.

Shields, J. (1962). *Monozygotic Twins*. Oxford: Oxford University Press.

Shostak, D.A., & McIntyre, C.W. (1978). Stimulus-seeking behavior in three delinquent personality types. *Journal of Consulting and Clinical Psychology, 46,* 582.

Siddle, D.A., Nicol, A.R., & Foggitt, R.H. (1973). Habituation and overextinction of the GSR component of the orienting response in antisocial adolescents. *British Journal of Social and Clinical Psychology, 12,* 303–308.

Siegel, R.A. (1978). Probability of punishment of behavior in psychopathic and non-psychopathic offenders. *Journal of Abnormal Psychology, 87,* 514–522.

Silver, A.W. (1963). TAT and MMPI Psychopathic Deviate scale differences between delinquent and nondelinquent adolescents. *Journal of Consulting Psychology, 27,* 370.

Smith, R.F. (1976). Person perception in the antisocial personality: An exploratory study. *Dissertation Abstracts International, 36*(9-B), 4710.

Smith, R.J. (1978). *The psychopath in society.* New York: Academic.

Smith, R.J., & Griffith, J.E. (1978). Psychopathy, the Machiavellian, and anomie. *Psychological Reports, 42,* 258.

Stafford-Clark, D., Pond, D., & Lovett Doust, J.W. (1951). The psychopath in prison: A preliminary report of a co-operative research. *British Journal of Delinquency, 2,* 117–129.

Stein, K.B., Gough, H.G., & Sarbin, T.R. (1966). The dimensionality of the CPI Socialization Scale and an empirically derived typology among delinquent and nondelinquent boys. *Multivariate Behavioral Research, 1,* 197–208.

Stern, J.A., & McDonald, D.G. (1965). Physiological correlates of mental disease. In P.R. Farnsworth (Ed.), *Annual review of psychology.* Palo Alto, CA: Annual Reviews.

Stock, D. (1949). An investigation into the interrelations between self-concept and feelings directed toward other persons and groups. *Journal of Consulting Psychology, 13,* 176–180.

Stricker, L.J. (1978). Review of the Eysenck Personality Questionnaire. In O.K. Buros (Ed.), *The eighth mental measurements yearbook.* Highland Park, NJ: Gryphon.

Suedfeld, P., & Landon, P.B. (1978). Approaches to treatment. In R.D. Hare & D. Schalling (Eds.), *Psychopathic behavior: Approaches to research.* Chichester, England: Wiley.

Swinn, R. (1961). The relationship between self-acceptance and acceptance of others: A learning theory analysis. *Journal of Abnormal and Social Psychology, 63,* 37–42.

Symkal, A., & Thorne, F.C. (1951). Etiological studies of psychopathic personality. *Journal of Clinical Psychology, 7,* 299–316.

Syndulko, K. (1978). Electrocortical investigations of sociopathy. In R.D. Hare & D. Schalling (Eds.), *Psychopathic behavior: Approaches to research.* Chichester, England: Wiley.

Tamayo, A., & Raymond, F. (1977). Self-concept of psychopaths. *Journal of Psychology, 97,* 71–77.

Taylor, A.J.W. (1975). Correspondence. *Bulletin of the British Psychological Society, 28,* 285–286.

Teitelbaum, H., & Milner, P. (1963). Activity changes following partial hippocampal lesion in rats. *Journal of Comparative and Physiological Psychology, 56,* 284–289.

Tennen, H., & Eller, S.J. (1977). Attributional components of learned helplessness and facilitation. *Journal of Personality and Social Psychology, 35*, 265–271.

Tuovinen, M. (1974). Depressio sine depressione—An aspect of the antisocial personality. *Dynamische Psychiatrie, 7*, 19–31.

Ullmann, L.P., & Krasner, L.A. (1969). *A psychological approach to abnormal behavior.* Englewood Cliffs, NJ: Prentice-Hall.

Ursin, H. (1965). Effect of amygdaloid lesions on avoidance behavior and visual discrimination in cats. *Experimental Neurology, 11*, 298–317.

Vada, A.V. (1977). The relationship of locus of control to manipulative attitudes and behavior of imprisoned sociopaths. *Dissertation Abstracts International, 38* (6-B), 2892.

Vaillant, G.E. (1975). Sociopathy as a human process: A viewpoint. *Archives of General Psychiatry, 32*, 178–183.

Velicer, W.F., & Stevenson, J.F. (1978). The relation between item format and the structure of the Eysenck Personality Inventory. *Applied Psychological Measurement, 2*, 293–304.

Wachs, T.D. (1977). The Optimal Stimulation Hypothesis and early development: Anybody got a match? In I. Užgiris & F. Weizmann (Eds.), *The structuring of experience.* New York: Plenum.

Warren, A.B., & Grant, D.A. (1955). The relation of conditioned discrimination to the MMPI Pd personality variable. *Journal of Experimental Psychology, 49*, 23–27.

Wechsler, D. (1958). *The measurement and appraisal of adult intelligence* (4th ed.). Baltimore: Williams & Wilkins.

Welsh, G.S. (1952). An anxiety index and an internalization ratio for the MMPI. *Journal of Consulting Psychology, 16*, 65–72.

Wheeler, Jr., C.A. (1973). *The relationship between psychopathy and the weak automatization cognitive style.* Unpublished doctoral dissertation. Tallahassee, Florida: Florida State University.

White, R.W. (1959). Motivation reconsidered: The concept of competence. *Psychological Review, 66*, 297–333.

Widom, C.S. (1974). Interpersonal conflict and cooperation in psychopaths. *Dissertation Abstracts International, 34*(7-B), 3480–3481.

Widom, C.S. (1976). Interpersonal conflict and cooperation in psychopaths. *Journal of Abnormal Psychology, 85*, 330–334.

Widom, C.S. (1978). An empirical classification of female offenders. *Criminal Justice and Behavior, 5*, 35–52.

Woodworth, R.S. (1958). *Dynamics and behavior.* New York: Holt.

Wortman, C.B. (1975). Some determinants of perceived control. *Journal of Personality and Social Psychology, 31*, 282–294.

Wyckoff, L.B. (1952). The role of observing response in discrimination learning, Part 1. *Psychological Review, 59,* 431–442.

Zucker, I., & McCleary, R.A. (1964). Perseveration in septal cats. *Psychonomic Science, 1,* 387–388.

Zuckerman, M. (1971). Dimensions of sensation seeking. *Journal of Consulting and Clinical Psychology, 36,* 45–52.

Zuckerman, M. (1974). The sensation seeking motive. In B.A. Maher (Ed.), *Progress in experimental personality research,* Vol. 7. New York: Academic.

Zuckerman, M. (1975). *Manual and research report for the Sensation Seeking Scale.* University of Delaware, Department of Psychology.

Zuckerman, M. (1978). Sensation seeking and psychopathy. In R.D. Hare & D. Schalling (Eds.), *Psychopathic behavior: Approaches to research.* Chichester, England: Wiley.

Zuckerman, M. (1979). *Sensation seeking: Beyond the optimal level of arousal.* Hilldale, NJ: Erlbaum.

Zuckerman, M., Bone, R.N., Neary, R., Mangelsdorff, D., & Brustman, B. (1972). What is the sensation seeker? Personality trait and experience correlates of the Sensation Seeking Scales. *Journal of Consulting and Clinical Psychology, 39,* 308–321.

Zuckerman, M., Kolin, E.A., Price, L., & Zoob, I. (1964). Development of a Sensation-Seeking Scale. *Journal of Consulting Psychology, 28,* 477–482.

Author Index

Subject Index

About the Author

Dennis M. Doren is the Forensic Clinical Director at the Mendota Mental Health Institute in Madison, Wisconsin. He is a member of the American Psychological Association, a diplomate from the American Board of Administrative Psychology, a listed provider on the National Register of Health Service Providers in Psychology, and a former honorary member of the International Differential Treatment Association. Dr. Doren received his Ph.D. from Florida State University in 1983. He has given presentations across the country on the treatment of psychopathy and the effective management of verbal aggression from clients.